To Larry

Then Came Trump

Robert R. Owens (signature)

Dr. Robert Owens

© 2017 by Robert R. Owens PhD

ISBN-13:978-1542729550

ISBN-10:1542729556

All rights reserved solely by the author. No part of this book may be reproduced in any form without the permission of the author.

Dedicated to The Donald, the billionaire man of the people, the real-life King of Queens who captured lightening in a jar, forged a movement by the force of his will, defied the establishment, and took America by storm.

CONTENTS

Preamble

Dispatch One......Chicago on the Potomac..........................1

Dispatch Two......A Government of Fallible Men to Rule Fallible Men..6

Dispatch Three......A Rose By Any Other Name..............10

Dispatch Four......Don't Tell Someone Else......................17

Dispatch Five......Down the Memory Hole.......................21

Dispatch Six......Good-bye America it Was Good to Know You...25

Dispatch Seven......Happy Days Are Here Again Again ..42

Dispatch Eight...... History is the Story of Life 47

Dispatch Nine......Hitler Mussolini FDR and Obama 52

Dispatch Ten......How Many Nails Does it Take to Seal a Coffin? 61

Dispatch Eleven......How Strange Can It Get? 65

Dispatch Twelve......If It Isn't America What Is It? 71

Dispatch Thirteen......Socialism is the Problem Capitalism is the Answer 77

Dispatch Fourteen......The Empire Swallowed the Republic..80

Dispatch Fifteen......The Great Disconnect.........................85

Dispatch Sixteen......The Solutions to Our Broken Institutions are in the Constitution 89

Dispatch Seventeen......To Write the Future Read the Past..101

Dispatch Eighteen......Useful Idiots and the Theater of the Absurd 108

Dispatch Nineteen......We Are a Conquered Nation 111

Dispatch Twenty......What Can't Happen Here Did 117

Dispatch Twenty-one...... What Happens When Progressives Tax (and Spend) 123

Dispatch Twenty-two......Who Voted For That? 132

Dispatch Twenty-three......Why Do I Say the Constitution Failed? 137

Dispatch Twenty-four......Why Do They Lie to Us Over & Over? 143

Dispatch Twenty-five......Why Does America Have a Written Constitution? 152

Dispatch Twenty-six......Why Empires Fall 163

Then Came Trump

Dispatch Twenty-seven......America First 172

Dispatch Twenty-eight......America Rising 183

Dispatch Twenty-nine......American Pravda and New York's Sixth Crime Family 185

Dispatch Thirty......Avast There's an Iceberg Ahead 190

Dispatch Thirty-one......Back When I Was a Boy 193

Dispatch Thirty-two......Bart Simpson For President 202

Dispatch Thirty-three......Bitter Clingers Hang On 206

Dispatch Thirty-four......Then Came Trump 211

Dispatch Thirty-five......Trump Earthquake Causes Democrat Tsunami 215

Dispatch Thirty-six......Trump or Clinton Life or Death .237

Dispatch Thirty-seven......Trump Tames Billary 231

Dispatch Thirty-eight......Trump Triumph Now Do What You Said You Would Do 236

Dispatch Thirty-nine......Trump Triumph to Dream the Impossible Dream 240

Dispatch Forty......Trump Trumps Never Trump 246

Dispatch Forty-one......Trump Vote a Vote For Hope 251

Dispatch Forty-two......Who Do You Believe When You Can't Believe Anyone? 256

Dispatch Forty-three......Why Should Obama Declare Martial Law? 260

Dispatch Forty-four......Why do Progressives Want a Recount They Know They Will Lose? 264

Dispatch Forty-five......Donald Dumps Bubba Dashes Dowager's Dreams 268

Dispatch Forty-six......Crooked Hillary 269

Dispatch Forty-seven......Obama the Bad Santa 273

Dispatch Forty-eight......The December Revolution 274

Dispatch Forty-nine......Trump Offices Attacked by Thugs..278

Dispatch Fifty......Trump the Chumps and Choose the Heroes 279

Dispatch Fifty-one......Trump Triumph Tour Takes America by Storm 281

Dispatch Fifty-two...... Trump's Gettysburg Address Needs Secret Sauce to Succeed 284

Conclusion

Dispatch Fifty-three......Are We as Dumb as They Think We Are? 287

Dispatch Fifty-four......Do You Have Hope? 292

Dispatch Fifty-five......How Do We Get Back to Where We Were? 296

Dispatch Fifty-six......A Parallel Universe Without Progressives 305

Dispatch Fifty-seven......Trump Makes America Great Again – Why Wait? 308

Dispatch Fifty-eight......The Hope That Does Not Disappoint 313

Endnotes 319

Then Came Trump

Preamble

Dispatch One

Chicago on the Potomac

Back in the Dream Time, elders were honored because of their accumulated knowledge, if Pops knew a better way to saddle horses that knowledge helped Junior since he saddled horses. Today if Pops knows how to tune-up cars what good is that when cars don't need to be tuned-up anymore? Now the old are relegated to extolling their own relevance while exclaiming, "I've never seen that before." Doddering ancients who use their cell phones merely to talk wonder why their grandchildren never answer their emails as Gen Z tweet each other: "Don't trust anyone over 15."

The world is moving so fast not only is today tomorrow's yesterday the generations are living in different todays today as we continue to charge our Chinese living standard to our grandchildren. Gen X and Y parents with their once hip lap-tops under their arms stare in wonder as their pre-teen Gen Zs text with one hand while Wii skydiving in the backseat. For these new additions to middle-age who're just old enough to remember Star Trek imagine Captain Kirk visiting Captain Picard pointing at Commander Data and saying, "What's that?"

After years of being treated as if the Wisdom of the Ages were as relevant as Confucius in a fortune cookie now that we have Chicago on the Potomac the wisdom gained in the City that Works is suddenly spot-on. Of course George the Second's doctrine of pre-emptive war made one old saying make sense beyond the Southside, "Never start fights but if you have to hit someone back first once in a while that's all right." Then again ACORN before it morphed into numerous faceless organizations with the same mission and different names or just became part of the nomenclature exemplified the everlasting relevance of Chicago's best known adage, "Vote early and vote often."

With the Democrats large-and-in-charge even when they lose elections, Windy City Proverbs may help many understand what kind of change we've stepped in. Such as "Everybody cheats so if you don't cheat you're a cheater," or "What's mine is mine, what's yours is negotiable." Maybe the taxman could use, "They must not have wanted it they didn't have their hand on it." Looking at our Congress, "If you're going to get mad at thieves you'll never have any friends" comes to mind. Thinking of the proposed Green Home Efficiency Inspectors we may one day deal with when buying or selling a home are reminiscent of the Chicago Fire

Marshal conscientiously telling a business owner, "We'll save the city some gas money if we just do the inspection right here in my office," while patting his desk indicating where to place the money.

The most transparent administration in history started off with some Southside swag calling the biggest earmark in history a stimulus, continued the virtuoso performance calling ward-healers czars and followed a time-honored Second City tradition in Al Franken's endless Minnesota recount by finding a bag of votes. Who says you can't go home again? They may turn the old neighborhood into Yuppie Heaven by knocking down the middleclass housing and putting up three-story imitation Victorians but right here right now the machine that gave no-show jobs to half the wise-guys on the corner as well as Michelle at the hospital is in the process of not just fixing tickets but fixing everything else. The political descendants of Big Bill Thompson, Richard the First and Richard the Second parlayed community organizing into a national organization that should make the Five Families green with envy.

Having fixed the economy, health care, hate-crimes, immigration, and cap-and-trade BHO has also had the opportunity to fix the highest court in the land. In the Chicago justice system lawyers give out printed pricelists stating how much acquittals cost verses dismissals and the old saying concerning courthouses goes, "It may say justice on the outside but that doesn't mean there's any on the inside." Since the Democratic Machine and their Me-To Republican allies rubber-stamped Mr. O's picks for the A-Team how do the prospects for judicial restraint and the Constitution look? Fine if you fit the profile for the protected or promoted classes not too good if you naively look for that lady wearing the blindfold and holding the scales. Well at least we have Chief Justice Roberts there to stop the train on its way to totalitarianism, oh wait, we don't.

Joining the sisterhood on the bench, Ms. Sotomayor feels her gender and her race make her uniquely qualified to reach wise decisions and believes international law should be consulted when weighing appeals. She should feel right at home with the former chief counsel for the ACLU Ruth Bader Ginsburg who apparently believes American Citizenship is the right of all mankind. In one decision she said, "You would have a huge statelessness problem if you don't consider a child born abroad a U.S. citizen."[i]

Ah justice, what is it good for? Or as they say in Chi-town, "How much justice can you afford?" The difference between Chicago Prime and Chicago on the Potomac is in the original version Mayors serve for life, or as long as they want, followed by a power struggle. Hopefully in the DC version we will get a change in 2017. I wonder if it will be a Bush or a Clinton.

Then Came Trump

Vive la Différence! Or as the French also say, the more things change the more they stay the same.

Dispatch Two

A Government of Fallible Men to Rule Fallible Men

In America today a debate rages concerning the legitimate role of government. Currently the Federal Government is controlled by a group of politicians who consider themselves the ideological descendants of the Progressive Movement.

Beginning in the 1890's the Progressives led by Theodore Roosevelt and Woodrow Wilson championed the idea that it was time to progress past America's old ways of doing things. They felt the traditions, forms, and style of American governance and society should break-out of the mold provided by the Constitution by casting it as a "living Breathing Document" that could be remolded to meet the desires of every generation.

They believed, and their descendants still believe, it is the behavior of men that defines who they are. This contrasts with our Founders who believed that it is instead the nature of men that provides this definition. Our Founders expressly stated that they believed humanity has been endowed by the Creator with rights.

They felt that these rights are inalienable, meaning they are humanity's by virtue of existence. In other words, these rights have not been earned by man they've been given by God and since they haven't been given by government, government can't legitimately take them away. Instead of existing for its own right, the reason for government is to protect these natural rights. It's the need for the order, security and liberty for the pursuit of happiness, which justifies the establishment and continuation of government.

Thus, a government of the people, by the people and for the people should be one based upon the nature of man. It's in this context that the voice of the people could almost be called the voice of God for if the Creator implanted this nature and these rights within humanity the collective expression freely arrived at and freely expressed should bring to the fore those who will respect and guard these rights.

If this is true then the will of the majority should always be the surest way to ensure the continued existence of man's natural rights. If we had a nation of perfect people this would be true; however, in establishing and maintaining government we don't deal with perfect people we deal with people as they are with all the imperfections and prejudices nurture superimposes upon nature. People who don't educate themselves enough to exercise self-leadership become the pawns of demagogues and the voice of God is perverted into the voice of the world.

Even the Founders, a grouping singular in the history of men concerning the brilliance of their intellects and the purity of their motives knew they couldn't trust themselves to form or maintain a government of fallible men to rule over fallible men. They knew that history is filled with examples of charismatic leaders who've proven that while you can fool all of the people only some of the time it's possible to fool enough people to take over a country. Then once you've fooled a plurality of voters to take over you can make fools of everyone doing whatever you like for as long as you like. This is why the protection of freedom is a limited government.

Power must be concentrated enough to provide order, security and liberty; however, if unrestrained power is given to a majority the opportunity exists for a faction to gain control and use it for purely partisan ends. Thus our Founders rejected direct democracy in favor of the federal model of divided sovereignty and the republican principle of both direct and in-direct representation. That the source of authority emanates from the people and the constituent States is demonstrated in several ways.

The Constitution itself was referred to delegates chosen by the States. In the American government as initially designed the people were represented directly by the House of Representatives and the States by the Senate.

The executive was elected indirectly by the people and the states through the Electoral College. The members of the judicial branch are appointed by the executive with the advice and consent of the Senate.

This process of allowing democratic choice within a framework of restraint was designed to create a government based upon the premise of inalienable rights yet cognizant of the fallible nature of mankind. A government powerful enough to ensure the security necessary to guarantee those rights, yet retrained enough not to trample them. Many of the Progressive innovations of the last 100 years have upset this delicate balance moving us from the government envisioned by the founders to the one we have today.

The Seventeenth Amendment mandates the direct election of the Senate. This left the States without any voice in the Federal Government. It also opened the door for a combination of factions acting as an unrestrained majority seeking the benefit of some at the expense of others. Often those who take the limits off government seek unlimited power for themselves. We must follow the guide of our ancestors for the good of our posterity. We must resist the temptation to seek security through government rather than security from government.

Dispatch Three

A Rose By Any Other Name

The main lesson we learn from History is that we don't learn from History. The lack of historical perspective is, I believe, one of the major contributing factors in America's current state.

People don't realize that all of these novel fixes our collectivist leaders are shoving down our throats with regard to health care have been tried multiple times before. Or that they have failed every time.

People don't realize that preemptive imperial wars of aggression and suppression have been disguised as endless wars for peace since Sargon the Great marched out of Akkad to found the first known empire.

Running true to form most people, apparently including our national leaders both political and military and the news anchors for the Corporations Once Known as the Mainstream Media, do not realize that ISIS is not an aberration in Islamic History.

Neither are the other forms of Islamic terrorist groups which have plagued the world since the late 1960s when Palestinian secular movements such as Al Fatah and the Popular Front for the Liberation of Palestine (PFLP) began to target civilians outside the immediate arena of conflict. These were self-proclaimed secular groups. As pointed out by Rand's Bruce Hoffman, in 1980 two out of 64 groups were categorized as largely religious in motivation; in 1995 almost half of the identified groups, 26 out of 56, were classified as religiously motivated; the majority of these espoused Islam as their guiding force.

Political versus Fundamentalist Islam

Political Islam, as opposed to fundamentalist or neo-fundamentalist Islam, posits a worldview that can deal with and selectively integrate modernity. In contrast, fundamentalist Islam calls for a return to an ontological form of Islam that rejects modernity; groups such as ISIS, Al Qaeda and the Egyptian Islamic Jihad are representative of fundamentalist Islam.[ii]

A Note on State Sponsors of Religious Terror Groups

Unlike the "secular" national, radical, anarchist terrorism which have been sponsored by states such as Libya, Syria, Iraq, Cuba, North Korea, and behind the scenes by the former Soviet camp, most of the religious Islamic terrorist groups have never been sponsored by states. Many Egyptian organizations emerged from the Egyptian domestic landscape. Algerian groups likewise were not sponsored by foreign states. Hezbollah certainly can be viewed as an Iranian surrogate, but other movements, while open to state assistance, remain operationally and ideologically independent. ISIS is different in that it has declared itself to be a state.[iii]

This brings us to the willful disregard of easily accessible knowledge which brings all of our political and cultural leaders to constantly say:

- That the forces of ISIS and other Islamic terrorist organizations are not Islamic.
- That these groups have somehow hijacked Islam or that they are merely criminals hiding behind Islamic names and slogans.

For one thing who are we to judge another's faith? If someone says they are followers of Muhammed who are we to say they aren't? If someone says they are doing their best to live by their interpretation of the Koran who are we to say they aren't?

This is one of the reasons it is so hard to get even the most "moderate" of Muslims to denounce ISIS and the other Islamic Terror organizations. Even if they personally disagree with their theology and their methods there is enough in their declarations of faith that align with traditional strains of Islam. It would be like a Catholic saying a Pentecostal isn't a Christian because they have differing views of the actions of the Holy Spirit in the modern day.

This refusal to admit the Islamic nature of these groups disarms the West. We cannot understand what they want, what they do, or why they have such a strong hold on the lives of so many. Another aspect of our official blindness that prevents us from confronting this clash of civilizations appropriately is the oft repeated mantra that those Muslims who support the radicals is a tiny group, often mentioned at 1%. We are also reminded often that

1.6 billion people make up the Muslim world. If this second figure is correct the tiny minority of the first figure translates to 16 million people.

Sixteen million people[iv] willing to fight to the death, blow themselves up, or financially support them is larger than any army ever fielded by Hitler, Mussolini, Tojo, or Stalin. Obviously this is a threat that should be taken seriously. It should not be dismissed by ignoring what they say about themselves. Imagine if the leaders of the western democracies had bothered to read Hitler's Mein Kampf and believe that he meant what he said. They could have stopped him when he marched into the Rhineland with no trouble whatsoever. Instead they ignored what he said and fifty million people paid with their lives.

Today we stand in a similar place. We ignored Osama Bin Laden when he declared war on America[v] in 1988 and 1996 with disastrous consequences. Now we are ignoring the inherent attraction of those who claim the Islamic world as their own when we say they are not motivated by their religion. It strips us of the ability to understand them, their objectives, their appeal, and their tactics.

Another disservice our leaders are foisting on us is the other mantra of their secular religion that Islam is a religion of peace. This flies in the face of historical reality. Islam did not initially spread as Christianity did by the power of its message and the blood of its martyrs. Islam spread as a conquering religion.[vi] Muhammed conquered[vii] Medina and Mecca, forced unity on the disparate Arab tribes before bursting forth from the Arabian Peninsula and spreading through military conquest and forcible conversions.

Rod Dreher in the American Conservative has done a masterful job of asking two important questions, "Is ISIS Islamic? How would we know?" [viii] Much of what follows is excerpted from his penetrating analysis.

To take one example:[ix] In September, Sheikh Abu Muhammad al-Adnani, the Islamic State's chief spokesman, called on Muslims in Western countries such as France and Canada to find an infidel and "smash his head with a rock," poison him, run him over with a car, or "destroy his crops." To Western ears, the biblical-sounding punishments—the stoning and crop destruction—juxtaposed strangely with his more modern-sounding call to vehicular homicide. As if to show that he could terrorize by imagery alone, Adnani also referred to Secretary of State John Kerry as an "uncircumcised geezer."

Adnani was not merely talking trash.[x] His speech was laced with theological and legal discussion. His exhortation to attack crops directly echoed orders from Muhammed[xi] to leave well water and crops alone—unless the armies of Islam were in a defensive position, in which case Muslims in the lands of Kuffar, or infidels, should be unmerciful, and poison away.

The reality is that the Islamic State is Islamic.[xii] Yes, it has attracted psychopaths and adventure seekers drawn largely from the disaffected populations of the Middle East and Europe. But the religion preached by its most ardent followers derives from coherent and even learned interpretations of Islam.

Virtually every major decision and law[xiii] promulgated by the Islamic State adheres to what it calls, in its press and pronouncements and on its billboards, license plates, stationery, and coins, "the prophetic methodology,"[xiv] which means following the prophecy and example of Muhammad in punctilious detail. Muslims can reject the Islamic State; nearly all do. But pretending that it isn't actually a religious, millenarian group, with theology that must be understood to be combatted, has already led the United States to underestimate it and back foolish schemes to counter it. We'll need to get acquainted with the Islamic State's intellectual genealogy if we are to react in a way that will not strengthen it, but instead help it self-immolate in its own excessive zeal.

Princeton scholar Bernard Haykel contends[xv] that the ranks of the Islamic State are deeply infused with religious vigor. Of partial Lebanese descent, Haykel grew up in Lebanon and the United States. Haykel regards[xvi] the claim that the Islamic State has distorted the texts of Islam as preposterous and sustainable only through willful ignorance. "People want to absolve Islam," he said.[xvii] According to Professor Haykel, "It's this 'Islam is a religion of peace' mantra. As if there is such a thing as 'Islam'! It's what Muslims do, and how they interpret their texts."[xviii] Those texts are shared by all Sunni Muslims, not just the Islamic State. "And these guys have just as much legitimacy as anyone else"[xix] Haykel.

In Haykel's estimation,[xx] the fighters of the Islamic State are authentic throwbacks to early Islam and are faithfully reproducing its norms of war. This behavior includes a number of practices that modern Muslims tend to prefer not to acknowledge as integral to their sacred texts. "Slavery, crucifixion, and beheadings are not something that freakish [jihadists] are cherry-picking from the medieval tradition,"[xxi] Haykel said. Islamic State fighters "are smack in the middle of the medieval tradition and are bringing it wholesale into the present day"[xxii] says Haykel.

According to one thought passed along by Rod Dreher what we call "Islamic fundamentalism" or "Islamic extremism" is so hard to defeat because it is so clearly rooted in Islamic history and Scripture. To tell the followers of ISIS that they are "un-Islamic" in their practices when they are doing, or trying to do, exactly as the Prophet and his early followers did, is a hard sell to fellow Muslims. It is also the kind of self-imposed blindness that stops us from effectively knowing what we are dealing with.[xxiii]

If we ignore what we know due to political correctness how will it ever be possible to do what needs to be done? If we refuse to name something does that mean it isn't what it claims to be? A rose by any other name would smell as sweet, and an Islamic Fundamentalist is a follower of Muhammad no matter what we say or how we say it. There are none so blind as those who will not see, and when the blind follow the blind they both end up in the ditch.

Dispatch Four

Don't Tell Someone Else

I'm thinking about changing my economic strategy. My parents were raised in the Roosevelt Depression and they taught me to work hard, save money, and pay for what I wanted. I was a deficit hawk when being a deficit hawk wasn't cool' Now that it isn't even an option why should I stay at the party when there's no one left to dance with?

In our new Omerica I think I'll join the winning side and try spending more than I make every day for the rest of my life and see how that works out. If I can just manage to get to where I owe so much that I'm too big to fail I can start really living large on federal handouts, excuse me bailouts, excuse me stimulus. Won't that be sweet? I'll hold seminars on "How to Borrow Your Way to Wealth," or "If You'll Take a Check I'll Take Two Please." What a great racket, excuse me scheme, excuse me program. And technically it's not a shell game if you don't use shells.

According to a USA Today study back in 2009 at the beginning of the present Imperial Presidency American taxpayers assumed an additional $55,000 per household for federal spending and promises in the just the last 12 months of the Bush Debacle. That represents a 12% increase in the deficient just in George II's final year in office and the media tells us he's a conservative.[xxiv] Of course he's the kind of conservative who can also use modern double-speak. I think this one should be above the door to his multi-million dollar presidential library down in Dallas, "I've abandoned free-market principles to save the free-market system"[xxv] This spending spree raised the per household federal debt to $546,668 which is four times the average personal debt for all mortgages, car loans, credit cards combined. Instead of "Don't Tread on ME" perhaps we should have flags that proclaim, "Send Me the Stuff and Send the Bill to Someone Else"

Don't tell Someone Else but this means our runaway government assumed a staggering $6.8 trillion in new obligations during the government created crash of 2008 alone. Then along came Obama. His explosion of excess when added to the creatively hidden realities of the federal entitlement programs brings poor old Someone Else's debt load (including unfunded liabilities) to the incomprehensible total over 100 trillion. That's trillion with a "T."[xxvi]

Some might say, "Wait a minute! This guy is way over board! Our national debt is *only* 19 trillion and change." I wish I could convince myself it was only $18 trillion that would help me sleep at night. However, government books are so over-cooked they make Enron and

WorldCom look as honest as the day is long. The real number doesn't just cover what we've borrowed so far but what we've promised to pay in the future minus what we might conceivably raise to offset future borrowing. When you lump that all together you end up with the $1oo trillion or some other such ridiculous number.[xxvii]

At least we can tell Someone Else that all this national shopaholicism isn't being wasted buying $7,000 toilet seats and $800 hammers its buying things we really need. Remember the stimulus, the one that ended the Great Recession? It paid for such needed items as: $97 million for a program that was already cancelled at Los Alamos National Laboratory. In the interests of national defense our government decided to replace old nuclear warheads with new ones. The rocket-scientists in the planning department said they needed two new buildings to produce the necessary plutonium components. Then the program was cancelled.

Never fear government is here and when has the lack of common sense ever gotten in the way of a good boondoggle? Along came our earmark-free stimulus and the $97 Million enters stage-left. Now that the money was there of course we had to spend it otherwise who would get stimulated. So the construction continued for buildings that were no longer needed. At least all these shovel-ready jobs have the economy purring along like a well-oiled machine even if they weren't as shovel-ready as our Dear Leader thought.

Remember the GM Bailout? Now there was a deal that just couldn't lose.   It inspired the following joke.

A man walks into a bank to open a checking account the teller says, "I have good news and bad news." The man asks, "What's the good news?" The teller says, "When you open an account with us you can have either a new toaster or 1000 shares of GM stock." "What's the bad news?" "We're all out of toasters." No one would buy GM stock which is why it fell to the 1$ range and our Glorious Leader decided to spend money that was authorized under TARP to buy up toxic assets to instead buy GM. So out comes Uncle Sugar's checkbook and out goes billions of Someone Else's money to buy the majority share in a company that was estimated to turn a profit when?

How could this ever fail? It turned out after all the celebrations of success that Someone Else lost $11.2 billion on that deal.[xxviii] And how is the resurrected auto giant? In 2014 GM recalled more cars than they made[xxix] and while they are closing plants in America they are building them overseas.[xxx]

What dolts we were working and saving when all you have to do is want something, charge it to Someone Else and shazam you get the stuff and Someone Else gets the bill. That Someone Else sure is a generous person aren't they? There's only one problem with this perpetual-motion money machine. When you look in the mirror Someone Else is looking back.

Dispatch Five

Down the Memory Hole

How can we possibly know the motive of the perpetrator of the Orlando Massacre? It is a mystery to the President, the Attorney General, his whole administration, and their cheerleaders in the Corporations Once Known as the Mainstream Media. Forget that the killer called 911 and pledged allegiance to ISIS. This has been redacted from the government transcripts so it has been effectively dropped down the Memory Hole. Forget that according to survivors he was shouting Allah Akbar as he shot his victims. Forget that while he was in the midst of his killing spree he logged into Facebook and pledged his loyalty to ISIS and threatened more attacks on the civilized world. How can we possibly know what his motive was?

If political correctness and the playbook of the Progressives stop us from accepting the evidence of reality which floods our vision we have become the object of the old saying, "There are none so blind as those who will not see."

Our Dear Leader and his minions refuse to label our enemy. It did not start with them. After 9-11 George II declared war on terror instead of declaring war on Radical Islamic Terrorists. It made me wonder at the time why on December 8, 1941 we didn't declare war on sneak attacks? BHO goes on and on lecturing us that what we call something doesn't mean anything. If what we call our enemy doesn't matter than why does the Obama regime insist on calling them ISIL instead of calling them ISIS as everyone else in the English speaking world does?

Instead of having enough respect for the victims, survivors, and their families to actually address who killed and wounded our fellow citizens or how to actually prevent such horrific incidents in the future the Progressives turned the whole Orlando terrorist attack into a platform for their own agenda of nullifying the Second Amendment.

Instead of focusing on the danger of radicalized Muslims who want to strike a blow for their Caliph let's focus our sights instead on banning the AR-15 even though the shooter didn't use an AR-15. If as the President says more people die in bathtubs die in bathtubs than they do in terrorist attacks why don't we ban bathtubs?[xxxi]

How to explain these misconnects between reality and the relentless long march the Progressives have orchestrated from a free republic to central government leviathan. From a nation of laws based upon a constitution carved in stone to a nation based on men with a living document written in the sand. The Progressives have systematically used education, media, and the courts to indoctrinate, cajole, and hijack the people into accepting a truncated vision of the Constitution. It was written to secure the rights of the people and to limit the power of the central government. Just look at a few comments by our Founders and framers with regard to the Second Amendment: "What is the militia? It is the whole people except for few public officials." And "To disarm the people is the best and most efficient way to enslave them," George Mason, Father of the Bill of Rights.[xxxii] "Laws that forbid the carrying of arms ... disarm only those who are neither inclined nor determined to commit crimes ... Such laws make things worse for the assaulted and better for the assailants; they serve rather to encourage than to prevent homicides, for an unarmed man may be attacked with greater confidence than an armed man" From Thomas Jefferson's Commonplace Book.[xxxiii]

What did the early courts have to say: "The right of a citizen to keep and bear arms has justly been considered the palladium of the liberties of the republic, since it offers a strong moral check against the usurpation and arbitrary power of rulers, and will generally, even if they are successful in the first instance, enable the people to resist and triumph over them." Joseph Story U.S. Supreme Court Justice 1833.[xxxiv]

From these monuments to freedom in a by-gone era our free republic has progressed or devolved into this centrally-planned politically correct social democratic republic sliding down the chute into the dust bin of History. In politics perception is reality and as Lenin said, "A lie told often enough becomes the truth." Keeping this in mind we can look at a killer who adamantly and repeatedly tells us exactly why he committed his crimes and we shouldn't be surprised when our leaders and their propaganda media arm tell us over and over there is no way we can know his motives. Truth has fallen down the memory hole.

We are a conquered and occupied nation. We just don't know it yet.

So what can we do?

Keep the faith. Keep the peace. We shall overcome.

Dispatch Six

Good Bye America It Was Good to Know You

It used to be that as one grew older their experience developed wisdom that could help guide succeeding generations. Today the world moves too fast. In some ways my 10 year old granddaughter knows more intuitively about computers than I do after working online since there was an online.

My father grew up plowing with mules as had his father and his grandfather and so on back to houses with no floors, no running water and no electricity. While they had passed wisdom down for uncounted generations what they had to say to the flower children of America's prosperity seemed hopelessly out of date just as what we have to say to the children of the Millennials seems like gibberish from the dark Ages.

One thing however remained a constant. We were all Americans. We all believed in the Land of the Free and the Home of the Brave. We not only expected our freedoms we came to take our heritage for granted. Today most people can tell you more about their local sports teams than they can about their government or the History of America. None of us gets the luxury of living in the country we grew up in yet in the past we could at least look forward to living in one that shared the same values and generally the same goals.

Today as our values swirl the drain and our goals have morphed from freedom to free access to government largess we are staring into the maw of an existential crisis that threatens to leave our children with the proverbial bowl of pottage for which we traded their future.

What is this issue that dramatically portends the ultimate doom of the America in which most of us grew up? As a British politician once said, "Demographics is destiny." [xxxv]

It used to be if the politicians were out of step with the voters the voters threw them out at the next election. Now our politicians have decided to import new voters who will support them and submerge us.

Just when you thought we were safe from the latest version of the Children's Crusade there is another surge of unaccompanied minors breaking on our borders like a tsunami. The second wave of unaccompanied illegal immigrant children has begun, with more than 3,000 of them surging across the Mexican border into the U.S. last month — the highest rate since the peak of last summer's crisis and a warning that another rough season could be ahead.

Immigration officials warned that they expected another surge as the weather improved. Although the numbers are down some 40 percent compared with last year's frenetic pace that sparked a political crisis for the Obama administration, fiscal year 2015 is shaping up to mark the second-biggest surge on record.

If this sounds ominous for us, never fear our ever vigilant Big Brother has a solution. Why don't we just spring for a free flight, education, health care and food stamps ad infinitum?

To facilitate the often treacherous process of entering the United States illegally through the southern border, the Obama administration is offering free transportation from three Central American countries and a special refugee/parole program with "resettlement assistance" and permanent residency.

Under the new initiative the administration has re-branded the official name it originally assigned to the droves of illegal immigrant minors who continue sneaking into the U.S. They're no longer known as Unaccompanied Alien Children (UAC), a term that evidently was offensive and not politically correct enough for the powerful open borders movement. The new arrivals will be officially known as Central American Minors (CAM) and they will be eligible for a special refugee/parole that offers a free one-way flight to the U.S. from El Salvador, Guatemala or Honduras. The project is a joint venture between the

Department of Homeland Security (DHS) and the State Department.

Specifically, the "program provides certain children in El Salvador, Guatemala and Honduras with a safe, legal, and orderly alternative to the dangerous journey that some children are undertaking to the United States," according to a DHS memo obtained by Judicial Watch this week. The document goes on to say that the CAM program has started accepting applications from "qualifying parents" to bring their offspring under the age of 21 from El Salvador, Guatemala or Honduras. The candidates will then be granted a special refugee parole, which includes many taxpayer-funded perks and benefits. Among them is a free education, food stamps, medical care and living expenses.[xxxvi]

I often wonder since we cannot know who or where the illegals are off in the shadows how do conveniently locate them to apply for programs, give interviews, attend inaugurations, or do anything else. Then again they do gather in large numbers to demonstrate for more rights. You would think the TV lights would at least brighten up the shadows a little bit.

Since it wouldn't be sporting to have so many people living, eating and breeding in America and not allow them to vote our visionary masters have that one figured out as well.

New York City is routinely described as a "global hub", a place so thoroughly penetrated by international capital and migration that it seems at once within and without the United States. It is the center of American commerce and media, but its politics, demographics and worldly outlook make the Big Apple an outlier.

New York may be about to become even more distinct. The left-leaning New York City council is currently drafting legislation that would allow all legal residents, regardless of citizenship, the right to vote in city elections. If the measure passes into law, it would mark a major victory for a voting rights campaign that seeks to enfranchise non-citizen voters in local elections across the country. A few towns already permit non-citizen residents to vote locally, but New York City would be by far the largest jurisdiction to do so.

Under the likely terms of the legislation, legally documented residents who have lived in New York City for at least six months will be able to vote in municipal elections. Reports suggest that the city council is discussing the legislation with Mayor Bill de Blasio's office, and that a bill might be introduced as soon as this spring.

While the legislation stands a good chance of sailing through the council and even winning the approval of the mayor, the prospect of New York City enfranchising its residents has stoked controversy. Many Americans find the idea of non-citizen voting entirely unpalatable and fear that it undermines the sanctity and privilege of citizenship.

Advocates for non-citizen voting in New York City argue that it would right a glaring wrong. Invoking the ancient American battle cry of "no taxation without representation", they point to the enormous numbers of non-citizen residents who pay taxes, send their children to public schools, are active members of their communities, but have no say in local elections. This could add up to as many as one million voters.

Let's see no voter ID allowed. No purging of dead people from the voter lists allowed. Non-citizens voting is allowed can illegal alien voting be far behind? Of course they would never be allowed to vote in a presidential election, no how no way…..;--)

And how are they supposed to get to the welfare office, the emergency room or the post office to pick up their check from the IRS for not paying taxes (Earned Income Tax Credit) without a driver's license? Oh wait the America Last crowd has a fix for that too.

A surge of undocumented immigrants seeking driver's licenses has surprised the California Department of Motor Vehicles, pouring in at twice the rate officials expected and underscoring massive interest in the new program.

Just three months after driver's licenses became available to immigrants living in California illegally,[xxxvii] the product of legislation advocates had pursued fruitlessly for years before prevailing and passing Assembly Bill 60 in 2013, 493,998 have sought licenses. The number has surprised officials who spent months bracing for an influx of new customers by hiring staff, opening new DMV offices and extending hours.

"The interest in this program is far greater than anyone anticipated," DMV Director Jean Shiomoto said in a statement.[xxxviii]

In preparing to offer the new licenses, the DMV estimated that about 1.4 million immigrants would apply over the course of three years. The new figures show they have handled one-third of that expected total in three months, a rate double what the DMV expected, although the official estimate of the total number of eligible applicants remains the same. About 203,000 people have received licenses.

Following the trail to the Fundamentally Transformed Amerika of course brings us proudly to motor-voter, that legacy from the Clinton administration, another gift that just keeps on giving.

Local and state government officials are registering non-U.S. citizens as valid voters — even when the non-citizens say they are not Americans on their voter registration forms, a former Justice Department attorney tells The Daily Caller.[xxxix]

J. Christian Adams, a former United States Department of Justice official in the Civil Rights Division will show the Supreme Court in a brief later this month that non-citizens are registering to vote through the government's motor voter program. The motor voter act became law during the Clinton administration as an easier way to register voters through their local Department of Motor Vehicles offices, but Adams says the program is failing to weed out those who are not American citizens.

At least our educational system will teach our children what America is all about? They will instill in them a decent appreciation for our system, our History and our values.

Oh wait a minute the Denver Public School system is allowing immigrants who have resided illegally in the United States since they were children to teach in its classrooms under a relaxed employment policy advanced by the Obama administration, district officials said this week.[xl]

Denver has hired teachers in the program as part of its participation with Teach for America, which places teachers in low-income schools, many of whom are recent college graduates without a background in education.

Fred Elbel, director of the Colorado Alliance for Immigration Reform, an organization that opposes granting any type of legal status to such immigrants, criticized the program.

"There are at least 20 million Americans who either do not have a full-time job or are underemployed. This includes teachers," he said. "It is unlikely that most of the illegal aliens with (DACA) status are trained, qualified and certified as educators."

So if the illegals are teaching our children what do you think they learn about illegal immigration? Oh excuse me I mean Undocumented Voters.

Now that I think about it the status for some of our visitors is changing. These aren't illegal aliens they are refugees. This gives them a special status according to our blue helmeted world government over at the U.N.

Take New Hampshire as an example. The number of refugees arriving annually in New Hampshire has waned in recent years, down from a peak of 559 in 2009 to 345 in 2014. However, those numbers represent a small fraction of the total number of refugees resettled nationally. During the last fiscal year, for example, 7,214 refugees arrived in Texas, 6,108 in California, 4,082 in New York, 4,006 in Michigan and 1,941 in Massachusetts. Connecticut and Maine resettled slightly more than New Hampshire; Vermont and Rhode Island resettled slightly fewer.

What rights are we obligated by the U.N. to provide our reclassified visitors? It can't be much right? Here is the official list from the Study Guide of the Rights of Refugees:

Articles 12 - 30 of the Refugee Convention set out the rights which individuals are entitled to once they have been recognized as Convention refugees:

- All refugees must be granted identity papers and travel documents that allow them to travel outside the country
- Refugees must receive *the same treatment as nationals of the receiving country* with regard to the following rights:
    - Free exercise of religion and religious education
    - Free access to the courts, including legal assistance
    - Access to elementary education
    - Access to public relief and assistance
    - Protection provided by social security
    - Protection of intellectual property, such as inventions and trade names
    - Protection of literary, artistic and scientific work
    - Equal treatment by taxing authorities

- Refugees must receive *the most favorable treatment provided to nationals of a foreign country* with regard to the following rights:
    - The right to belong to trade unions
    - The right to belong to other non-political nonprofit organizations
    - The right to engage in wage-earning employment
- Refugees must receive *the most favorable treatment possible, which must be at least as favorable to that accorded aliens generally in the same circumstances,* with regard to the following rights:
    - The right to own property
    - The right to practice a profession
    - The right to self-employment
    - Access to housing
    - Access to higher education
- Refugees must receive *the same treatment as that accorded to aliens generally* with regard to the following rights:
    - The right to choose their place of residence
    - The right to move freely within the country
    - Free exercise of religion and religious education

- Free access to the courts, including legal assistance
- Access to elementary education
- Access to public relief and assistance
- Protection provided by social security
- Protection of intellectual property, such as inventions and trade names
- Protection of literary, artistic and scientific work
- Equal treatment by taxing authorities[xli]

Being a nation of immigrants I am sure the average American is totally on board with these policies. Maybe not, despite President Obama's efforts to cool the nation's views on illegal immigrants storming over the U.S.-Mexico border, Americans have reached a new level of anger over the issue, with most demanding a more aggressive deportation policy and reversal of an interpretation of the 14th Amendment that currently grants citizenship to kids of illegals born in the U.S.

A new Rasmussen Reports survey released Monday also finds Americans questioning spending tax dollars on government aid provided to illegal immigrants. A huge 83 percent said that anybody should be required to prove that they are "legally allowed" to be in the country before receiving local, state or federal government services.[xlii]

Overall, the poll is bad news for the White House because it shows sustained, and in some cases, elevated anger and frustration over the surge in undocumented immigrants in the United States. For example, 62 percent told the pollster that the U.S. is "not aggressive enough" in deporting those illegally in the United States. Just 15 percent believed the administration's current policy was "about right" and 16 percent said it was "too aggressive."

That 62 percent number is a jump from a year ago when it was 52 percent.

When asked if the baby of an illegal born in the United States should automatically become a U.S. citizen, as is now the law, 54 percent said no versus 38 percent who said yes.

In another area that seems to test American patience with the administration, 51 percent said that illegal immigrants who have American born children should not be exempt from deportation.

No matter how the haters try to stop it at least this tidal wave drowning America in the third world is all being done legally, or is it?

Take the celebrated case of a Federal Judge trying to staunch the flow down in Texas. President Obama's new deportation amnesty will remain halted, a federal judge in Texas ruled Tuesday night in an order that also delivered a judicial spanking to the President's lawyers for misleading the court.

Judge Andrew S. Hanen, who first halted the amnesty in February, just two days before it was to take effect, said he's even more convinced of his decision now, particularly after Mr. Obama earlier this year said he intends for his policies to supersede federal laws.

Judge Hanen pointed to Mr. Obama's comments at a February town hall when the President warned immigration agents to adhere to his policies or else face "consequences."

"In summary, the chief executive has ordered that the laws requiring removal of illegal immigrants that conflict with the 2014 DHS directive are not to be enforced, and that anyone who attempts to do so will be punished," Judge Hanen wrote.[xliii]

"This is not merely ineffective enforcement. This is total non-enforcement," the judge continued, saying that Mr. Obama's own descriptions of how he is carrying out his policies have hurt his case.[xliv]

Mr. Obama in November announced a new amnesty for illegal immigrant parents whose children are either U.S. citizens or legal permanent residents. The amnesty could apply to as many as 5 million illegal immigrants.

Texas and 25 other states sued to stop Mr. Obama, and Judge Hanen sided with them, finding that they suffered an economic harm from the policy, granting them standing in court, and then finding that the President broke the law in bypassing Congress to announce his policy.

The administration has appealed Judge Hanen's ruling, but also asked the judge to reconsider.

On Tuesday the judge not only refused to reconsider, but also said the administration misled him when it said no part of the amnesty had been implemented, and the lawyers bungled their attempt to try to repair the damage by filing an "advisory" with the judge early last month.[xlv]

Since November, the administration had been granting a three-year amnesty to illegal immigrant Dreamers under the new policy. That's a year longer than the two-year program Mr. Obama announced for the Dreamers in 2012.

More than 100,000 applications were approved for the three-year amnesty between Nov. 21 and the February date when Judge Hanen halted the program.

"Whether by ignorance, omission, purposeful misdirection, or because they were misled by their clients, the attorneys for the government misrepresented the facts,"[xlvi] the judge said, adding that he was stunned the government waited for two more weeks after his ruling to inform him that the applications had already been processed. In addition, the DHS broke the judge's order moving forward in approving amnesty applications despite injunction Texas argues that had it known applications were being processed, it would have taken extra legal steps to try to halt the program earlier.

Judge Hanen said he may still issue sanctions against the government for misleading him though he declined to strike the government's pleadings, which would have essentially closed the case and granted victory to Texas.[xlvii]

The judge said that while that may be warranted, it would do a disservice to the weighty issues at stake in the case, including fundamental issues of presidential power.[xlviii]

What about that passport to everything else a legal Social Security number? That has to be well regulated to make sure none of our uninvited guests can gain unfettered access to the entire social network we have built and paid for, doesn't it?[xlix]

The Obama administration has issued more than half a million new Social Security Numbers (SSN) to illegal immigrants granted amnesty under President Obama's Deferred Actions for Childhood Arrivals program.[l]

In a letter to Sens. Sen. Jeff Sessions (R-AL) and Ben Sasse (R-NE), exclusively obtained by Breitbart News, the Social Security Administration (SSA) reveals that by the end of Fiscal Year 2014 the Obama administration "had issued approximately 541,000 original SSNs to individuals authorized to work under the 2012 Deferred Action for Childhood Arrivals (DACA) policy since its inception" in 2012.[li]

What do we face in America today?

- A government dedicated to importing enough voters to achieve unassailable dominance.
- A government that is out of control, ignoring laws and trampling on the rights of its own citizens in favor of those who have crashed the gate.
- If the Constitution was established to guarantee Americans a limited government what can we say except that at this moment in American History the Constitution Failed.

Looking at the sad state of our Republic about all I have left to say is, "Good bye America it was good to know you."

Dispatch Seven

Happy Days Are Here Again Again

So long sad times
Go long bad times
We are rid of you at last

Howdy gay times
Cloudy gray times
You are now a thing of the past

Happy days are here again
The skies above are clear again
So let's sing a song of cheer again
Happy days are here again

Can you believe it the Bush recession has been over for more than five years. According to the government figures unemployment is down.[lii] As a matter of fact according to the Progressive Project President Obama has brought America sixty one straight months of booming economic growth and full employment.[liii] According to our Progressive leaders this is the greatest recovery and the strongest boom in American History.[liv] Just look with only billions upon billions of new fiat money each month for sixty one months the stock market is up, and everything is coming up roses.[lv] There is a flat screen on every wall, a smart phone in every hand, and flying cars just can't be that far away. Why, the economy is doing so good that twenty somethings are retiring at twenty-two to Mom's basement and living the high life.

The Bush wars in Iraq and Afghanistan have either been won or soon will be or as the winning slogan said, "GM is alive and Osama Bin Laden is dead." The Arab Spring has toppled tyrants and the glorious leading from behind of the administration's foreign policy savants has ricocheted from the faculty lounge to the UN. Doesn't it just feel like another American Century?

The Fed keeps pumping and the Big Board keeps jumping. The NSA watches us all without a warrant, and the man who tells us about it is a traitor. Congress has to sue the President in an attempt to get him to enforce laws unless of course he wants to change a law unilaterally. The Court strikes down unconstitutional move after unconstitutional move by the adjunct instructor in the Oval Office. Yet he continues to issue decree after decree with the force of law.[lvi] The IRS is used to suppress the votes of Conservatives, its leaders either lying to Congress or pleading the Fifth while Attorney General Holder refused to appoint a special prosecutor just as he refused in Fast and Furious and Benghazi. Of course if you want to require a photo id to vote you're a racist attempting to suppress the vote while you need a photo ID to get into the DNC. There's nothing to see here so move along.

Common Core is poised to take our educational system to higher heights. After more than 100 years of Progressive Education and generations of Federal intrusions into local school boards America now successfully spends more per capita on education than any other country. The self-esteem of our students ranks as the highest in the world even as our grades slide. In other words our students are doing poorly, but they think they are doing well.

It reminds me of a foreman in a factory who was in one of my management classes. He shared an incident in his shop. A young man was hired as a material handler who wore his pants down around his knees. He constantly had to use one hand to hold up his pants while using the free hand to handle material. When the foreman asked him, "Don't you think you could get more done if you used both hands?" the young man answered, "No I'm doing all right." The job may not get done but at least he feels good about what he's doing. Is this the American Way in the New Normal?

Russia swallows Crimea, China launches its first aircraft carrier and starts building a second while creating islands out of nothing and claiming the entire South China Sea, the Islamic State declares itself to be the Caliphate some of us were thought crazy to predict. Oh Happy Day! Once again America is respected in the world after that cowboy Bush brought us so low. Reagan said it was once again Morning in America and now we have Mourning in America as the fruit of Progressive policies, and cum bi ya diplomacy leads us from crisis to crisis. Then again we should never let a good crisis go to waste said President Obama's first Chief of Staff before heading to Chicago to strengthen the gun laws.

Looking forward there is good news and bad news. The good news is that thanks to that paragon of progressivism, FDR, there are term limits on the presidency. The bad news is our southern sieve and the import-a-voter program brings in thousands of undocumented democrats everyday as Flat Broke Hillary and the transition team waits in the wings with self-proclaimed Native American Elizabeth Warren as an understudy.

I used to say, "We made it through the Second World War, and we can make it through Bill Clinton." Then I said, "We made it through the Cold War we can make it through Bush the Younger." Now I wonder, "If we threw away Iraq and we're about to throw away Afghanistan, Texas, New Mexico, and Arizona how will we survive another year of rule by decree with a Republican Congress that has gone over to the dark side?"

We may not be in Kansas anymore and we may have followed the white rabbit through the looking glass but at least illegal immigrants can now get driver's licenses in California, Colorado, Connecticut, Illinois, Maryland, Nevada, New Mexico, Utah, Vermont, and Washington, as well as Washington, D.C. These states are estimated to have an illegal immigrant population of 4,120,000 combined. Can anyone say "Motor Voter" or coming to a neighborhood near you soon. How can this ever go wrong with millions of undocumented Democrats and Hillary, or as I like to call her, "The Nail in Our Coffin" and the Predator-in-Chief ready to turn the White House into a Gentleman's Club.

Altogether shout it now
There's no one
Who can doubt it now

Then Came Trump

So let's tell the world about it now
Happy days are here again

Your cares and troubles are gone
There'll be no more from now on

Happy days are here again
The skies above are clear again
So, Let's sing a song of cheer again

Happy times
Happy nights
Happy days
Are here again! Again!!

Just in case you hadn't noticed.

Dispatch Eight

History is The Story of Life

The older we get the more of our lives become History. Perhaps that is why it slowly eventually becomes interesting to many people; we can remember so much more of it. The future slides into the present. The present slides into the past. Our lives are the history of the future.

The average American has no Historical perspective. To most people History began the day they were born and it will end when they do. Without a historical perspective we live constantly in an ever progressing NOW and now can always be shaped and molded by whoever has the loudest megaphone at the moment. This puts the lives of the low information citizen in the hands of the establishment and their media mouthpieces.

So many students say, "History is boring, just names and dates" yet if History is boring than so is life, because History is the story of life. It is nothing more or less than the accumulated stories of the lives of people just like us who have lived at different times in what might as well have been different worlds.

These different worlds are the scaffold upon which our own world exists and if we ignore the framework that holds us up we imagine that we are afloat on a sea of forgetfulness beginning each epoch with no guidance from the collected wisdom of those who have gone before. And if we choose ignorance as our starting point can we wonder what will be our end?

What passes for education today doesn't help much, and in many ways it just muddies the water. The History we are taught in secondary school is often sugar coated or slanted through the eyes and opinions of someone who has been run through the progressive stamping plant that is contemporary teacher training. Either we get an uncritical, "America right or wrong!" or "America's always wrong!" depending on the slant of the education bureaucracy in the area.

After decades of teaching History to America's best and brightest I have sadly come to the conclusion that as time goes by people not only know less and less about History but also what they do know isn't so. It is only when we start to look at alternative views that we find there has always been a great debate as to what happened, how it happened, why it happened, and what it all means. To most of the snowflake generation and even to those older who have swilled the progressive kool-aide it is a micro aggression to try to expose them to anything that contradicts or even conflicts with the mantra of Al Gore's man-made global warming cult or the anti-colonial views of the Obama zombies. Yet it is these alternative views that make History expansive, exciting, interesting, and informative. Without them it isn't education it is indoctrination.

Every society and culture has always taught what might be called a glorified History that explains why they exist and should exist as a distinct group. When a country stops teaching this to their young in a few generations it is hard for the people to justify in their own minds why they are who they are and why they should continue to be a distinct people. This leads inevitably to a crisis that usually portends the end. Things are being left out of our History books, purged you might say. What isn't remembered will be forgotten. That which is not written, is not preserved, passed down or remembered is the dust in the dustbin of History.

History is the best opportunity we have to learn from the mistakes of others. If we ignore these or we never learn of them we face the inevitable reality of repeating these mistakes over and over.

A case in point:

The socialist economics of the USSR and the inefficiencies it caused brought about the implosion of the Soviet empire. After that fall America rushed headlong into socialism itself. After almost 50 years of resisting communism, spending trillions of dollars and hundreds of thousands of lives lost or destroyed how did Americans fall for the siren song of, "From each according to his ability to each according to his need"? How did the Cold Warriors morph into interchangeable drones, cogs in a socialist utopian pyramid scheme? They didn't realize the snake oil the Progressives were selling was the same thing all the other socialists have been selling since the 19th century. They couldn't see that the hell holes of Cuba and Venezuela are the inevitable result of collectivism carried to its predictable dead end. They had no historical perspective.

Having followed the hope and change of the pied piper Barack Obama, America is teetering on the edge of the abyss. If enough of our fellow citizens bolstered by the best imported voters available and all the dead people in Chicago give Hillary and the Clinton crime family another shot at plundering this country we may well topple over following Rome and Britain into that aforementioned dust bin of History.

It may just be a matter of time until we join the Soviets on the trash heap of History. I remember that we woke up one morning and the USSR was arguably the strongest nation on earth and unarguably the largest, and by the time we went to bed it had disappeared. Since then we have worked hard to limit competition and extend benefits while our self-satisfaction has risen everything else is in decline. Maybe what we need is some Glasnost and Perestroika?

We can't know what we don't know but we can know that we don't know. I first discovered History when I was nine years old, and I realized I didn't know what had happened in the world before I had arrived. I set off on a journey that has now lasted fifty-eight years. I read and study History on a daily basis. I look for perspectives that may not match my own. I try to extend my understanding by looking at the world from many different viewpoints, and often I find that what I thought yesterday isn't what I think today. Not that History has changed, but my understanding of it has. And with this evolving understanding comes new ways to move through this puzzle factory we call life.

I heartily recommend anyone who wants to make it through the maze and find the cheese study History so you will learn, someone always moves the cheese.

Dispatch Nine

Hitler Mussolini FDR and Obama

Many people today feel as if President Obama has been leading America covertly into the Socialism Bernie is overtly proclaiming. Many feel that they are no longer living in the America of their youth. To understand how we got here it is necessary to understand how we got here.

History not only allows us the opportunity to learn from the mistakes of others it also provides us with a mirror to show us how we are continuing the mistakes of others. The present does not appear like a virgin birth in a vacuum it is the child of the past. The America of today was born in the progressivism of the 1890.

Teddy Roosevelt started the progressive ball rolling. His place holder William Howard Taft kicked the can down the road a little further. Woodrow Wilson trampled over the Constitution to create the framework of tyranny. Then after Silent Cal Coolidge and the interlude of the 1920s, the Crash of 29 provided the golden opportunity for Progressives to capture the government and impose upon a willing America its regimented dream of central planning at home and intervention abroad: the welfare/warfare state.

On May 7, 1933, just two months after the inauguration of Franklin Delano Roosevelt, the New York Times reporter Anne O'Hare McCormick wrote that the atmosphere in Washington was "strangely reminiscent of Rome in the first weeks after the march of the Black Shirts and of Moscow at the beginning of the Five-Year Plan. America today literally asks for orders." The Roosevelt administration, she added, "envisages a federation of industry, labor and government after the fashion of the corporative State as it exists in Italy."[lvii]

The broad-ranging powers granted to Roosevelt by Congress, before that body went into recess, were unprecedented in times of peace. Through this "delegation of powers," Congress had, in effect, temporarily done away with itself as the legislative branch of government. The only remaining check on the executive was the Supreme Court. In Germany, a similar process allowed Hitler to assume legislative power after the Reichstag burned down in a suspected case of arson on February 28, 1933.[lviii]

In the North American Review in 1934, the progressive writer Roger Shaw described the New Deal as "Fascist means to gain liberal ends."[lix] He wasn't hallucinating. FDR's adviser Rexford Tugwell wrote in his diary that Mussolini had done "many of the things which seem to me necessary."[lx] Lorena Hickok, a close confidante of Eleanor Roosevelt who lived in the White House for a spell, wrote approvingly of a local official who said, "If [President] Roosevelt were actually a dictator, we might get somewhere."[lxi] She added that if she were younger, she'd like to lead "the Fascist Movement in the United

States."[lxii] At the National Recovery Administration (NRA), the cartel-creating agency at the heart of the early New Deal, one report declared forthrightly, "The Fascist Principles are very similar to those we have been evolving here in America."[lxiii]

Roosevelt himself called Mussolini "admirable"[lxiv] and professed that he was "deeply impressed by what he has accomplished."[lxv] The admiration was mutual. In a laudatory review of Roosevelt's 1933 book *Looking Forward*, Mussolini wrote, "Reminiscent of Fascism is the principle that the state no longer leaves the economy to its own devices.... Without question, the mood accompanying this sea change resembles that of Fascism."[lxvi] The chief Nazi newspaper, *Volkischer Beobachter*, repeatedly praised "Roosevelt's adoption of National Socialist strains of thought in his economic and social policies"[lxvii] and "the development toward an authoritarian state"[lxviii] based on the "demand that collective good be put before individual self-interest."[lxix]

Soon after having taken his second Oath of Office in January 1937, President Roosevelt, in a conversation with a speechwriter, articulated his belief that the limits on governmental power that were enshrined in the U.S. Constitution were impediments to the transformative social and economic policies he wished to implement:

"When the chief justice read me the oath and came to the words 'support the Constitution of the United States,' I felt like saying: 'Yes, but it's the Constitution as I understand it, flexible enough to meet any new problem of democracy -- not the kind of Constitution your court has raised up as a barrier to progress and democracy.'"[lxx]

FDR chose to attack the depression with his so-called New Deal: a series of economic programs passed during his first term in office. These programs greatly expanded the size, scope, and power of the federal government, giving the President and his Brain Trust near-dictatorial status. "I want to assure you," Roosevelt's aide Harry Hopkins told an audience of New Deal activists in New York, "that we are not afraid of exploring anything within the law, and we have a lawyer who will declare anything you want to do legal."[lxxi]

Personally Roosevelt never had much use for Hitler, but Mussolini was another matter. "I don't mind telling you in confidence,' FDR remarked to a White House correspondent, 'that I am keeping in fairly close touch with that admirable Italian gentleman." Rexford Tugwell, a leading adviser to the president, had difficulty containing his enthusiasm for Mussolini's program to modernize Italy: "It's the cleanest ... most efficiently operating piece of social machinery I've ever seen. It makes me envious"[lxxii]

Why did contemporaries see an affinity between Roosevelt and the two leading European dictators while most people today view them as polar opposites? We all suffer from Presentism which means that people read history backwards: they project the fierce antagonisms of World War II, when America battled the Axis, to an earlier period, the 1930s. At the time, what impressed many observers, including as we have seen the principal actors themselves, was a new style of leadership common to America, Germany, and Italy.[lxxiii]

Many of Roosevelt's ideas and policies were entirely indistinguishable from the fascism of Mussolini. In fact, Jonah Goldberg writes in *Liberal Fascism*, there were "many common features among New Deal liberalism, Italian Fascism, and German National Socialism, all of which shared many of the same historical and intellectual forebears." Like American progressives, many Italian Fascist and German Nazi intellectuals championed a "middle" or "Third Way" between capitalism and socialism. Goldberg further explains:

> "The 'middle way' sounds moderate and un-radical. Its appeal is that it sounds unideological and freethinking. But philosophically the Third Way is not mere difference splitting; it is utopian and authoritarian. Its utopian aspect becomes manifest in its antagonism to the idea that politics is about trade-offs. The Third Wayer says that there are no false choices—'I refuse to accept that X should come at the expense of Y.' The Third Way holds that we can have capitalism and socialism, individual liberty and absolute unity."[lxxiv]

I don't know about anyone else but I was taught in grade school and high school that America no longer had a capitalist economy. Instead America had combined capitalism and socialism into what we were taught was now a mixed economy. And that was back in the 1950s and 1960s.

In *Three New Deals* the German cultural historian Wolfgang Schivelbusch states "To compare is not the same as to equate. America during Roosevelt's New Deal did not become a one-party state; it had no secret police; the Constitution remained in force, and there were no concentration camps; the New Deal preserved the institutions of the liberal-democratic system that National Socialism abolished." But throughout the '30s, intellectuals and journalists noted "areas of convergence among the New Deal, Fascism, and National Socialism." All three were seen as transcending "classic Anglo-French liberalism"—individualism, free markets, decentralized power.[lxxv]

Since 1776 liberalism had transformed the Western world. As The Nation editorialized in 1900, before it too abandoned the old liberalism, "Freed from the vexatious meddling of governments, men devoted themselves to their natural task, the bettering of their condition, with the wonderful results which surround us"[lxxvi]—industry, transportation, telephones and telegraphs, sanitation, abundant food, electricity. But the editor worried that "its material comfort has blinded the eyes of the present generation to the cause which made it possible."[lxxvii] Old liberals died, and younger liberals began to wonder if government couldn't be a positive force, something to be used rather than constrained.

Others, meanwhile, began to reject liberalism itself. In his 1930s novel *The Man Without Qualities*, Robert Musil wrote, "Misfortune had decreed that...the mood of the times would shift away from the old guidelines of liberalism that had favored the great guiding ideals of tolerance, the dignity of man, and free trade—and reason and progress in the Western world would be displaced by racial theories and street slogans."[lxxviii]

The dream of a planned society infected both right and left. Ernst Jünger, an influential right-wing militarist in Germany, reported his reaction to the Soviet Union: "I told myself: granted, they have no constitution, but they do have a plan. This may be an excellent thing."[lxxix] As early as 1912, FDR himself praised the Prussian-German model: "They passed beyond the liberty of the individual to do as he pleased with his own property and found it necessary to check this liberty for the benefit of the freedom of the whole people,"[lxxx] he said in an address to the People's Forum of Troy, New York.

American Progressives studied at German universities. Schivelbusch writes, and "came to appreciate the Hegelian theory of a strong state and Prussian militarism as the most efficient way of organizing modern societies that could no longer be ruled by anarchic liberal principles."[lxxxi] The pragmatist philosopher William James' influential 1910 essay "The Moral Equivalent of War"[lxxxii] stressed the importance of order, discipline, and planning.

Schivelbusch finds parallels in the ideas, style, and programs of the disparate regimes even their architecture. "Neoclassical monumentalism," he writes, is "the architectural style in which the state visually manifests power and authority." In Berlin, Moscow, and Rome, "the enemy that was to be eradicated was the laissez-faire architectural legacy of nineteenth-century liberalism, an unplanned jumble of styles and structures." Washington erected plenty of neoclassical monuments in the '30s, though with less destruction than in the European capitals. Think of the "Man Controlling Trade" sculptures in front of the Federal Trade Commission, with a muscular man restraining an enormous horse. They would have been right at home in Il Duce's Italy.[lxxxiii]

Intellectuals worried about inequality, the poverty of the working class, and the commercial culture created by mass production. They didn't seem to notice the tension between the last complaint and the first two. Liberalism seemed inadequate to deal with such problems. When economic crisis hit, in Italy and Germany after World War I and in the United States with the Great Depression, the anti-liberals seized the opportunity arguing that the market had failed and that the time for bold experimentation had arrived.

Trace all that to today. We have a president who entered office comparing himself to FDR,[lxxxiv] a president who said he aspired to be a transformative leader,[lxxxv] a president who has promised to fundamentally transform America, and we can see that the New Deal is alive and well even if the Republic is not.[lxxxvi]

Fifty years of reading History on a daily basis has taught me one thing: we do not learn the lessons of History. Look about us and find the great examples of socialism. Mostly you will have to look in the dustbin of History although Venezuela provides a perfect example of where economies go when robbing Peter to pay Paul becomes national policy.

A soviet dictator, Nikita Khrushchev told us:

"We will take America without firing a shot ... we will bury you!"[lxxxvii]

"We can't expect the American people to jump from capitalism to communism, but we can assist their elected leaders in giving them small doses of socialism, until they awaken one day to find that they have communism."[lxxxviii]

"I once said, 'We will bury you,' and I got into trouble with it. Of course we will not bury you with a shovel. Your own working class will bury you."[lxxxix]

"We do not have to invade the United States, we will destroy you from within."[xc]

No one gets to live in the world they grew up in --- time moves too fast. We could however preserve and pass on the country we grew up in --- unless of course we don't.

Dispatch Ten

How Many Nails Does it Take to Seal a Coffin

How many lopsided trade deals does it take to teach a nation they are being sold down the river? Apparently it takes one more than we have.

After months of secrecy President Obama has the chutzpa to throw the thing online and challenge people to read it.[xci] Saying "Along with the text of the agreement, we've posted detailed materials to help explain it. It's an unprecedented degree of transparency — and it's the right thing to do."[xcii]

Sounds great doesn't it? How open. How accessible. Give it a quick read and let's get on with the job of selling out our heritage for a bowl for oatmeal.

The next time you have a few moments free between jobs why not give it a go. It is only 5,544 pages containing 2,056,560 words which is according to the Daily Caller:

- 3.18x longer than the King James Bible
- 5.77x longer than the Affordable Care Act
- 1.63x longer than the entire Harry Potter series
- 3.73x longer than the entire Lord of the Rings trilogy

- 1.06x longer than the entire Game of Thrones series
- 4.33x longer than the entire works of Shakespeare
- 2.65x longer than the New Oxford American Dictionary 3rd Edition

Just take a little break from trying to make ends meet while you compete with workers around the world making ten dollars a day and make a decision about whether we should take another bite of the free trade apple. Of course no matter what you decide the twin headed party of power in Chicago on the Potomac is going to shove this give away of American jobs and prosperity down your throat.

TPP is an agreement between the United States and 11 other countries – Australia, Brunei, Canada, Chile, Japan, Malaysia, Mexico, New Zealand, Peru, Singapore, and Vietnam. China is not a party to this treaty.

According to Public Citizen:[xciii]

The TPP would expand the North American Free Trade Agreement (NAFTA) "trade" pact model[xciv] that has spurred massive U.S. trade deficits and job loss, downward pressure on wages, unprecedented levels of inequality and new floods of agricultural imports. The TPP not only replicates, but expands NAFTA's special protections for firms that offshore U.S. jobs. And U.S. TPP negotiators literally used the 2011 Korea FTA – under which exports have fallen and trade deficits have surged – as the template for the TPP.[xcv]

In one fell swoop, this secretive deal could:

- offshore American jobs and increase income inequality,
- jack up the cost of medicines,
- sneak in SOPA-like threats to Internet freedom,
- empower corporations to attack our environmental and health safeguards,
- expose the U.S. to unsafe food and products,
- roll back Wall Street reforms,
- ban Buy American policies needed to create green jobs,
- and undermine human rights.

Although it is called a "free trade" agreement, the TPP is not mainly about trade. Of TPP's 29 draft chapters, only five deal with traditional trade issues. One chapter would provide incentives to offshore jobs to low-wage countries. Many would impose limits on government policies that we rely on in our daily lives for safe food, a clean environment, and more. Our domestic federal, state and local policies would be required to comply with TPP rules.[xcvi]

So if the stagnant or falling wages of the last few decades have left you feeling as if you haven't given enough hold on because the DC Leviathan is about to ask for more.

I would now make a plea for everyone to call their senators and congressman but does anyone believe that would make a difference. This is just another milestone on the road to the 3rd world by those who seek to fundamentally transform America. Then along comes Hillary, the nail in our coffin.

Then Came Trump

Dispatch Eleven

How Strange Can It Get?

Some people believe in the Six Degrees of Separation Theory: the idea that everyone in the world is separated from everyone else by six links. Some people believe all of us are in this thing together, and that diversity is our strength and I am he as you are he as you are me and we are all together.

Even if we are all connected in ways we cannot know I believe the world is filled with strangers. Take a ride and as you pass through country, town, and city you are constantly presented with the faces of people you will never know, and all of whom have lives and families that will never know you or your life or your family. Every day we see people we have never seen before and will never see again. They rise out of the mist beyond the pale of our personal knowledge and immediately are submerged again never to rise again. Our only connection will forever be that one fleeting moment when we moved through a single frame of the separate sagas which are our lives.

Unlike Cain I do believe we are our brother's keeper, and unlike Scrooge I believe we should help our brothers in need instead of seeing them boiled with their own pudding and buried with a stake of holly through their hearts. However, unlike the rhetoric of Marx, Lenin, President Obama, Hillary Clinton, and Bernie Sanders I do not believe that life should operate on the basis of from each according to their ability to each according to their need, or as we say in America today, spreading the wealth around.[xcvii] In other words, I am not a socialist. I believe in personal liberty, individual freedom, and economic opportunity. Sadly I find myself out of phase with the Progressive Clique which has successfully maneuvered its way to power using the education system, the media, government handouts, and uninformed, uninvolved, and emotional voters.

Out of phase or not, I believe in the equality of opportunity which gives everyone a shot at success as opposed to the equality of outcome which our Dear Leader and his fellow-travelers wish to foist upon us, and which gives everyone the assurance of mediocrity.   No matter the consequence, no matter the sacrifice we must stand up for what we believe or we will stand by while our nation is transformed into what we won't be able to believe is still called the United States of America.[xcviii]

Day by day the bean counting pencil pushers who make up the nameless faceless bureaucracy grind out rule after rule and regulation after regulation with the force of law.

President Obama's signature piece of legislation, Obamacare, churns out thousands upon thousands of pages of federal requirements all meant to fill in the blanks in a 2600 page bill that we had to pass to find out what was in it.[xcix]

Hope and change has become bait and switch. In the last presidential election Mr. Obama wasn't even trying to win votes from those who disagree with him. He wasn't trying to change minds. He was blatantly buying votes. He was betting that generations of entitlements had finally birthed the lumpen proletariat that his theories of government proclaim must exist for History to reach its summit. He bet his second term on the belief that there were enough people dependent upon the government that they would vote for a handout instead of voting for a hand up. He bet that America had been dumbed down enough and bribed enough to trade our heritage of freedom for the yoke of a guaranteed something instead of the opportunity for everything.

Class warfare, penalizing success, dividing America into interest groups and voter blocks this was the strategy Mr. Obama thought would win as he worked to build a coalition of leftist intellectuals and those convinced they were disenfranchised. Looking at the polls it appeared he had the solid core of 40+% who will vote for a Democrat even if he is the devil himself. The question was would the unengaged and uninformed voters when combined with the illegals and the dead who at least get to vote in

Chicago be enough for him to win? In the end it didn't matter when Romney decided to take the last month of the campaign off after throwing the last few debates.

Can you imagine what a third Obama term (or as some call it Hillary's first term) will look like won on the basis of her promise to double down on social democracy, a complete disregard for the balance of power, and a desire to totally transform America? What will be left of the America we have known? How would we ever get back to where we came from? No entitlement once enacted has ever been repealed. The size of government never shrinks. The power it usurps from the people and the States is never surrendered and the check and balance of the Supreme Court will be frozen into a Progressive rubber stamp.

A world filled with strangers keeps getting stranger all the time. No matter how many degrees of separation we should never be as divided as our Progressive Leaders try to portray us. We are Americans, and we can do better than this. Reject the siren song of free entitlements which are never free, and embrace the liberty our forefathers won for us. Let us renew our great experiment in human freedom and strive to see our nation rise again to be the last best hope of man that it is meant to be. The shining city on a hill that can light the way to a future worthy of free men and women held together by unity. Not a falling empire of competing special interests cobbled together as a ruling coalition led by an elitist clique who promotes separation and hyphenated Americans.

Even if it takes more than six degrees of separation to connect to others what does it matter how connected we are to people around the world if we are in terminal disagreement with our fellow Americans? As a nation we are divided between those who want to strive to achieve and those who thrive because they receive. The Progressives have bred generations of passive takers who believe they are entitled to the fruit of others' labor. They pay no taxes so they don't care how high taxes go. They have no conception of paying for what they have, so they don't care about the national debt. They see America as a vending machine, so they don't believe in our unique place in History. They desire a shabby world of bread and circuses based on equality of outcome, so they don't long to be all they can be.

Those of us who want America to be what America has been and what it should be, the home of the brave and the land of the free can't let divisions divide us anymore! We must unite to save liberty or we will stand alone at the end of the day. We may be strangers to one another. We may not know each other but if we are fellow believers in the personal liberty, individual freedom, and economic opportunity we must unite over what connects us to save what has always made us E PLURIBUS UNUM.

Either that or we admit we are merely strangers in a strange land looking around at the social and cultural turmoil of today wondering how strange can it get.

Dispatch Twelve

If It Isn't America First What Is It?

The very words "America First" have gained a social stigma accorded few things in American History; things such as "McCarthyism," or "America for Americans," or "Reverse Discrimination." These words that have been made politically incorrect by the media wing of the Progressive Republocrat Party.

The original America First Committee was painted with the broad brush of anti-Americanism for opposing America's entrance into WW II. The committee was established on September 4, 1940, by Yale Law School student R. Douglas Stuart, Jr. along with several other students, including future President Gerald Ford, future Peace Corps director Sargent Shriver, and future U.S. Supreme Court justice Potter Stewart. Future President John F. Kennedy contributed $100, along with a note saying "What you all are doing is vital."[c] It also attracted many national leaders such as General Robert E. Wood, the aviator Charles A. Lindbergh, and Senator Gerald P. Nye. The committee was dissolved on December 10, 1941 after the Japanese attack on Pearl Harbor brought America into the war.

This was no insignificant student organization staging rallies on a few campuses. At its peak, America First claimed 800,000 due-paying members in 450 chapters. This was a mass movement of Americans who believed that entering WW II would not be in America's best interests. Whether subsequent events lead you to believe that this was a correct position, it was a heartfelt belief of many and was certainly not based on anything other than seeking what they thought was best for America: America First.

Today we face another situation that many believe should lead us to the passionate cry for America First!

What is this situation? Is it the disastrous foreign and domestic policies of the current administration? While the first of these is forfeiting our position as world hegemon and the latter is eroding our economy and submerging our population in a migration invasion these are not the issues I am addressing today.

The issue that has me ready to climb on the rooftops and unfurl the flag of America First is the false god of free trade which has been the golden calf for the last four administrations. Ever since George the First declared that we were instituting a New World Order in 1991 America has been aggressively chasing free trade deals with nations from all over the world.[ci]

Using fast track authority to negotiate, wherein Congress cedes their authority to amend, international trade deals such as NAFTA, CAFTA, and KORUS FTA, the United States has opened its markets without tariffs or other barriers.

This has led to a massive flight of American industry overseas. Savvy industrialists could immediately see the value in manufacturing overseas with lower labor costs and less regulation as long as they still had unfettered access to the American market. Other countries also saw their new competitive advantage. They could subsidize home industries and then dump their products below cost on the American market until they wiped out their American competitors, captured the niche, and then raise the prices again. A good example of this is what Japan did to the American TV industry or what India and China have done to textiles.

Is this free trade? No it is free in only one direction. These foreign nations still restrict their markets to American goods. They also subsidize their industries and dump their products below cost as described above. Some might say this is good. Let foreign tax payers subsidize our purchases. Look at the great deals we are getting. Now everyone can have a flat screen, a smartphone, and a laptop.

However, it doesn't seem like such a good deal if you drive through backroads America and you see the shuttered factories: the abandoned remnants of what was once the greatest manufacturing nation in the History of the world. It doesn't seem like such a good deal when you look at all the millions of American workers who have lost manufacturing jobs that paid a living wage and have had to accept a lower paying job in the service industry or have adjusted to living on the dole.

We have allowed politicians who masquerade as statesman to follow their belief that free trade will bring about world peace. This belief can be traced back more than two hundred years and began to make a mark in the world with the repeal of the Corn Laws in Great Britain in 1846. This led eventually to the British Empire embracing free trade. They did this believing it would give them a competitive advantage, since at the time they were the number one industrial nation on earth.

However, it acted in the reverse and within a half century America and Germany both with heavily protected markets passed up Britain and took the lead in manufacturing.

Today America is following the British Empire. We have opened our markets and are being supplanted as the industrial leader of the world by China which protects its markets. The question is, are we going to follow the British Empire into the trash heap of History? Or are we going to make the hard choices, shoulder the heavy burden, and re-industrialize America so we can once again stand alone as the industrial behemoth that bestrides the world?

If we believe as my favorite president once said, "After all, the chief business of the American people is business" then we should rise up and demand that our leaders quit sacrificing American jobs and American living standards on the altar of their free trade idol.

For if the business of America is business we must stop the fire sale of our manufacturing sector to foreign nations, many of whom are actually hostile to us. We must remember that the duty of our government is to protect and enhance the lives and fortunes of Americans. It is not to promote world peace, raise the standard of living for the citizens of other nations, or create a world government. We are not an international aid agency. We are not a free trade advocacy lobbyist before the court of world opinion. We are the United States of America, and all our policies should work for the benefit of Americans first.

It is easy to complain. It is easy to say what others are doing is wrong. It is harder to offer concrete suggestions for how things should be done. Here are my suggestions for a way to re-industrialize America, end the Great Recession, and improve the living standards of Americans.

I call my program Equitable Trade. I advocate for 100% reciprocity in trade and 100% equity in international commerce.

Under this program America should deal with other nations on a case by case basis predicated on how they deal with us. We should impose tariff for tariff, fee for fee, and fine for fine. Domestically I call for an end to all subsidies. Let the forces of the market prevail. At the same time any nation that subsidizes their industries should face a tariff on the subsidized good equal to the subsidy.

Diplomatically the complimentary policy should be a return to the traditional American position. Established by George Washington during his administration and enshrined in his farewell address farewell address, "The great rule of conduct for us in regard to foreign nations is in extending our commercial relations, to have with them as little political connection as possible." With Jefferson, "Peace, commerce and honest friendship with all nations--entangling alliances with none, I deem [one of] the essential principles of our government, and consequently [one of] those which ought to shape its administration."[cii]

So if it isn't America first what is it? It is politicians seeking their own fame, their own counsel and their own benefit. It is those who want to be citizens of the world betraying those of us who are proud to be citizens of the United States of America. If we don't stand up for what we believe do we think anyone else will? If we don't rise up and demand that the leaders of America consider America first they will continue to consider America last. How do you think that will work out for your children and grandchildren?

Will we be the first generation of Americans to leave our posterity a nation poorer than the one we inherited? We will be unless we join together and declare it must be America First!

Dispatch Thirteen

Socialism is the Problem Capitalism is the Solution

In the long and dismal History of human bondage an unbroken chain of command economies and tyrants has kept their boot on the neck of humanity.

Then came the American experiment, the spirit of 76, the miracle at Philadelphia, and for brief moment in the hours of human bondage the flame of freedom flickered and then blazed, lighting the way to a new age: the Age of Liberty. Unfettered by central planning and tyranny the ingenuity and enterprise of man brought forth in two short centuries more innovation and accomplishment than the previous eons of slavery.

Then the shackles were re-forged by the Progressives who want the power to dictate the lives of others for goals they say are for the betterment of others but which are in reality merely tools they use to gain power. Through manipulation of the media and control of education the Progressives gained the tacit approval of the general population. Most people were too busy working and living their lives to keep their attention on the wider society. The prosperity freedom had created bred generations of people who began to take it for granted. Today after years of bread and circus cycles of neglect we have a mass of citizens who follow like sheep to the slaughter or lemmings to the cliff anywhere the Progressive puppet masters portray as the next free entitlement.

Founded upon a limited government, today we have an imperial president who rules by decree as we pretend that the Constitution is still in force. We live in a dysfunctional oligarchy that is masquerading as a functional republic. We flounder and lurch from one crisis to the next on the world stage because we are divorced from our principles and hypnotized into believing we actually still stand for freedom when we actually are a front for multi-national corporations and international banks. A giant hobbled by pygmies unable to understand that by discarding our heritage of personal liberty, individual freedom, and economic opportunity we have made ourselves no different from every other plunder empire that has fallen from Rome to Britain.

We have descended into mediocrity by adopting the same over regulated, "from everyone according to the ability to everyone according to their need" pathology that doomed the commissars with their five-year plans, their gulags, and iron curtains. Whenever this rob from the rich to give to the poor looting of producers to support non-producers runs into trouble, which is whenever they run out of other people's money, they blame Capitalism: the goose that lays the golden eggs. In a classic bait and switch the Progressive collectivists offer freedom and deliver regulations. They offer prosperity and deliver stagnation, inflation, and economic ruin. Our rob Peter to pay Paul pied pipers blame capitalism when in reality Socialism is the problem and Capitalism is the solution.

This progressive slide into the dustbin of History will only be reversed by applying the opposing force of freedom. This must include freedom of action, freedom of association, of speech, thought, and the freedom to excel.

If we outlaw failure with a security net of social programs we ensure that some will turn it into a hammock. When we open the borders and welcome the world should we really watch in disbelief as the programs our elected masters have implemented turn the greatest nation the world has ever known into a third world hellhole saluting the stars and stripes and repeating like a robot, "We're number one!"

Dispatch Fourteen

The Empire Swallowed the Republic

Take a look at the size of the defense budget in America today as a percentage of federal spending.

In 2015 it accounted for 53.71% of the entire budget.[ciii] Now try to image what would happen to our economy if that spending was stopped and not immediately replaced by other federal spending. See the problem? We may have been warned by President Eisenhower about the military industrial complex. However the thing he forgot to tell us was that the military industrial complex had already won and that we as a nation are dependent on military spending which is dependent on continuing crisis, wars, and garrison duties around the world.

In other words when our most idealistic sing give peace a chance while they are giddy in their idealism, if we chose to follow their advice it would lead us all to depression.

What is the result of all this?

The Empire has swallowed the Republic.

How can we know that? What guide is there to evaluate if this is so?

Garet Garret, that great critic of the New Deal revolution which changed America forever outlined the characteristics of empire:

(1) Rise of the executive principle of government to a position of dominant power

(2) Accommodation of domestic policy to foreign policy

(3) Ascendancy of the military mind

(4) A system of satellite nations for a purpose called collective security, and,

(5) An emotional complex of vaunting and fear.[civ]

There are other versions of this metric used to recognize an empire.[cv]

1. Imperial boundaries – there is a distinction between imperial and non-imperial space.

2. Dissolution of equality – subordinates are considered to be "client states" or "satellites." In other words international relations are not between equals, but between a "center" and a "periphery."

3. The existence of most empires has been due to a mix of chance and contingency – most empires do not arise due to "will to empire" (imperialism) or a grand strategy, but rather a series of circumstances that lead to increased power and control of people and/or territories.

4. The capacity for reform and regeneration – empires do not need to necessarily hold to the qualities of the original situation in which it was conceived. Often they

become independent of the values/qualities of the founder(s).

5. Inability to remain neutral in relation to the powers in its sphere of influence – empires will retaliate if there is an attempt at independence or non-participation on the part of its subordinates.

Ask yourself, are any of the current crop of presidential candidates from either side of the government party talking about ending America's crushing commitment to empire?

If we would bring our troops home, use them to guard our borders, and held in reserve to protect our genuine interests we would have all the money we need to do anything we want.

Whichever guide for recognizing an empire you choose one of these or any of the many others available America transitioned long ago from a peaceful nation of farmers, shop keepers, and mechanics into a worldwide empire projecting power for many reasons, few of which have anything to do with either our vital interests or our security. We have garrison troops in over one hundred nations. We are spending billions building infrastructure for people who burn it down while our own nation crumbles.

We are spending ourselves into the poor house for nations that hate us. Which brings us back to the problem imagined in the beginning of this essay: what would happen to our economy if that spending was stopped and not immediately replaced by other federal spending?

The answer to this question is found in a fundamental need in the American psyche: the need for a mission. Today our mission is portrayed as being the world's unipolar hegemon involved in everything everywhere a roll completely inappropriate and incompatible with a free republic. History is littered with the dust left behind by republics that have tried it and found themselves becoming slave states with imperial dictators on their way to being debtors who collapse in economic ruin. Look at Athens. Look at Rome. If they could not avoid this, how can we?

I know many will try to broad brush these thoughts with the stain of isolationism or America First. For one, I am not advocating for isolation because I advocate for peace and trade with all. And secondly, I don't think there is anything wrong with Americans thinking of America first.

Here is my solution. End our occupation of Europe and Korea. Stop the endless war in Afghanistan. Close every military base in the world that does not directly protect the Homeland. Build effective walls on our borders and use our returning troops to garrison them. Instead of providing military aid to other nations refit, retrain, and retain our own military so that it is unthinkable that anyone would challenge us.

And what shall be our new national goal?

Let us dedicate ourselves to once again becoming not only the preeminent space faring nation but also the nation that sets its sights on the active exploration and colonization of the Solar System. I believe if we build the Starship Enterprise in earth orbit no one would dare becoming the target for its phaser banks. The technology that would evolve from a renewed move into space would expand our lives and offset the cost.

Today we are a dysfunctional republic masquerading as a functional democracy. Tomorrow we may be an operating oligarchy with the veneer of a republic. Following this trajectory how long will it be until we are a third world hellhole that used to be the United States of America.

As Garet Garret, told us "There are those who still think they are holding the pass against a revolution that may be coming up the road. But they are gazing in the wrong direction. The revolution is behind them. It went by in the Night of Depression, singing songs to freedom."[cvi]

Jettison the empire to save the republic!

Dispatch Fifteen

The Great Disconnect

Chaos is the mother of tyranny. Chaos reigns when people operate in confusion and disorder. It is a state in which behavior and events are not controlled by reason. Today we are faced with a government and an elite controlled media that lie to the people and then lie about lying. They operate as if the country is theirs to run and ruin for their own personal enrichment. Chaos is a time like today when life makes little sense and we are force-fed such gobbledygook as the economy is booming, President Obama has outperformed Reagan when it comes to job creation and investment, inflation is under control, unemployment is at 4.9%.[cvii] Over here in reality we are fighting endless wars for peace, working people are being squeezed between stagnant wages and rising prices, and almost as many able-bodied people have dropped out of the workforce[cviii] as there are people working.[cix] This is chaos. This is the seedbed of tyranny.

Our tyrants-in-training have captured the government and the economy, created a dependent class [cx]of motor voters,[cxi] convinced people that a continually growing debt is sustainable and turned the government into the one who picks winners and losers instead of a free economy. The slow slide down a slippery slope has accelerated into a precipitous procession over a predictable precipice. To those who have seen this coming it is like watching a slow motion train wreck. The coming destruction is not mitigated in the least by decades of warning by the watchmen on the walls.

How is this evolving progression from individual freedom, personal liberty, and economic opportunity into a centrally-planned collectivist corporatist regime possible?[cxii] It is built upon the alliance of perpetually re-elected political hacks, crony capitalists, and corrupt unions aided and abetted by a sycophant media?

Why have the descendants of the Founders, the Framers, and the Revolution fallen for the same swan song that has led so many others before us down the primrose path to authoritarianism, totalitarianism, despotism, and collapse? I believe it is because the average American has no frame of reference. If we don't know what has gone before how can we understand what is? Or plan for what might be?

If we don't know where we came from it is impossible to predict where we are going. Therefore it is helpful to learn how the world became the way it is so that we can work to make it the way we think it should be, for without the past the present will never come into focus and the future will be nothing more than a mist that someone else will bring into focus. History consists of perspectives from the present projected onto facts from the past. While the facts are often disputed the perspectives tend to become quasi-religious dogma expressed as political opinions wherein the present uses the past to shape the future. Examples would be increasing the minimum wage [cxiii] is good for the working poor, infrastructure stimulus is good for the economy,[cxiv] or preemptive war [cxv] is good for peace. [cxvi]

An important thing to realize across the board in Historical studies is a truism often maligned and sometimes even used as an insult but true nonetheless, everyone is the center of their own world and everyone experiences life from where they stand, and all attempts to speak of "the" experiences of THE people are fabrications that may be agreed upon by scholars but has little relationship to what any one person may experience.

As we mature it is easier to gain an appreciation of History since we have an ever increasing personal experience with the past with which to analyze our present and to project our future.

America's lack of historical perspective and lack of understanding the basics of civics and economics has led to what I call the Great Disconnect. Here is the condition which we all encounter on a daily basis that exemplifies this educationally instilled mental pathology: How many people do you meet who vote for politicians diametrically opposed to everything they believe in? From everything they say you would imagine they must vote for party X then you find out they are rabid supporters of party Y which is against everything they are for, and they can't stand the politicians of party X which supports everything they believe in. This is what I call the Great Disconnect.

A historical perspective is the antidote for this pathology.

In essence what I am talking about is using history to build a platform of the past to be a launching pad for the future. We are currently mortgaging the future to pay for the excesses of today. We are spending money that has not been earned by people who have not been born to subsidize the current creature comfort of those who don't care who pays as long as they get what they want. It is unfortunate for the generations of the future for they will be forced to live in a world that we have created. Our parents conquered the world and left the nation inherited by the Boomers as the sole colossus who bestrides the tides of time. We have wasted the accumulated wealth of two hundred years, created a far flung empire we cannot afford to garrison, and turned a noble experiment in human freedom from a city on a hill into dysfunctional republic functioning as an entrenched oligarchy masquerading as a democracy.

If we had only learned from the mistakes of others, if we had only seen in the sudden collapse of the USSR that we too could follow hubris and collectivism from victory to defeat. Unfortunately it appears the only lesson we have learned from History is that we don't learn the lessons of History and this is the Great Disconnect.

Dispatch Sixteen

The Solutions to Our Broken Institutions Are In the Constitution

America is facing a crisis. As a matter of fact we are in such a constant state of crisis that I should be using the plural crises but that sounds silly and looks improbable. As do the policies which have pushed us to this point.

- Open borders erase what being an American means.

- Strangulation regulation that prohibit growth and punish productivity.

- Free Trade giveaways that send our industry and jobs overseas.

- Taxation that makes us long for the tax rates that started the Revolution.

- Attacks on police, on every right guaranteed, not granted, guaranteed by the Bill of Rights.

- An internal war on our own energy sector in the name of a mythical man-made global warming.

- An administration that fans the flames of racial and social divides for political advantage.

- A political class made up of the perpetually re-elected of both parties that sits like a twin headed bird of prey atop a corporatism system rigged to reward the connected and ignore the rest.

How could any of this fail…..to end America's 240 year old experiment in human freedom? The institutions of our government are broken. However, there is a solution, and it is in the Constitution.

First of all the system was built to provide checks and balances. Each branch, the legislative, the executive, and the judicial were meant to counterbalance each other so that no one branch could usurp the power of the other two.

The Evansville Bar Association in its annual recognition of Constitution Day in 2015 summed it up well;

Although the terms "Separation of Powers" and "Checks and Balances" are not found in the Constitution, these principles are key to its vitality. As George Washington wrote in February of 1788, the two great "pivots upon which the whole machine must move" are: (1) "the general Government is not invested with more Powers than are indispensably necessary to perform the functions of a good Government[,]" and (2) "these Powers are so distributed among the Legislative, Executive, and Judicial Branches, that [the Government] can never be in danger of degenerating into a monarchy or any other despotic or oppressive form, so long as there shall remain any virtue in the body of the People." As recently as 2011, the Supreme Court affirmed that these principles were "intended, in part, to protect each branch of government from incursion by the others. The structural principles secured by the separation of powers protect the individual as well."

Congress has abdicated its powers to unelected bureaucrats and the courts have decided that is the order of the day. Generation Opportunity covers this well when they say;

One of the reasons that elections are such so important is because legislative representatives are responsible to create federal laws that impact every one of their constituents.

This is not a task to be taken lightly, which is why voters must dedicate time to research candidates before heading to the voting booth. But few people realize that there are unelected individuals who create regulations that govern everything from what type of light bulb you are allowed to use, as well as how much water your toilet may flush. According to an article published by the Competitive Enterprise Institute (CEI), no one is entirely sure how many government agencies actually exist, not even the government knows the exact number.

For instance, in the appendix of the Administrative Conference of the United States, there are 115 agencies listed with a disclaimer saying, "[T]here is no authoritative list of government agencies."

The federal government has grown so large that no one can even keep track of it anymore. Worse still, each of these agencies are filled with unelected people who take on legislative authority to interpret laws passed by Congress.

Although Congress is prohibited from "delegating" its legislative function to another branch of government, Courts have consistently held that federal agencies may create their own rules as long as an "intelligible" principle can be discerned from the original statute in question.

In other words, if Congress passes a law that regulates a particular industry or action, unelected federal bureaucrats are given almost unchecked power to create whichever rules (or crimes associated with the conduct in question) that they please.

Here's an example: When Congress passed the Clean Air Act Amendments of 1977, it mandated that certain environmental standards must be imposed on the states, but it hardly clarified what those standards were, or how they were to be enforced.

One of the components of the Act mandated states to establish a permit program that regulates, "new or modified major stationary sources" of air pollution. That seems simple enough, except that Congress never properly defined what qualified as a "stationary source."

Therefore, the Environmental Protection Agency was left with the task of defining what a "stationary source" meant. Additionally, the original legislation never detailed what the penalty would be for breaking any of the statutes created by the new amendments, leaving it open to interpretation by the EPA.

This predicament led to the 1984 landmark case of Chevron U.S.A., Inc. v. Natural Resources Defense Council, Inc., where the Supreme Court held that federal agencies have authority to interpret statutes which they are in charge of administering.

This meant that the EPA now had legal authority to determine what would be considered a "stationary source" of air pollution.

Since the Chevron Doctrine applies to all government agencies, the opportunities for abuse are endless. Government is only legitimate when it derives its powers from the consent of the governed. When we give legislative powers to unelected government officials we completely disregard the core American belief of consensual representation.

In other words we elect legislators to make laws and they make general laws like, "We want clean water," and then they let unelected bureaucrats fill in the blanks with the force of law.

Here is how it works. Everyone wants clean water so the legislators pass their "We want clean water," law and they come back to their constituents and campaign on "I brought you clean water." Then the EPA issues a regulation that says you can't build on wet lands. The EPA gets to decide what wet lands means which consequently gives them De Facto control over any piece of property they say is a wet land. Then when voters complain to their congressional representative, who voted for the law and bragged about it, that they can't build their house on a lot that is obviously dry the legislator becomes indignant. They tell their constituents, "We'll just see about this!" Then they have an aide send a strongly worded letter to the EPA that makes no difference whatsoever.

Problem solved. Pat the denizens from fly-over country on the head and leave the matter in the hands of the commissars who have inherited the rule of what was once a representative republic. This way the hack can get back to his real job of raising money and getting re-elected.

This abdication of responsibility on the part of the legislature is the root cause of our problems because it has led to or facilitated the rise of the imperial presidency wherein many presidents have expanded the power of the executive until today we have an elected monarch who rules by decree unchallenged by Congress and unfettered by the will of the people.

Although the imperial presidency by no means began with the present occupant of the White House, to many Barack Obama has pushed the envelope beyond any discernable constitutional limits and has become the prime example of this phenomenon.

According to the Christian Science Monitor;

President Obama's use of executive action to get around congressional gridlock is unparalleled in modern times, some scholars say. But to liberal activists, he's not going far enough.

Obama, a former constitutional law lecturer, was once skeptical of the aggressive use of presidential power. During the 2008 campaign, he accused President George W. Bush of regularly circumventing Congress. Yet as president, Obama has grown increasingly bold in his own use of executive action, at times to controversial effect.

The president (or his administration) has unilaterally changed elements of the Affordable Care Act (ACA); declared an anti-gay-rights law unconstitutional; lifted the threat of deportation for an entire class of undocumented immigrants; bypassed Senate confirmation of controversial nominees; waived compliance requirements in education law; and altered the work requirements under welfare reform. This month, the Obama administration took the highly unusual step of announcing that it will recognize gay marriages performed in Utah – even though Utah itself says it will not recognize them while the issue is pending in court.

Early in his presidency, Obama also expanded presidential war making powers, surveillance of the American public, and extrajudicial drone strikes on alleged terrorists outside the United States, including Americans – going beyond Mr. Bush's own global war on terror following 9/11. But more recently, he has flexed his executive muscle more on domestic policy.

In the process, Obama's claims of executive authority have infuriated opponents, while emboldening supporters to demand more on a range of issues, from immigration and gay rights to the minimum wage and Guantánamo Bay prison camp.

To critics, Obama is the ultimate "imperial president," willfully violating the Constitution to further his goals, having failed to convince Congress of the merits of his arguments. To others, he is exercising legitimate executive authority in the face of an intransigent Congress and in keeping with the practices of past presidents.

It also leads to the tyranny of the courts. Unelected lawyers with life tenure decide what is and what is not constitutional often with the vaguest references to the

Constitution itself. Disregarding what are clearly enunciated rights such as the one to keep and bear arms while finding such nonexistent rights such as the right to dispose of unborn children. The Justices of the Supreme Court have abrogated unto themselves unlimited power to turn our Constitution which was supposed to be written in stone into a living letter written in sand. Or as one Chief justice said, Chief Justice Charles Evans Hughes once said, "We are under a Constitution, but the Constitution is what the judges say it is." Or as the website Western Journalism describes it;

Our federal judiciary has become, arguably and disturbingly, an oligarchy. When they rule on the "constitutionality" of an issue, it is assumed to be the final say in whether a vote of Congress or the vote of the people via referendum or initiative is legitimized or annulled. This is not how the Supreme Court and its substrata of appellate courts were intended to operate, nor is it de facto the way it should be.

The federal judiciary, as it has evolved, has unchecked and unlimited power over the nation by either of the other branches—the executive or the legislative—or even the people. Its members are not accountable to the citizenry, since most of their appointments are for life, and they cannot be removed from the bench by a vote of the people they purportedly serve. Their ruminations and the results of their decisions are insular, and they often trump the will of the people with regard to key social issues. Their decisions are presumed to be final, even though they may be at odds with the democratic majority of our citizens.

Herein lies the fundamental problem about the present construct of our federal judiciary as it has evolved since the founding. If, as stated in the 10th Amendment, all "rights and powers" not specifically itemized in the Constitution are held by the people collectively or by the states, what right does a court have to negate the will of the people? As it relates especially to key cultural issues like abortion, public religious displays, and definitions of marriage, should not the final court be the court of public opinion, rather than an oligarchy of judges insulated from, and not accountable to, the citizenry? In most of these cases, state courts have ruled, and appeals are then made to the federal judiciary.

Thomas Jefferson portended this judicial despotism: "To consider the judges as the ultimate arbiters of all constitutional questions [is] a very dangerous doctrine indeed, and one which would place us under the despotism of an oligarchy. Our judges are as honest as other men and not more so. They have with others the same passions for party, for power, and the privilege of their corps. Their maxim is boni judicis est ampliare jurisdictionem [good justice is broad jurisdiction], and their power the more dangerous as they are in office for life and not responsible, as the other functionaries are, to the elective control."

These situations exist because Congress abdicates its authority to unelected bureaucrats of the federal nomenclature, it refuses to stand up to the runaway executives and refuses to reign in the Supreme Court.

The first could be accomplished by passing a law rescinding the ability of bureaucracies to issue regulations that have the force of law without congressional approval.

The second could be accomplished as they were with President Nixon, hearings which could lead to impeachment.

And the third is constitutionally provided for in Article 3, Section 2, Clause 2 which states, "In all Cases affecting Ambassadors, other public Ministers and Consuls, and those in which a State shall be Party, the supreme Court shall have original Jurisdiction. In all the other Cases before mentioned, the Supreme Court shall have appellate Jurisdiction, both as to Law and Fact, with such Exceptions, and under such Regulations as the Congress shall make." Congress should exercise its power to limit the jurisdiction of the courts. The Constitution provides that Congress is authorized to establish those federal courts subordinate to the Supreme Court and set forth their jurisdiction. Congress also has the power to limit the jurisdiction of the Supreme Court and regulate its activities. Accordingly, Congress should exercise this authority to restrain an activist judiciary.

If Congress would step up and be what we elect them to be We the People could once again become more than just an empty phrase from History in a discarded document that once sought to form a more perfect Union, establish Justice, insure domestic tranquility, provide for the common defense, promote the general welfare, and secure the blessings of liberty to ourselves and our posterity. If our representatives will represent us instead of themselves and their cronies we would find that the solutions to our broken institutions are in the Constitution.

Dispatch Seventeen

To Write the Future Read the Past

Unfortunately most of what we are taught in History survey classes in American schools consists of simplistic formulas. Formulas designed to persuade those forced to attend the government controlled education mills that they should ride the same ideological hobby horses as whoever currently has the power to select textbooks and prescribe curricula. Whether it was the rabidly pro-American imperial History of yesteryear that pushed lines such as, "We never started a war and never lost one," and "We turned a raw wilderness into a civilized nation." or, if it is the rabidly anti-American propaganda of today spouting lines such as, "America was founded by deists who used serial genocide and economic fascism to steal a nation, pollute the earth, and poison the sea" neither are correct. Both versions are merely two sides of an extremely myopic view which does not seek to discover nor promote the truth but instead seek to mold the next generation into what they think will be foot soldiers in their own crusade.

History, if it has any value at all is that it fulfills two goals. First, the study of History should provide context. A text without a context is a pretext and we must have context so we can understand how we as a people became who we are, how the world became what it is, and where it might go next. Secondly, the study of History should help us learn from and hopefully avoid the mistakes made by those who have gone before so we can leave a better world to those who come after. However, as stated above, these are rarely the goals of History education. The reason why is summed up in a joke only Historians seem to get.

Objectivity.

Most people in the world believe objectivity exists. They act as if the stories presented in survey of history classes are "the facts ma'am and nothing but the facts." I was once part of this blissful herd. I was a self-taught Historian before I took the plunge and studied to become a card carrying member of the profession. I was captured by the allure of History when I was nine years old. Nothing in the world made any sense. What I was taught and saw at home conflicted 180 degrees from what I was taught at church. What I was taught at church conflicted 180 degrees from what I was taught at school. What I saw on the streets appeared real because it seemed to be the way the world actually worked, but it was out of synch with my home my church and my school. Not knowing myself well enough to know that I am a person who operates best when things make sense and the world appears orderly I was confused and uncomfortable living in a world so out of joint.

Consequently when I learned in the third grade that there were histories of the world available I latched on to them like a drowning man latches on to a life preserver. I began reading History books every day. They became my raft in a swirling sea of confusion creating an orderly world of sequential reality that I used to build my bridge to the first positive value of History, gaining a coherent understanding of how we as a people became who we are, how the world became what it is, and where it might go next. However, I was a rebellious child, a child who never moved to the second value of History. I never learned to profit from the mistakes of those who went before. Following those in my family who went before I walked out of traditional education at age sixteen figuring I knew enough to make my way in the world. Twenty plus years of manual labor later I thought it might be a good idea to finish my education.

When I finished my Bachelor degree in History I realized that a Bachelor degree in History is good for two things, it can help you become the manager of the electronics department at Wal-Mart and it opens the door for a Master Degree in History. Since I was determined to become a History professor, I chose the latter. On my first day of graduate school this budding self-taught Historian had to grit my teeth as a professor told our class, "There are no facts, and History is only what Historians say it is."

Of course I had to run up after class to argue, "How can you say there are no facts? Look at the Vietnam War. We know it happened. We know when it started and when it ended. Those are facts and we can know them!" After listening calmly to my impassioned tirade the professor quietly said, "Maybe there's another side to that story."

This rude awakening sent me on a journey of discovery: searching for the other side of the story. Along the way I contributed my first chapter in a History book. My research helped me realize there is more than one side to every story. There are often conflicting facts, overlapping timelines, and always another way to look at everything. The truth of this is displayed in an endless series of quotes. Napoleon once said, "History is a set of lies agreed upon."[cxvii] Voltaire said, "History is a pack of lies we play on the dead."[cxviii] Ambrose Bierce said, "God alone knows the future, but only an historian can alter the past."[cxix] And one of my favorite philosophers, Anonymous sagely added, "The certainty of history seems to be in direct inverse ratio to what we know about it."[cxx]

What is the purpose of this self-revealing stroll down memory lane? It isn't for the purpose of either self-actualization or confession. Both of those goals were achieved long ago. It is instead my attempt to lead you my loyal reader (for those will be the only ones left after such a lesson in historiography) to the second value of the study of History. I am encouraged by the multitudes of people who are today engrossed in this study. So many of the recently awakened yearn to know the History of America, they long to know how our Constitution was written by whom and why. I am here to remind everyone we need to look at all sides, consider every angle, and remember everyone has a point of view, even Historians, and objectivity is in reality subjectivity in a grey flannel suit.

Remember that second value of History? It should help us learn from and hopefully avoid the mistakes made by those who have gone before so we can leave a better world to those who come after. If we merely exchange the unabashedly anti-American lenses of the present for the unquestioning pro-American lenses of the past we will be blind to what we really need to see.

The complexity of reality defies the easy interpretations of partisan politics. Has America always been right? No, the jingoistic refrain of "My country right or wrong" will lead those who blindly salute it into supporting what is wrong as easily as what is right. Has America always been wrong? No, the view currently used to indoctrinate the youth in our public schools which sees America as an imperialistic power that used genocide, racism, and naked aggression to build a hegemonic empire forget all the good America has accomplished. This view presents an America bent on maintaining the privileges of the rich over the rights of the poor and leads those who imbibe its venom into ignoring that America was founded as the world's greatest experiment in personal liberty and economic freedom.

Both views are too simplistic for people who want to break free of the matrix and see the world for what it truly is: a struggle between those who wish to control mankind for their own benefits and those who wish to see man set free so he can become all that he may be.

This is a call for those who have taken the bread and circus blinders off their eyes not to replace them with another set. Today we don't have to rely on what we have been taught. We can use the Internet as a portal into every perspective imaginable, histories beyond counting, and all the great works of mankind. Read broadly, study extensively and think for yourself. Don't exchange the purveyors of self-serving pap on the left for the purveyors of self-serving pap on the right. Open both ears, hear both sides, use the mind God gave you, and find the center path.

America has done some things wrong. America has done some things right. When it all is brought to the scales, when enough is seen to grasp the big picture, it is the non-objective view of this Historian that America has provided more freedom for more people than any other country that has ever existed. It is also my opinion that powers of anti-freedom have sought to regain control since the Revolution, and if those who have been too busy working and raising families don't spend enough time to learn what History teaches we will soon earn the reward for the failure to hold on to the past. We will lose the future.

Dispatch Eighteen

Useful Idiots and the Theater of the Absurd

Recently I had the opportunity to spend some time with a person who would easily qualify as one of Lenin's useful idiots. Here is a man who grabbed the brass ring. Not by government intervention. Not by being one of the bigtime crony capitalists who rig the system that chooses winners and losers. No, he had achieved success and fortune through his own ingenuity and hard work. And for this I have always respected and commended him.

Why would I call such a hard working successful entrepreneur a useful idiot? Because last night at a friendly meal he went on and on about how to be fair we needed to outlaw the law of supply and demand when it comes to housing, healthcare, and food. He went on and on and on, as he often does about how society should count more than individuals. He paused for a moment to cast damning accusations of heartlessness on real estate developers and the greed which infects others. Then he went on to his standard praise for other countries that take care of their people and aren't soiled by the deplorable capitalism of America.

All this from a man who made his fortune by employing others to work in his factory, retired early, has a million dollar estate in an exclusive area of Norther California, an apartment in Italy, and enough money to live comfortably in both places. All this, from a man who benefited from the law of supply and demand in his own industry, a man who went to great lengths to regain the Italian citizenship his grandparents had forsaken so he could take advantage of EU citizenship but doesn't pay his income tax in Italy to help support its failing social safety net.

Growing tired of the endless hypocrisy I asked if the law of supply and demand should have been suspended in his industry. No, he didn't think that would have been right. Comparing that and suspending it for real estate developers was comparing apples to oranges he said not seeing the dichotomy or the conundrum such double think created.

I then asked if it was fair that the owner of a factory should get to retire early and live a life of leisure while the people who toiled in his factory to make him rich were still working. That was a different issue all together, he asserted. I then asked if we are talking about suspending the law of supply and demand for certain industries just to be fair why fairness wasn't extended to the rewards people receive from their work. I was just trying to muddy the issue he protested.

I then asked why is it fair that one person who worked all their life got to retire with a 401K, a pension, and social security while another person only received social security. In the name of fairness shouldn't we all receive the same thing, I asked. Yes, that would be fair said the man living off much more than social security.

As of now I haven't heard that he is going to give up his intercontinental jet-set life style and join the 99% down here in Obama's economy struggling to navigate the New Normal. I do however believe after actively supporting Bernie and his campaign for an openly declared socialist America he is now supporting Hillary and her stealth campaign for the same thing.

As a postscript suspending the law of supply and demand is about as possible as suspending the law of gravity. If there are two widgets they are worth this much. If there are 2,000 widgets they are worth that much. A follows B, just as sure as day follows sunrise. I wonder when the useful idiots will start arguing against that. Why should day always follow sunrise? That just isn't fair to the night. Then again if they elect Hillary "The Nail in our Coffin" Clinton night might just begin to follow sunrise after all.

Wouldn't that be fair?

I wonder if my socialist acquaintance enriched by capitalism has any rope to sell. I think Hillary is asking for donations to buy some. Wait, is that Goldman Sachs on the line?

Dispatch Nineteen

We Are a Conquered Nation

It's time to take the gloves off. For decades I have been writing that the Progressives who have ruled our nation since 1988 have been using every tactic at their disposal to transform America from the indispensable nation to a disposable dystopia. I have railed against the open border mass immigration importation of Democrat voters that has swamped our culture and warped our electoral process.

I have long believed we have passed the tipping point and the reason I keep on is so that when my grandchildren turn to their children living in a third world hell hole that was once the richest most powerful nation on earth they can say, "At least your Great Grandfather tried to let people know what was coming." For this reason I have written the History of the Future. For this reason I ran a quixotic campaign for the Virginia State Senate in a gerrymandered district that was drawn for and belonged to a man famous for attending less than fifty percent of the Senate's meetings and sleeping through much of those. I won every vote that was not his by birth and lost by two to one. However in that campaign I was free to say the things politicians can never say.

I told people that it was time for the States to stand up and bring federalism back from the brink of extinction. That it was time to demand real money instead of fiat currency that destined to bring us to financial ruin. I told them that it was time to declare English the official language for education, ballots, and government forms. I called for a ten year moratorium on all immigration so that those who were already here legally could be assimilated. I called for a vigorous enforcement of the laws against hiring illegals with massive fines for anyone who violated them. Coupling this lack of work with a denial of all government benefits so that our illegal population would self deport and go home. I called for the imposition of a 10% tariff on imported manufactured goods so that the native industries could be protected and the income could fund tax cuts for Americans.

That was my platform. It was well received and well supported outside the areas of the district where public support was not the major industry. It went down to a rousing defeat.

Over the years anyone who has read this column knows that I have called the two government parties two sides of the same coin and two heads on the same bird of prey. I have pointed out that no matter which party is in power we end up with a bigger federal government, more laws, more taxes and more undocumented democrats. Signaling that we have passed the tipping point in 2012 we re-elected the biggest spending president in American History in the midst of a recession he has successfully turned into the New Normal whose actual platform was a bigger federal government, more laws, more taxes, and more undocumented democrats. The handwriting isn't on the wall, because there is no wall, because the executive branch has refused to build it even though the legislative branch mandated it and funded it. The handwriting is in columns like this and in the works of Pat Buchanan, Anne Coulter, Mark Steyn, and the words of Rush Limbaugh, Glenn Beck, and countless other watchmen on the walls.

However, even though Americans have and are listening. Conservative radio talk is ubiquitous; Fox has buried CNN and MSNBC. Coulter, Styen, Levin, and many others write multiple best sellers. The documentaries of Dinesh D'Souza break box office records. Yet the political class continues to be re-elected to rule exactly in the opposite direction.

Socialism is dying everywhere in the world except in America. Our progressive conquerors use the agencies of the imperial executive branch to harass, tax, prosecute, and spy. We are watched, regulated and held back at every step. They have used free trade to export our manufacturing base changing us from the arsenal of democracy into the marketplace for a communist dictatorship. Crony capitalists walk away with billions, billions more disappear in federal rounding errors, and banks are bailed out as the Creature from Jekyll Island inflates bubble after bubble.

It isn't time to roll over and go back to sleep. People woke up in 2010 when the Tea Party was born. I was there at the birth. I went to the rallies. I spoke at the meetings. I attended the conventions and supported the candidates that swept the House in 2010. What happened? Those brave new world conservatives that had just turned out Nancy Pelosi went to Washington, voted to make John Boehner the Speaker of the House, renewed the Patriot Act, and then passed continuing resolution after continuing resolution to keep the money rolling and the government growing.

Knowing what was coming I wrote and published *The Constitution Failed* in October of 2010, which is a book many people still reject merely because of the title. They erroneously think I am saying the document itself is a failure or that it was flawed from the beginning when what I am really saying is the execution of it has failed. The thumbnail sketch being, "If the Constitution was written for the express purpose of giving us a limited government and we now have an unlimited government it has failed."

I am not saying that it didn't bring us the most freedom and the greatest opportunities any people in the History of the world have ever had. It did. I am not saying that it didn't allow America to rise from 13 struggling states on the edge of the world to the greatest nation History has ever known. It did. What I am saying is that if our founding document guarantees us a limited government, individual freedom, and economic opportunity, and we are now laboring in the Progressives New Normal as the NSA watches our every move and listens to our every conversation something is very wrong here.

Everywhere I go and everyone I speak to seems to know intuitively how to solve our problems. Seal the border, cut off the free meals, and the illegal immigration problem will solve itself. Stop immigration long enough for the millions of legal immigrants to become culturally American. We all came from somewhere else, and after a generation, or at most two, we are all Americans because the old melting pot was allowed to work instead of the Progressive smelting pot that is Balkanizing America. Everyone can see we need to protect our industry and do everything we can to foster its resurgence. Everyone knows we need more domestic energy not less, less regulation not more, and that the healthcare system was healthier and more affordable before the Affordable Care Act.

Everyone everywhere can see these things, or at least a vast majority of native born Americans can. Yet does anyone honestly believe that the perpetually re-elected or their carbon copy replacements are going to shut down the nomenclature in OZ, the casino in New York, or the giveaway to China? Everyone everywhere can see we are on a crash course to nowhere on the express to the dustbin of History. The best people can say is it will last long enough for them to continue living the high life.

This is not the case. I began this plea by saying it's time to take the gloves off and it is. The economy is heading for the biggest crash we have ever known. Our foreign policy or lack thereof is leading us to international humiliation. The immigration invasion is leading us to the third world.

Believing that once a people lose their freedom there is no way to restore it by internal means without a complete collapse of the ruling superstructure as happened in the Soviet Union I am soon bringing out a new book, *Political Action Follows Political Philosophy*. While every author hopes his books will sell, this is a book I plant as seed for our descendants. It is a distillation of the Enlightenment political theory upon which our freedoms and our Constitution were founded as expressed against the background of the events which led to their demise: The History of the Future.

As I close today I pray for the freedom of all, and I counsel: keep the peace, keep the faith, we shall overcome.

Dispatch Twenty

What Can't Happen Here Did

Revolutions happened in other countries. That great slave house of nations the USSR, their satellite countries in Eastern Europe and Asia, African countries and of course those banana republics somewhere down south but one thing is for sure, it can't happen here. Following in the footsteps of giants who have used these prophetic words of Sinclair Lewis I want to examine how it did happen here.

In the America of George Washington, Thomas Jefferson, and James Madison, the America we inherited from our forefathers, we knew that there could never be a revolution. We had the Constitution with its checks and balances, its separation of powers, and its Bill of Rights. These were rock solid, carved in stone, and strong enough to preserve the Republic and safe guard the freedom of its people.

Besides the American people would not stand for some wannabe dictator and his brown, black, or whatever color shirt followers marching through the streets and into the White House. The sons of the Pioneers wouldn't sit still for any attempt to curtail limited government, personal freedom, or economic opportunity. No way! No how! Others might accept censorship, surveillance, and rigged elections but not us, not Americans. We had fought wars to defend our independence, wars to defeat totalitarianism; we had even fought wars to spread freedom. No, we wouldn't quietly allow homegrown tyrants to grasp the levers of power.

It sounds so comforting, "It can't happen here." If you take a beginning Political Science class in either High School or College you will learn how the government works. How bills become laws, how the legislature is made up of the freely elected representatives of the people, how the President runs the executive branch and the Supreme Court sits atop the judicial branch. You will learn about the Declaration of Independence and how the Constitution was written to replace the Articles of Confederation which were too weak to work. Yes, you will learn all about how it's supposed to work.

In most schools you will also learn that the Constitution is a "living Document" that can be re-interpreted to fit every generation and every age. The results of 100 years of re-interpretation have led us to the brink of ruin and me to recommend that the study of the Constitution should be moved from Political Science to History since what rules us today is legal precedent and bureaucratic regulation. The courts use foreign laws[cxxi] and traditions to interpret our laws and traditions.[cxxii] The legislature passes laws they don't read filled with thousands of pages of vague platitudes and goals that the bureaucrats fill in with no oversight and the force of law. And the President does whatever he wants and no one says a thing.

So how did America fall for the second oldest con in the world, "Give me your freedom and I'll give you security?"

Those who wished to gain power had no ideology or theology which inspired them. They only sought power for power's sake. They espoused whatever populist themes gave them the broadest support. To bring as many interest groups as possible into their coalition they embraced an "I'm okay you're okay" relativity that rejected absolutes and extoled the fringe as the mainstream.

And all the while the decedents of the blacksmiths and farmers who once congregated on corners to discuss the latest political pamphlet or to debate the merits of economic policy snoozed on the couch waking up long enough to go to work or watch the game.

The Revolutionaries of the New America first took root in the faculty lounges of academia providing the intellectual and cultural cover for an American movement that promoted the opposite of everything America stood for. From the classrooms of our colleges, came the next generations of teachers, journalists, lawyers, artists, and politicians. Soon it was common knowledge that our once rock-solid Constitution was a Living Document to be twisted and changed whenever those in power found the need.

From here it was just a matter of time until a revolution was accomplished through evolutionary change. Once the centers of power were secure in Washington, Hollywood, and in the media the trickle of change became a torrent and the torrent became a tsunami. Two wings on the same bird of prey, perpetually re-elected representatives from the twin headed party of power pander to the lowest common denominators, buying votes, using taxes to punish enemies and tax money to reward friends.

Our tyrants-in-training have captured the government and the economy, created a dependent class of motor-voters, convinced people that a continually growing debt is sustainable and turned the government into the one who picks winners and losers instead of a free economy. The slow slide down a slippery slope has accelerated into a precipitous procession over a predictable precipice. To those who have seen this coming it is like watching a slow motion train wreck. The coming destruction is not mitigated in the least by the decades or warning.

Our prideful boast of it can't happen here has become a heart wrenching analysis of how it did happen here. How did the Progressives capture our land and subvert our Republic? They did it gradually inch by inch, step by step. When they lost a round they held their gains and as soon as possible recovered their long march toward a fundamentally transformed nation.

How they changed it brings us to the question, "How do we change it back?"

Violent revolt is both repugnant and obviously suicidal to people who understand that once that genie is out of the bottle there is no way to know which way it will go, except that the odds are heavily against it ever landing back in a stable land of limited government and personal freedom. The power of the state is overwhelming. Millions of shot guns, pistols, and even those terrible assault rifles we are constantly being lectured about would make no headway against Abrams tanks and F-18s.

There are only two ways to have a successful peaceful revolution. One: the vast majority of the people must go on strike and refuse to operate as a society until the changes have been made. Or two: it must happen gradually line upon line verse upon verse always keeping the goal in sight and moving forward at every opportunity. In other words we must do to the new establishment what they did to the old: not overthrow it. Supplant it and replace it in the hearts and minds of the people.

We can rest assured that all people at all times eventually yearn for freedom thus the stage is set by the very nature of man that God imprinted on us in His creation. Free choice is the natural state of man and in the end we will return to it. This pall of totalitarianism which is falling like a shadow across the land will one day awake to find the light of liberty cannot be quenched forever.

What should we do? Education is the key. If you are not a teacher become one. Learn to show yourself approved. Teach anyone who will listen of freedom, of the true History of the American experiment. Become involved in any way you can to retake control of our education system so that we can train the coming generations to love freedom, truth, justice, and the American way.

And don't lose hope. God created us to be free and though tyrants always seek to ensnare people in their self-serving systems we will one day be free again. Draw near to God and He will draw near to you. Remember what we thought couldn't happen here did, and what they think can't happen to them will. Freedom will rise from the ashes, and one day the light of liberty will once again burn brightly in America the beautiful.

Dispatch Twenty-one

What Happens When Progressives Tax (and Spend)

As Rush Limbaugh so rightly pointed out, "No nation has ever taxed itself into prosperity."[cxxiii]

So many people have accepted the argument that progressive taxation is just, necessary, and fair, so I know this article will offend many. Hopefully it will also make a few people reconsider their acceptance of policy. Many who are vehemently opposed to socialism, collectivism, and all the other trappings of the centralized corporate state believe that any injustice that might result from a free society would and should be mitigated by a policy of progressive taxation. The government through its education arm and the politicians through their media arm have used both hands and done a superb job.

It hasn't only been dumbing down it has also been indoctrination convincing the patient that it makes sense to cut off both legs to keep them from running amuck. However; as James Madison said, "Knowledge will forever govern ignorance, and a people who mean to be their own governors, must arm themselves with the power knowledge gives. A popular government without popular information or the means of acquiring it, is but a prologue to a farce or a tragedy or perhaps both."[cxxiv]

The easiest thing to do would be to ignore this 800 pound elephant. As the cop on the block says when something has happened and there is most definitely something to see, "Move along there's nothing to see here." However as the Historian of the Future that would be irresponsible. For it is in the mass acceptance of this inherently unfair coercive action as fair that the base of democratic irresponsibility forms the basis for the towering structure which is the Progressive State.

For generations this once unconstitutional procedure for wealth distribution has been accepted without question. This was not always the case.

James Madison, the Father of the Constitution, had some interesting things to say about unequal taxation. Such as in his Essay on Property, March 29, 1792, "That is not a just government, nor is property secure under it, where the property which a man has in his personal safety and personal liberty, is violated by arbitrary seizures of one class of citizens for the service of the rest."[cxxv] And "A just security to property is not afforded by that government, under which unequal taxes oppress one species of property and reward another species: where arbitrary taxes invade the domestic sanctuaries of the rich, and excessive taxes grind the faces of the poor."[cxxvi]

In Europe which is often the source and first scene of the crime when it comes to the Socialist/Utopian schemes foisted on the uninformed and unsuspecting American public, when progressive taxation was first proposed during the French Revolution the classical liberal Anne-

Robert-Jacques Turgot, said, "One ought to execute the author and not the project."[cxxvii]

During the socialist led revolutions of 1848 Karl Marx and Friedrich Engels frankly proposed "a heavy progressive or graduated income tax"[cxxviii] as one of the measures by which, after the first stage of the revolution, "the proletariat will use its political supremacy to wrest, by degrees, all capital from the bourgeois, to centralize all instruments of production in the hands of the state."[cxxix] And these measures they described as "means of despotic inroads on the right of property, and on the condition of bourgeois production ... measures ...which appear economically insufficient and untenable but which, in the course of the movement outstrip themselves, necessitate further inroads upon the old social order and are unavoidable as a means of entirely revolutionizing the mode of production."[cxxx]

According to John Chamberlain in 1961, "It was Marxian socialism—'From each according to his abilities, to each according to his needs—which fathered the great attack on proportional tax equity: a 'heavy graduated income tax' is a salient feature of the Communist Manifesto of 1848. But the Marxians would have made little headway if non-Marxian economists had not come unwittingly to their support with the theory that 'it is not equal to treat unequals equally.' In cases of charity, this is undoubtedly true, but no comprehensive legal system can be reared on a rule which begins by regarding everybody as an exception."[cxxxi]

After these proposals for income redistribution had been dismissed out of hand by economic experts and thinking people as inherently unfair they were smuggled in as supposedly rational arguments based on the need or desire to spread the sacrifice equally. Those who presented this type of argument were careful to stress that they were not interested in income redistribution and that any progression beyond a modest scale should of course be condemned. Opponents tried to point out that once the principle of progression was accepted there was no limit to which the progression could be pushed. These opponents were said to be maliciously distorting the argument and showing a lack of confidence in democratic rule. Even today the watch word for the advocates of progressive taxation is that everyone should pay their fair share. This fair share is never defined.

The countries of Europe led by Prussia fell first to this pernicious scam. In the 1910 and 1913 respectively Great Britain and then the United States bought into the lie that inequality in taxation provides equality in sacrifice. At first the rates were moderate. In Great Britain they started at 8.5 % and In America at 7%. However within 30 years the top rates were 97.5% and 91 %. Within one generation that which its proponents said would never happen and its opponents said was inevitable came to pass.

This radical change in the rates and the progressive nature of the tax changed not only the degree but also the character of what was taking place. This soon became a vehicle for income distribution and nothing more. Social engineering based on the communist dictum "From each according to his ability to each according to his need." This is all based upon the difference between greed and envy. Greed wants more and will do what is necessary to attain it. Envy wants what someone else has and will do what is necessary to take it.

To solve the problem of greedy people making more than others, envious people created a system to take what the greedy had earned.

One of the foundation stones of the continuing support by the general non envious public for this institutionalized theft is the belief that the high rates levied on the rich make an indispensable contribution to the total revenue of the nation. This is an illusion. If all the assets of the rich were expropriated in their entirety they would not cover the profligate spending of the political class.

In 2011 Steve McCann pointed out, "Using the latest statistics from the IRS, in 2004 there were 2.7 million adults with a net worth above $1.5 million. If the government were to seize all the wealth above the $1.5 million threshold, Washington would realize a one-time windfall of $4.0 Trillion -- and no one would again attempt to accumulate wealth. Assuming it was applied to the national debt (unlikely with the Left in charge as they would spend it) the national debt would only be reduced from $14.5 Trillion to $10.0 Trillion."[cxxxii] And that would be a once in a lifetime score. Today the debt stands above 19 trillion.

In 2012 John Stossel noted, "If the IRS grabbed 100 percent of income over $1 million, the take would be just $616 billion. That's only a third of this year's deficit. Our national debt would continue to explode."[cxxxiii]

According to the non-partisan Tax Foundation's David Logan, "Even taking every last penny from every individual making more than $10 million per year would only reduce the nation's deficit by 12 percent and the debt by 2 percent."[cxxxiv] In any event according to Parkinson's Law, "The expenditures of the State always rise to meet potential income."

According to F. A. Hayek:

"The real reason why all the assurances that progression would remain moderate have proved false and why its development has gone far beyond the most pessimistic prognostications of its opponents is that all arguments in support of progression can be used to justify any degree of progression. Its advocates may realize that beyond a certain point the adverse effects on the efficiency of the economic system may become so serious as to make it inexpedient to push it any further. But the argument based on the presumed justice of progression provides for no limitation, as has often been admitted by its supporters, before all incomes above a certain figure are confiscated and those below left untaxed. Unlike proportionality, progression provides no principle which tells us what the relative burden of different persons ought to be. It is no more than a rejection of proportionality in favor of a discrimination against the wealthy without any criterion for limiting the extent of this discrimination."[cxxxv]

J. R. McCulloch expressed the problem with progressive taxation in this way, "The moment you abandon the cardinal principle of exacting from all individuals the same proportion of their income or of their property, you are at sea without rudder or compass, and there is no amount of injustice and folly you may not commit."[cxxxvi]

When will the insanity of unequal = equal stop? It will never end because there is no ideal rate of progression that can be demonstrated by any type of formula. There is never a reason why "a little more than before" should not always be represented as just and reasonable.

Looking to the end result Alexis de Tocqueville told us long ago, "The American Republic will endure until the day Congress discovers that it can bribe the public with the public's money."

Hayek assures us that this is not a general attack upon democratic principles. It is instead the revelation that democracy must be guided by principles or it will founder on the shoals of expediency and the illusion of rationality.

Hayek expressed it well, "It is no slur on democracy, no ignoble distrust of its wisdom, to maintain that, once it embarks upon such a policy, it is bound to go much further than originally intended. This is not to say that "free and representative institutions are a failure" or that it must lead to "a complete distrust in democratic government, but that democracy has yet to learn that, in order to be just, it must be guided in its action by general principles. What is true of individual action is equally true of collective action except that a majority is perhaps even less likely to consider explicitly the long-term significance of its decision and therefore is even more in need of guidance by principles. Where, as in the case of progression, the so-called principle adopted is no more than an open invitation to discrimination and, what is worse, an invitation to the majority to discriminate against a minority, the pretended principle, of justice must become the pretext for pure arbitrariness."[cxxxvii]

So what's the answer? First it should be obvious that the majority should not be able to impose a tax rate that it does not pay. Secondly the maximum rate of taxation should be tied to the % of the GDP devoted to government. If the government is absorbing 25% of the economy no rate higher than 25% should be allowed. If in the case of a war or other national emergency the rate of government cost rises the rate could rise, and when it falls the rate should fall.

Raising tax rates as a way to solve the debt problem just doesn't work. Looking at the 1950s when the rates were higher than they are today Hayek pointed out, "How small is the contribution of progressive tax rates (particularly of the high punitive rates levied on the largest incomes) to total revenue may be illustrated by a few figures for the United States and for Great Britain. Concerning the former it has been stated (in 1956) that the entire progressive super-structure produces only about 17 per cent of the total revenue derived from the individual income tax'-or about 8.5 per cent of all federal revenue,-- and that of this half is taken from taxable income brackets up through $16,000-$18,000, where the tax rate approaches 50 per cent (while] the other half comes from the higher brackets and rates."[cxxxviii]

When Congress was debating the 16th Amendment to allow for individual income taxes Massachusetts Rep. Samuel McCall stated, "The character of the argument which had been made leads me to believe that the chief purpose of the tax is not financial, but social. It is not primarily to raise money for the state, but to regulate the citizen and to regenerate the moral nature of man. The individual citizen will be called on to lay bare the innermost recesses of his soul in affidavits, and with the aid of the Federal inspector, who will supervise his books and papers and business secrets, he may be made to be good, according the notions of virtue at the moment prevailing in Washington."[cxxxix]

To paraphrase Parkinson's Law, "Government spending always rises to exceed revenues."

So what happens when Progressives tax? They tax us into poverty.

AND

Spend us into insolvency.

Dispatch Twenty Two

Who Voted For That?

Who voted for an immigration policy whose purpose is to change the racial, ethnic and cultural make-up of the United States? That is exactly what the Kennedy Immigration Bill of 1965 was designed to do and just what it has done.

Who voted for open borders and constant calls for amnesty for anyone who can drag themselves across the border? Has anyone else noticed that the estimate of how many illegals are in the United States has been stuck at 11 million for at least the last 11 years?

Who voted for anchor babies automatically gaining citizenship? This has led to birth tourism wherein pregnant women from all over the world fly in, have their babies, go home, and then Uncle Sugar is on the hook for these babies the rest of their lives. This entire fraudulent practice is based on a blatant misinterpretation of the 14th amendment. The correct interpretation based on original intent is readily available for anyone who can click a mouse.[cxl]

Contrary to the common knowledge of everyone successfully programed by the Corporations Once Known as the Mainstream Media and the public indoctrination centers once known as schools anchor babies are not found anywhere in the constitution. In fact they didn't even exist until 1982 when Justice Brennan slipped them into the footnote of a Supreme Court decision.[cxli] Notice I didn't say into a Supreme Court decision it is found only in a footnote.

And contrary to Bill O'Reilly and many other armchair lawyers this could be corrected without a constitutional amendment.[cxlii] All that is needed is a law which clarifies that Justice Brennan's footnote does not carry the force of law. It's kind of a no-brainer when you think about it.

Who voted for unlimited and unregulated abortion on demand? In 1973 the rogue Supreme Court out to remake America by fiat declared in Roe v. wade that all state laws regulating abortion were unconstitutional. Since that red letter day the blood of more than 57 million babies stains the hands of America. Our babies have been dismembered in the womb and had their skulls pierced with scissors as they were being born. Their bodies have been tossed like garbage into landfills, flushed down toilets, and sold for their organs.

Who voted for restricting the rights of lawful citizens to keep and bear arms? Over and over we hear about commonsense gun laws. Every one of these proposals does nothing to stop criminals from getting guns. They are criminals, so breaking the law is what they do. All of these proposals have just one result: they restrict the rights of law abiding citizens since they are the only ones who follow the laws.

When the Bill of Rights was added to the Constitution it was because the so-called Ant-Federalists refused to ratify the document without these first ten amendments. The statements of the Framers as enumerated in the Federalist Papers and the demands of the opposition as enumerated in the Anti-Federalist Papers makes it clear that the 2nd Amendment was meant[cxliii] to give the people the right to defend themselves against personal attack and against tyranny.[cxliv] Criminals love unarmed victims and tyrants love citizens who cannot resist their authority.

Who voted for Obamacare which destroyed the best healthcare system ever known to man and after six years we are told there are just as many people without insurance as there were before? Polls before its passage and since have consistently shown that the majority of the American people do not want this train wreck of a law. Yet despite our best efforts to make our opposition known this is shoved down our throats like a horse pill that chokes a patient to death before we find out it is really a placebo.

Who voted for our president to bow before despots and dictators? Never before in History has an American president bowed before a foreign leader or anyone else. Until the revolutionary presidency of Barak Obama it would have been considered shameful. No one ever imagined it would happen. Under the man determined to take America down a peg or two[cxlv] it hasn't happened, once or twice or even three times. On eight separate occasions our president has bowed before foreigners not only showing his respect for them but also showing his contempt for us.[cxlvi]

Who voted for the Fed to pump trillions of fiat money into Dodd-Frank banks too big to fail? Since the crash of 2008 the Federal Reserve has been printing money at an unprecedented rate. Where has all this monopoly money gone? To the banks too big to,[cxlvii] of course, through the happy-go-lucky-how-can-this-ever-fail money machine known as Quantitative Easing. What a friendly sounding name for a galloping printing press. All this supposed money is adding to the national debt and still no inflation. I think someone should tell the geniuses at the Fed what inflation is: more money chasing the same number of goods. No inflation means no raises for anyone except the plutocrats who run the crony capitalist institutions and the government people who print the money. No inflation, right. Has anyone been to the grocery store recently?

Who voted for an economy that instead of recovering has plateaued at a new normal with over 90 million[cxlviii] able bodied people out of the work force, only slightly more than 122 million[cxlix] working, and a government that calls this full employment? The government's own statistics show that approximately 62% of the workforce is working.[cl] To me that looks like 36% aren't working. Full employment is generally accepted as meaning, "The condition in which virtually all who are able and willing to work are employed." Does anyone see a problem with this picture?

Who voted for any of this?

Then Came Trump

Oh, wait a minute. Anyone who has voted for a Democrat in the last fifty years voted for all of this.

To paraphrase Sam Cooke

Don't know much about history
Don't know much biology
Don't know much about a science book
Don't know much about the French I took

Don't know much about geography
Don't know much trigonometry
Don't know much about algebra
Don't know what a slide rule is for

But I do know that if Progressives can fool you
And I know that if Progressives could fool me, too
What a wonderful world this would be

Just don't take the red pill. Whatever you do, don't take the red pill. Take the blue one. You'll feel much better as we slide into the dustbin of History.

Dispatch Twenty-three

Why Do I Say The Constitution Failed?

People often ask me, "How could you write a book entitled The Constitution Failed?"

If the Constitution was written to ensure a limited government and if today we have an unlimited central government my question is, "How can anyone contend that the Constitution hasn't failed?"

We know that for the last 100 years the Progressives have sought progress by changing the Constitution, which was written to establish unbreakable boundaries for government, without recourse to the amendment process. The Framers knew that without these boundaries government would grow into a millstone around the neck of the American people. Instead of a document establishing solid limits the Progressives say it is a living document that can be re-interpreted with each passing year evolving into whatever the current leaders may desire.

Our twin headed Progressive party of power expands and twists the General Welfare, the Commerce, and the Supremacy clauses to sanction any executive, legislative, judicial, or regulatory action they wish to impose whether it's a welfare state, energy policies, or the mandatory purchase of insurance. However, nothing is more symbolic of the current irrelevance of the Constitution to our leaders than the utter contempt they hold for the 9th and 10th Amendments.

Back during the original debate to ratify the Constitution these two sentinels of limited government were forced upon the proponents of a strong central government by those much maligned patriots the Anti-Federalists. The Constitution never would have been ratified without an assurance that the first order of business for the new government would be the ratification of the Bill of Rights. The capstone of these sacred rights is the 9th and the 10th Amendments which state:

The 9th Amendment, "The enumeration in the Constitution, of certain rights, shall not be construed to deny or disparage others retained by the people."

The 10th Amendment, "The powers not delegated to the United States by the Constitution, nor prohibited by it to the States, are reserved to the States respectively, or to the people."

I present the following examples of how our Progressive central government infringes upon the rights of the States and the people:

Term limits:

While in almost every instance that voters have had an opportunity to voice their opinion they have overwhelmingly approved term limits, and the courts have just as consistently overturned the will of the people. Through ballot initiatives and Constitutional amendments to State Constitutions the people have spoken, but instead of the voice of the people we hear the commands of the elites.

The Supreme Court in a classic five-to-four decision in U.S. Term Limits v. Thornton (1995) said the states don't have the authority to limit the terms of their own congressional delegations. They further ruled that unless the Constitution is amended neither the states nor Congress has the power to limit the number of terms members of Congress can serve.[cli] Dissenting Justice Clarence Thomas pointed out that the majority ignored the clear meaning of the Tenth Amendment.[clii] Since there is no explicit denial of the power to limit terms to the States in the Constitution the 10th Amendment clearly states this power is reserved to the States.

Immigration:

When the Governor and legislators of Arizona attempted to address the hundreds of thousands of illegal immigrants who are pouring over their borders with Mexico each year they first had to admit that the Federal Government was not enforcing their own laws. After the central government ignored their petitions and pleas for help for years the government of Arizona acted to protect their citizens.

Immediately, the Justice Department sued to block the law, contending it violates the U.S. Constitution. The Arizona law was subsequently struck down by the Federal Courts using the Supremacy Clause for their justification. Judge Richard Paez, said, "By imposing mandatory obligations on state and local officers, Arizona interferes with the federal government's authority to implement its priorities and strategies in law enforcement, turning Arizona officers into state-directed [Homeland Security] agents."[cliii] When it reached the 9th U.S. Circuit Court of Appeals a three judge panel said, "Congress has given the federal government sole authority to enforce immigration laws, and that Arizona's law violates the Supremacy Clause of the Constitution."[cliv] The Federal Government has abdicated its responsibility to protect Arizona from invasion and in their opinion a law that requires law enforcement officials to enforce the law goes too far.

The intrusive actions of the Transportation Security Administration (TSA):

Legislators in Texas decided to take action to protect their citizens from what many considered to be overly aggressive pat-downs. The reaction of the TSA to Texas attempting to protect their citizens from the molestation the Federal Agency calls a pat-down is indicative of the attitude our central government has towards any infringement of their absolute power. On their website *The TSA Blog* the gatekeepers of the air said, "What's our take on the Texas House of Representatives voting to ban the current TSA pat-down? Well, the Supremacy Clause of the U.S. Constitution (Article. VI. Clause 2) prevents states from regulating the federal government."[clv] This says it all. As far as our Federal masters are concerned there is no limit to their power.

Obamacare: Mandating action and penalizing inaction:

The Federal Government's successful attempt to enforce the mandatory purchase provisions of Obamacare alternately as authorized by the Commerce Clause and as a tax, depending on which argument they think a judge would uphold.[clvi] This massive invasion of personal liberty was challenged by 28 States as being beyond the bounds of the Constitution.[clvii] Two judges ruled it unconstitutional[clviii] and three have ruled it constitutional.

This provision wherein not taking an action is considered either engaging in commerce and thereby subject to regulation and that a non-action is taxable was ruled constitutional by a delusional Supreme Court. Which leads me to ask, what is left of our precious freedom? What other non-actions will now be under the power of the government. If a government can control our non-actions what does that say about their power over our actions?

By ignoring the unambiguous meaning of the 9th and 10th Amendments and by stretching and twisting the meanings of a few vague clauses the Progressive leaders of our Federal government have interpreted our Constitution to mean anything needed to do anything desired. Once the words lose their meanings, once the sentences can mean anything the Progressives want, what power does the Constitution have to limit government?

Ultimately this is a message of hope because I trust in the ability of the American people to solve any problem they confront. However, we have to admit there is a problem before we can solve it, and if we refuse to admit there is a problem we have no chance of solving it. The problem is our limited government has become unlimited and does whatever it wants. How can I say, "The Constitution Failed"? What I am saying is our system is broken, it is no longer functioning as designed, and we need a re-set button.

Dispatch Twenty-four

Why Do They Lie to Us Over and Over?

Joseph Goebbels, Hitler's Minister of Propaganda said, "If you tell a lie big enough and keep repeating it, people will eventually come to believe it. The lie can be maintained only for such time as the State can shield the people from the political, economic and/or military consequences of the lie. It thus becomes vitally important for the State to use all of its powers to repress dissent, for the truth is the mortal enemy of the lie, and thus by extension, the truth is the greatest enemy of the State."[clix]

Progressives and the Big Lie(s):

When faced with the highest levels of unemployment in American History why does the government trumpet a falling unemployment rate? In the face of overwhelming evidence of ineptness at best in Benghazi why do our hacks and their flacks insult us with answers like, "Dude this was two years ago!"[clx] With the obvious politicization of the IRS why does the president tell us there isn't even a smidgen of corruption in the IRS while professional bureaucrats who really run this country take the 5th, stonewall, and lie?[clxi]

The Corporations Once Known as the Mainstream Media regales us with oxymoronic statements such as, "Despite the unemployment rate plummeting, more than 92 million Americans remain out of the labor force."[clxii] The Great Recession grinds on in the lives of everyday working people while our leaders talk about a recovery that only benefits them and their cronies. If you live in Washington DC or the surrounding area you are probably doing fine, for the rest of us in fly-over country not so much.

The shoes in the Benghazi scandal continue to drop finally reaching the point where even go-along-to-get-along John Boehner finally agreed to allow the House to vote on the establishment of a select Committee so that this long simmering embarrassment could hopefully come to the truth. Then again, as our once and future Queen said, "What difference at this point does it make?" [clxiii]

A funny thing happened on his way to becoming the Speaker of the House after Boehner fell on his sword for the Progressive agenda House Majority Leader Kevin McCarthy said the entire Benghazi investigation was designed only to hurt Hillary's poll numbers. He blew his chance for the big seat but at least he completely discredited the committee which also advanced the Progressive agenda.[clxiv]

Remember the IRS scandal? The one that was swept under the carpet.[clxv]

Article 2 section 1 of the Articles of Impeachment filed against President Nixon was about the abuse of power. It stated, "He has, acting personally and through his subordinated and agents, endeavored to obtain from the Internal Revenue Service, in violation of the constitutional rights of citizens, confidential information contained in income tax returns for purposes not authorized by law, and to cause, in violation of the constitutional rights of citizens, income tax audits or other income tax investigation to be initiated or conducted in a discriminatory manner."[clxvi]

Now 40 years later, under the Obama regime, the taxman cometh.[clxvii] When massive harassment of conservative groups by the IRS came to light as reported in The Daily Caller (DC) we were told:

- **Progressives were targeted, too**

For months, Democrats and the media relied on the talking point that progressive groups also ended up on an IRS "Be on the Lookout" list while the agency was auditing and seizing information from conservative groups. But as The DC reported, IRS agents testified before the House oversight committee that the IRS scrutinized ACORN groups because it thought they were old groups applying as new ones; the group Emerge America was scrutinized for potential "improper private benefit;" and no evidence exists to prove that the IRS targeted any Occupy Wall Street group.

"Only seven applications in the IRS backlog contained the word 'progressive,' all of which were then approved by the IRS... [T]here is simply no evidence that any liberal or progressive group received enhanced scrutiny because its application reflected the organization's political views," according to an oversight committee staff report.

- **No White House involvement**

"Not necessarily the White House" was the phrase that some Democratic "strategist" used when attacking one of our Daily Caller stories on cable television last year. He meant that while the IRS may have been corrupt to its very Washington core, President Barack Obama and Valerie Jarrett have not yet been photographed sifting through tea party applications at a desk in the Lincoln Bedroom.

But we do know, however, courtesy of The Daily Caller's reporting, that Lerner exchanged confidential taxpayer information on conservative groups with White House officials including White House health-policy adviser Ellen Montz and Deputy Assistant to the President for Health Policy Jeanne Lambrew, who just happened to be the most powerful official on Obamacare implementation within the White House.

- **A couple of rogue agents in Cincinnati**

Ah, yes. The "WKRP in Cincinnati" Theory of 2013. You know the episode where the wacky characters in the Cincinnati office make a little "whoops" and take it upon themselves to target conservatives nationwide? A team of reporters from The New York Times, including dreamboat Nicholas Confessore, even went to bat for the administration on this theory last year, publishing a disgraceful article about Ohio-based "confusion" and "staff troubles" among "Low-level employees in what many in the I.R.S. consider a backwater."

But at least five different offices ranging from Chicago to Laguna Niguel, CA. engaged in this kind of "confusion," and the whole excuse got torn down like Riverside Stadium. A Cincinnati-based IRS official said that Washington "was basically throwing us under the bus."

- **Lerner can still cite the Fifth Amendment**

That's what her lawyer, Bill Taylor, wrote in a recent letter to Speaker of the House John Boehner and Majority Leader Eric Cantor, calling a possible contempt vote "un-American." But it's just not true. Lerner waived her Fifth Amendment privilege when she made a statement attesting to her innocence at a May 2013 oversight hearing. The oversight committee and U.S. House counsel both determined as much.

- **It could take years for the IRS to get all of Lerner's emails**

That's what new IRS Commissioner John Koskinen, who has been threatened with contempt himself, told oversight investigators. But the independent group Judicial Watch managed to obtain emails showing Lerner coordinating with the Department of Justice to potentially prosecute conservative activists. It only took Judicial Watch one Freedom of Information Act request to get that stuff. "Now I see why the IRS is scared to give up the rest of Lois Lerner's emails," said oversight member Rep. Jim Jordan. When they were found and they did show not only that the conservative groups were targeted but also that the IRS tried to cover it up, nothing happened except Louis Lerner continues to receive her massive pension of over $100,000 per year plus we have learned that she also earned Up to $129,000 in bonuses for her exemplary work.

- **Don't worry, federal government investigators are on top of things**

Eric Holder's Department of Justice tapped an Obama political donor to head its investigation. FBI investigators went months without contacting the conservative groups that were victimized by the IRS targeting, and leaked to the press that no criminal charges would be filed in relation to the case before much of the relevant information we currently have even came out.

The Obama administration's investigation of the scandal was such a joke that House Judiciary Committee Chairman Rep. Bob Goodlatte accused Obama and Holder of "undermining" investigators on multiple occasions, and joined with other House GOP leaders in calling for a special counsel to prosecute the case.

But if the investigation was a joke, here's the punchline: The Justice Department has been the only investigative body to ask Lois Lerner any questions, at an off-the-record "Q+A" that was not under oath.

- **Only tea party groups were targeted**

Good for the IRS for taking a firm stand against all those wacky tea party groups popping up out in

Palookaville trying to exercise their little "First Amendment rights." Bunch of Koch-funded rednecks.

But oh wait: The IRS also audited the Leadership Institute, founded by Morton C. Blackwell, which has been one of the Washington area's foremost conservative activist training organizations since 1979, even demanding personal information about the institute's college-aged interns. Oh yeah, and the IRS also told a pro-life group "you can't force your religion" and tried to stop pro-life activists from picketing Planned Parenthood clinics.

- **The targeting is over now**

Sure it is. Just ask Ron Paul and his group Campaign for Liberty's donors about that.

Now the latest update, despite a court order to the contrary the IRS has deleted hard drives that held critical evidence in the agency's on-going scandals.[clxviii]

And now the BIG LIE continues in the Benghazi scandal. The movie 13 Hours has come out. It is amazing and every American should see it. Written by and based upon the experiences of three of the surviving heroes this movie tells the story that has been hidden from us for so long. In the aftermath of the release the families of the victims have once again come forward and said that Hillary told them at the coffin ceremony that a video was the cause of the attack. She also said[clxix] that they would arrest the maker of the video.[clxx] Subsequently some of Hillary's emails which were only obtained through a Freedom of Information request, a law suit and a judge's order show that she knew this to be a lie at the time she used it to cover herself and the President at the time.[clxxi] She has admitted this is true at the discredited Benghazi hearings.[clxxii]

The families are saying Hillary lied.[clxxiii] Hillary is now saying that she never blamed the video and in essence that the families are lying.[clxxiv] Every news outlet is playing this like a "He said she said" debate. They are interviewing the families. Of course Hillary avoids interviews from anyone except her pet networks and their softball questions.

Here is my big problem with the big lie. One click of the mouse and you can pull up the YouTube video of Hillary at the coffin ceremony blaming the video.[clxxv] The maker of the video was arrested and is still in jail. The one who lied to the families, lied to the nation isn't in jail, isn't under a cloud of shame. No, they are now busy with the help of the Corporations Once Known as the Mainstream Media and their cable henchmen lying her way to the White House

Why do they lie to us over and over?

The easy answer is because they can. The major media has morphed from a watchdog to a lapdog barking on cue that everything is all right, there's nothing to see here, move along.

The best government money can buy has shown us that they can safely operate on the assumption that American voters choose their leaders based on the philosophy, "I know he's a liar but I like what he says."

But hey there's a game on tonight! Or as President Obama's body double Alfred E. Newman has been known to say, "What me, worry?"

Dispatch Twenty-five

Why Does America Have a Written Constitution?

Recently I spent some time with a person I respect highly, who is very intelligent, and who has thought about and reached conclusions concerning America's Constitution. This person, who is representative of many others, believes that a document written hundreds of years ago is meaningless in today's America. He cited the fact that many of the Framers were slave owners, they could not have imagined a nation of hundreds of millions, they could not foresee the technologically rich environment we call home, or the diverse population that now constitutes the body politic.

None of the things cited above can be refuted because they are all true.

First of all, what is a constitution? A constitution organizes, distributes and regulates the power of the state. A constitution sets out the structure of the state, the major state institutions, and the principles governing their relations with each other and with the state's citizens.

So, why do we have a written Constitution, and does this written Constitution still matter?

When the American Revolutionaries broke free from Great Britain they wanted to build their new nation on a solid foundation. They most assuredly did not want what they had just rebelled against, a monarchy or an unlimited government.

Did the British have a constitution? In the Eighteenth Century just as it is now Britain is unusual in that it has an 'unwritten' constitution: unlike the great majority of countries there is no single legal document which sets out in one place the fundamental laws outlining how the state works. Britain's lack of a 'written' constitution can be explained by its history. In other countries, many of whom have experienced revolution or regime change, it has been necessary to start from scratch or begin from first principles, constructing new state institutions and defining in detail their relations with each other and their citizens.

By contrast, the British Constitution has evolved over a long period of time, reflecting the relative stability of the British polity. It has never been thought necessary to consolidate the basic building blocks of this order in Britain. What Britain has instead is an accumulation of various statutes, conventions, judicial decisions and treaties which collectively can be referred to as the British Constitution. It is thus more accurate to refer to

Britain's constitution as an 'uncodified' constitution, rather than an 'unwritten' one.

The British Constitution can be summed up in eight words: What the monarch in Parliament enacts is law. This means that Parliament, using the power of the Crown, enacts law which no other body can challenge. Parliamentary sovereignty is commonly regarded as the defining principle of the British Constitution. This is the ultimate lawmaking power vested in a democratically elected Parliament to create or abolish any law. Other core principles of the British Constitution are often thought to include the rule of law, the separation of government into executive, legislative, and judicial branches, and the existence of a unitary state, meaning ultimate power is held by 'the center' – the sovereign Westminster Parliament.

In other words there is neither check upon nor balance to the power of the government. The entire shape, form, and substance of the government can change at any time by a simple majority vote of Parliament. To sum up: the British Constitution is a living document.

This is what caused the revolution. If you look at the list of particulars that are in the overlooked or forgotten part of the Declaration of Independence you see that many of these individual charges against the Monarch as the representation of the government are changes made by arbitrary and unilateral acts of Parliament.

- He has refused his Assent to Laws, the most wholesome and necessary for the public good.

- He has forbidden his Governors to pass Laws of immediate and pressing importance, unless suspended in their operation till his Assent should be obtained; and when so suspended, he has utterly neglected to attend to them.

- He has refused to pass other Laws for the accommodation of large districts of people, unless those people would relinquish the right of Representation in the Legislature, a right inestimable to them and formidable to tyrants only.

- He has called together legislative bodies at places unusual, uncomfortable, and distant from the depository of their public Records, for the sole purpose of fatiguing them into compliance with his measures.

- He has dissolved Representative Houses repeatedly, for opposing with manly firmness his invasions on the rights of the people.

- He has refused for a long time, after such dissolutions, to cause others to be elected; whereby the Legislative powers, incapable of Annihilation, have returned to the People at large for their exercise; the State remaining in the mean time (sic) exposed to all the dangers of invasion from without, and convulsions within.

- He has endeavoured (sic) to prevent the population of these States; for that purpose obstructing the Laws for Naturalization of Foreigners; refusing to pass others to encourage their migrations hither, and raising the conditions of new Appropriations of Lands.
- He has obstructed the Administration of Justice, by refusing his Assent to Laws for establishing Judiciary powers.
- He has made Judges dependent on his Will alone, for the tenure of their offices, and the amount and payment of their salaries.
- He has erected a multitude of New Offices, and sent hither swarms of Officers to harass our people, and eat out their substance.
- He has kept among us, in times of peace, Standing Armies without the Consent of our legislatures.
- He has affected to render the military independent of and superior to the civil power.
- He has combined with others to subject us to a jurisdiction foreign to our constitution, and unacknowledged by our laws; giving his Assent to their Acts of pretended Legislation:

- For Quartering large bodies of armed troops among us
- For protecting them, by a mock Trial, from punishment for any Murders which they should commit on the Inhabitants of these States
- For cutting off our Trade with all parts of the world
- For imposing Taxes on us without our Consent
- For depriving us in many cases, of the benefits of Trial by Jury
- For transporting us beyond Seas to be tried for pretended offences
- For abolishing the free System of English Laws in a neighbouring (sic) Province, establishing therein an Arbitrary government, and enlarging its Boundaries so as to render it at once an example and fit instrument for introducing the same absolute rule into these Colonies
- For taking away our Charters, abolishing our most valuable Laws, and altering fundamentally the Forms of our Governments
- For suspending our own Legislatures, and declaring themselves invested with power to legislate for us in all cases whatsoever

- He has abdicated Government here, by declaring us out of his Protection and waging War against us.

- He has plundered our seas, ravaged our Coasts, burnt our towns, and destroyed the lives of our people.

- He is at this time transporting large Armies of foreign Mercenaries to compleat (sic) the works of death, desolation and tyranny, already begun with circumstances of Cruelty & perfidy scarcely paralleled in the most barbarous ages, and totally unworthy the Head of a civilized nation.

- He has constrained our fellow Citizens taken Captive on the high Seas to bear Arms against their Country, to become the executioners of their friends and Brethren, or to fall themselves by their Hands.

- He has excited domestic insurrections amongst us, and has endeavoured (sic) to bring on the inhabitants of our frontiers, the merciless Indian Savages, whose known rule of warfare, is an undistinguished destruction of all ages, sexes and conditions.

The colonists tried to follow the procedures as they knew them to find relief within the system. But they were ignored and baffled as the system kept changing. They describe their experience dealing with the shifting sands of their revered living document in the following words.

In every stage of these Oppressions We have Petitioned for Redress in the most humble terms: Our repeated Petitions have been answered only by repeated injury. A Prince whose character is thus marked by every act which may define a Tyrant, is unfit to be the ruler of a free people.

Nor have We been wanting in attentions to our British (sic) brethren. We have warned them from time to time of attempts by their legislature to extend an unwarrantable jurisdiction over us. We have reminded them of the circumstances of our emigration and settlement here. We have appealed to their native justice and magnanimity, and we have conjured them by the ties of our common kindred to disavow these usurpations, which would inevitably interrupt our connections and correspondence. They too have been deaf to the voice of justice and of consanguinity. We must, therefore, acquiesce in the necessity, which denounces our Separation, and hold them, as we hold the rest of mankind, Enemies in War, in Peace Friends.

It was because of this failed effort to deal with a system that has no solid structure, a system that can change at the will of a simple majority that the Framers were determined to set our new nation on the solid rock of a written constitution. What did the Founders and Framers have to say?

George Washington said, "The basis of our political systems is the right of the people to make and to alter their constitutions of government. But the Constitution, which at any time exists, 'till changed by an explicit and authentic act of the whole people, is sacredly obligatory upon all. ... If in the opinion of the people the distribution or modification of the constitutional powers be in any particular wrong, let it be corrected by an amendment in the way which the Constitution designates. But let there be no change by usurpation; for though this in one instance may be the instrument of good, it is the customary weapon by which free governments are destroyed."[clxxvi]

Thomas Jefferson said, "Our peculiar security is in possession of a written Constitution. Let us not make it a blank paper by construction. ... If it is, then we have no Constitution."[clxxvii]

James Madison said, "Can it be of less consequence that the meaning of a Constitution should be fixed and known, than a meaning of a law should be so?"[clxxviii]

This is what we were founded upon and this is the philosophical underpinning for the originalist view of the constitution as championed by the late Supreme Court Justice Antonin Scalia.

What do the leading lights of the living document side of the argument have to say?

Woodrow Wilson said, "Living political constitutions must be Darwinian in structure and in practice. Society is a living organism and must obey the laws of life, not of mechanics; it must develop. All that progressives ask or desire is permission—in an era when 'development,' 'evolution,' is the scientific word—to interpret the Constitution according to the Darwinian principle; all they ask is recognition of the fact that a nation is a living thing and not a machine."[clxxix]

FDR said, "The United States Constitution has proved itself the most marvelously elastic compilation of rules of government ever written." [clxxx]

Supreme Court Justice Felix Frankfurter said, "The words of the Constitution ... are so unrestricted by their intrinsic meaning or by their history or by tradition or by prior decisions that they leave the individual Justice free, if indeed they do not compel him, to gather meaning not from reading the Constitution but from reading life."[clxxxi]

Supreme Court Justice Thurgood Marshall said, "I cannot accept this invitation [to celebrate the bicentennial of the Constitution], for I do not believe that the meaning of the Constitution was forever 'fixed' at the Philadelphia Convention ... To the contrary, the government they devised was defective from the start."

Supreme Court Justice Antonin Scalia summed up the end result of more than a century of Progressive constitutional stretching. "If we're picking people to draw out of their own conscience and experience a 'new' Constitution, we should not look principally for good lawyers. We should look to people who agree with us. When we are in that mode, you realize we have rendered the Constitution useless."[clxxxii]

Or to put it another way the Progressive's living document has gone a long way to changing the Constitution from something carved in stone to a mirage written in the sand. So why do we have a written constitution? In my opinion we need a written constitution so that the government cannot change the social contract with the wave of its hand or the passage of thousand page bills no one even reads.

So why do we have a written constitution?

To keep demagogues and tyrants from arbitrarily changing the rules by which we live. If you think this has worked see my book The Constitution Failed. As a professor of Political Science and as the Director of one of the largest Political Science Departments at any university I have long advocated that the study of the Constitution should be moved from Political Science to History because it has become merely an historical document and now has little to do with how our country is administered by the political class.

Does it still matter? Only if the citizens of this nation have the fortitude to rise up and demand that it matters.

Dispatch Twenty-six

Why Empires Fall

Although the generalization is usually applied to republics, according to Sir John Glubb, a British author and lecturer, most empires don't last longer than 250 years.

The nation	Dates of rise and fall	Duration in years
Assyria	859-612 B.C.	247
Persia	538-330 B.C.	208
(Cyrus and his descendants)		
Greece	331-100 B.C.	231
(Alexander and his successors)		
Roman Republic	260-27 B.C.	233
Roman Empire	27 B.C.-A.D. 180	207
Arab Empire	A.D. 634-880	246
Mameluke Empire	1250-1517	267
Ottoman Empire	1320-1570	250
Spain	1500-1750	250
Romanov Russia	1682-1916	234
Britain	1700-1950	250

Or as Sir John said in summation:

As numerous points of interest have arisen in the course of this essay, I close with a brief summary, to refresh the reader's mind.

(a) We do not learn from history because our studies are brief and prejudiced.
(b) In a surprising manner, 250 years emerges as the average length of national greatness.
(c) This average has not varied for 3,000 years. Does it represent ten generations?
(d) The stages of the rise and fall of great nations seem to be:
The Age of Pioneers (outburst)
The Age of Conquests
The Age of Commerce
The Age of Affluence
The Age of Intellect
The Age of Decadence.
(e) Decadence is marked by:
Defensiveness
Pessimism
Materialism
Frivolity
An influx of foreigners
The Welfare State
A weakening of religion.
(f) Decadence is due to:
Too long a period of wealth and power

Selfishness
Love of money
The loss of a sense of duty.[clxxxiii]

Does any of this sound familiar? In other words all empires rise and all empires fall. It is the luck of the draw or the happenstance of birth that situates us as spectators of the fall.

I know from experience as the Author of *The Constitution Failed* that if you question the viability of the American experiment even the most humble participant in that experiment becomes indignant. As I have been asked repeatedly, "How can you say, the Constitution failed don't you mean, we failed the Constitution?" This always elicits my response, "Is that a distinction without a difference?"

Since the declared and understood purpose to the writing and ratification of the Constitution was to create and sustain a limited government and since *We the People* now face an unlimited government I maintain we must face the painful reality that the Constitution has failed. With that failure the experiment in individual liberty, personal freedom, and economic opportunity is hurtling towards a destination with destiny as we become like all the other nations of the earth: a command economy with a permanent political class.

When did we start our slide from a limited government to a centrally-planned Leviathan masquerading as a utopian paradise?

The experiment jumped the tracks under the second president. John Adams signed the Alien and sedition Act and then used that act to arrest anyone who disagreed with him. This was not the beginning of our present slide into totalitarianism.

Abraham Lincoln waged total war against eleven States that sought to secede when the right to secede was not withheld from the states and the right to wage war against the States was not afforded to the Federal Government by the Constitution. He did however allow West Virginia to secede from Virginia without the approval of the Virginia government which is explicitly contrary to the Constitution. This was not the beginning of our present slide into totalitarianism.

In the midst of the banking crisis of 1932-33 FDR told America, "We have nothing to fear but fear itself." He should have told us that we had him and his Progressive agenda to fear, at least as far as the fundamental nature of the American Experiment was concerned.

Despite the fact that by 1932 the recovery from the crash of 1929 was well under way as evidenced by freight loadings that rose 20 percent, industrial production 21 percent, construction contract awards gained 30 percent, unemployment dropped by nearly one million, wholesale prices rebounded by 20 percent, and the battered stock market was up by 40 percent. David Stockman goes so far as to say, "the Hoover recovery would be celebrated in the history books even today if it had not been interrupted in the winter of 1932-1933 by a faux banking crisis which was entirely the doing of President-elect Roosevelt and the loose-talking economic statist at the core of his transition team."[clxxxiv]

At that time the banking crisis, as it was loudly and universally called, had Americans fearing that the economy was about to collapse. This has been called the failure of capitalism. However as David Stockman points out,

> The truth of the so-called banking crisis is that the artificial economic boom of 1914-1929 had generated a drastic proliferation of banks in the farm country and in the booming new industrial centers like Chicago, Detroit, Youngtown and Toledo, along with vast amounts of poorly underwritten debt on real estate and businesses.
>
> When the bubble burst in 1929, the financial system experienced the time-honored capitalist cure — a sweeping liquidation of bad debts and under-capitalized banks. Not only was this an unavoidable and healthy purge of economic rot, but also reflected

the fact that the legions of banks which failed were flat-out insolvent and should have been closed.[clxxxv]

How great was this meltdown? How many people lost everything in the bank failures? Was this a massive slide into a financial morass? As David Stockman summed it up, "Indeed, a single startling statistic puts paid to the whole New Deal mythology that FDR rescued the banking system after a veritable heart attack: to wit, losses at failed US banks during the entire 12-year period ending in 1932 amounted to only 2-3 percent of deposits. There never was a sweeping contagion of failure in the banking system."[clxxxvi]

Foreshadowing President Obama's first Chief of Staff Rahm Emanuel who said, "You never let a serious crisis go to waste. And what I mean by that it's an opportunity to do things you think you could not do before,"[clxxxvii] FDR used this crisis to forever change the very structure of American government.

FDR didn't introduce his sweeping changes in the dead of night. He campaigned on them. He said he would bring in a New Deal for all Americans and he did. As his first inaugural speech ended he laid his cards on the table, "It is to be hoped that the normal balance of executive and legislative authority may be wholly adequate to meet the unprecedented task before us. But it may be that an unprecedented demand and need for undelayed (sic) action may call for temporary departure from that normal balance of public procedure."[clxxxviii]

In these two sentences the new president announced that if he deemed it necessary to upend the balance of powers he would do so. He then threatened to do whatever he thought necessary in the 1933 version of President Obama's "We can't wait" proclamation.[clxxxix] Instead of saying, "I have a pen and I have a phone,"[cxc] FDR said, "But in the event that the Congress shall fail to take one of these two courses, and in the event that the national emergency is still critical, I shall not evade the clear course of duty that will then confront me. I shall ask the Congress for the one remaining instrument to meet the crisis—broad Executive power to wage a war against the emergency, as great as the power that would be given to me if we were in fact invaded by a foreign foe."[cxci]

Congress did not fight. They did not stand on their prerogatives as a co-equal branch. Instead they knuckled under and in 100 days created an alphabet soup of federal agencies to control everything from soup to nuts. America began its dramatic descent from freedom and liberty to servitude and regulation. With FDR's imagery of a war against an emergency America found itself at war with a recession which had already ended successfully turning it into the Great Depression which wouldn't end for eight more years.

Since that time we have declared war on poverty. Fifty years and several trillion dollars later and we have just as much poverty as before. We have declared war on drugs and hundreds of thousands of incarcerations and trillions of dollars later and the drug problem is worse than before. We have of course also been in either a hot or a cold war since 1941 and hundreds of thousands of lives and many trillions of dollars later we have less security than we had before.

All of this has led to an erosion of our individual liberty, personal freedom, and economic opportunity. The balance of power has all but dissolved as Congress ceded its power to the executive and the bureaucracy while nine Supreme Justices make all the final decisions.

The Constitution was written to set the foundations for how our nation should be ruled. The First Article of the Constitution established the Legislature and most of the document deals with the Legislature, obviously the most important part of our national government. The part that is closest to the people. Today that body has transferred its power and we are faced with an imperial presidency and a Supreme Court that has decreed itself to be the source and the summit of legitimacy.

John Locke, the inspiration of much that became our Constitution said in his Second Treatise of Civil Government, "The Legislative cannot transfer the Power of Making Laws to any other hands. For it being but a delegated Power from the People, they, who have it, cannot pass it over to others."[cxcii]

Yet this is what has happened and this is why we are no longer forging ahead at the vanguard of humanity. We are instead rapidly becoming the source of raw materials and a market place for the goods of others: a colony in all but name. Or as the saying goes, the borrower is slave to the lender.

Everywhere I go and everyone I speak with knows America is losing its edge, sliding down a Progressive rat hole into an over-regulated shabby future in the dustbin of History. At the same time everywhere I go and everyone I speak to says, "At least it won't happen in my day but I feel sorry for the generations coming after me."

Why do empires fall? Because they think they won't.

Then Came Trump

Dispatch Twenty-seven

America First!

I was raised by people who believed in "My country right or wrong." I was taught that America never started a war and never lost a war. Reading *Burry My Heart at Wounded Knee* and an honest appraisal of the War of 1812 disabused me of those two notions. While the jingoist attitude of blind acceptance and unreflective loyalty and unquestioning support for a sacred homeland are not descriptive of my life I am devoted to the enlightenment ideas enshrined in the Constitution.

I am a vocal proponent of the nation founded on the proposition that all men are created equal, that they are endowed by their Creator with certain unalienable Rights that among these are Life, Liberty, and the pursuit of Happiness. I am a proud supporter of the federal republic founded in order to form a more perfect Union, establish Justice, insure domestic Tranquility, provide for the common defense, promote the general Welfare, and secure the Blessings of Liberty to ourselves and our Posterity.

I am an avowed non-interventionist capitalist who believes passionately in individual liberty, personal freedom, and economic opportunity. I was a Republican all my life, working my first campaign ringing door bells for Nixon in 1960, supporting Goldwater, Reagan for Governor and then for president in 1976, 1980, and 84.

George H.W. Bush with his compassionate conservatism and new world order turned me off. Bob "It's my Turn" Dole discouraged me and after the Contract with America Congress veered off the rails and started pushing bigger government and crony capitalism I quit the party and became an independent. George the Second pushed me over the edge. I could no longer consider myself a Conservative because there was nothing left to conserve, so I began to style myself as a radical who believes in a return to limited government, individual liberty, personal freedom, and economic opportunity.

The Clinton interlude between the Bush bookends and the Obamanation I have viewed as akin to the Vichy regime in France during WW II. They were and are mere figureheads for the multinational corporations and international organizations to which they surrendered our independence doing their best to institutionalize the Corporate State.

I have long believed and advocated for the following policies.

Moratoriums on all immigration until those who are already here are assimilated. Initiate policies which will induce those who are here illegally to self-deport. These policies would include a cut off of public assistance and an E-verify law with teeth meaning significant fines for people who employ illegals and incarceration for those who have multiple offenses. In foreign policy, resigning as the policeman of the world by ending our far-flung system of bases in more than a hundred countries, leaving Europe and Korea to defend themselves, bringing our troops home, securing the border and our defenses with the strongest military in the world and stop intervening in places that are not in our national interest.

Yes, I know that these proposals will be called racist, xenophobic and anti-American by the open borders clique; however, to quote Ronaldus Magnus, "A nation that cannot control its borders is not a nation."[cxciii] They will also be opposed by the neo-con hawks as isolationist. I stand with Ron Paul when he says, "The Founders and all the early presidents argued the case for non-intervention overseas, with the precise goals of avoiding entangling alliances and not involving our people in foreign wars unrelated to our security."[cxciv]

Yes, I know tariffs will make prices rise for many goods. However, I also know that we need to rebuild our industrial base if we are to remain an independent nation capable of providing jobs for our people that support a middleclass lifestyle and a nation that can provide for its own defense.

Yes, I know that a non-interventionist resignation from being the policeman of the world is portrayed as a retreat and as abdicating our leadership of the world. I call it jettisoning the empire to save the republic.

These positions have been heretical within the globalist interventionist neo-con Republican Party of Bush, McCain, Krauthammer, and the National Review. However, today is a new day and perhaps there is a chance to right the Ship of State and resurrect the greatest experiment in human freedom in History before we plunge into the dustbin of History as another centralized collectivist utopia that will inevitably end up a dystopian nightmare.

Now we face a choice of historic proportions. Do we want Hillary "The Last Nail in Our Coffin" Clinton to complete the transfer of American sovereignty to international globalist cabals such as the WTO and the UN? Or are we willing to vote for the first candidate since Buchanan with the courage to even say, "America First"?

I am still an independent. I will not rejoin the Republican Party unless and until it has been purged of its globalist leadership. However, I have waited my entire life to hear a politician say what The Donald said in his speech of June 28, 2016 "Declaring America's Economic Independence."[cxcv] In this speech he outlines a program I can endorse 100%.

Mr. Trump said in that speech,

> This wave of globalization has wiped out our middle class.
>
> It doesn't have to be this way. We can turn it all around - and we can turn it around fast.
>
> But if we're going to deliver real change, we're going to have to reject the campaign of fear and

intimidation being pushed by powerful corporations, media elites, and political dynasties.

The people who rigged the system for their benefit will do anything - and say anything - to keep things exactly as they are.

The people who rigged the system are supporting Hillary Clinton because they know as long as she is in charge nothing will ever change.

The inner cities will remain poor.

The factories will remain closed.

The borders will remain open.

The special interests will remain firmly in control.

Hillary Clinton and her friends in global finance want to scare America into thinking small - and they want to scare the American people out of voting for a better future.

My campaign has the opposite message.

I want you to imagine how much better your life can be if we start believing in America again.

I want you to imagine how much better our future can be if we declare independence from the elites who've led us to one financial and foreign policy disaster one after another.

This is the message I have been waiting for all my life. This message is clear and direct. Trump often speaks off the top of his head. He speaks his mind and often says things which offend the politically correct media and by extension those who slavishly believe and follow the Progressive's multi-mouthed Pravda. However this speech was scripted. He used a teleprompter to deliver it and its text has been released as an official campaign document.

I know that in the divided America of the 21st century many who have followed the History of the Future for years will be angry with what I have to say next. Some may be surprised and some may be disappointed. However I have to do what I believe is the best for my country. Therefore, I have decided to endorse and support Donald Trump. Some may say you can't believe what he says. A man I greatly respect says, "All politicians lie. The good ones do it convincingly." That may be true.

Just as Eve did not sin because she believed the serpent and just as if you donate to a charity that you honestly believe will do good and they waste the money that is not your responsibility that is on them. I believe Donald Trump. I believe he honestly wants to make America great again, and I am 100% for that.

While I encourage everyone to read the entire speech or listen to it on YouTube[cxcvi] and it is too long to include verbatim in this article I want to end by sharing his trade program for rebuilding America.

A Trump Administration will change our failed trade policy - quickly

Here are 7 steps I would pursue right away to bring back our jobs.

One: I am going to withdraw the United States from the Trans-Pacific Partnership, which has not yet been ratified.

Two: I'm going to appoint the toughest and smartest trade negotiators to fight on behalf of American workers.

Three: I'm going to direct the Secretary of Commerce to identify every violation of trade agreements a foreign country is currently using to harm our workers. I will then direct all appropriate agencies to use every tool under American and international law to end these abuses.

Four: I'm going tell our NAFTA partners that I intend to immediately renegotiate the terms of that agreement to get a better deal for our workers. And I don't mean just a little bit better, I mean a lot better. If they do not agree to a renegotiation, then I will submit notice under Article 2205 of the NAFTA agreement that America intends to withdraw from the deal.

Five: I am going to instruct my Treasury Secretary to label China a currency manipulator. Any country that devalues their currency in order to take advantage of the United States will be met with sharply

Six: I am going to instruct the U.S. Trade Representative to bring trade cases against China, both in this country and at the WTO. China's unfair subsidy behavior is prohibited by the terms of its entrance to the WTO, and I intend to enforce those rules.

Seven: If China does not stop its illegal activities, including its theft of American trade secrets, I will use every lawful presidential power to remedy trade disputes, including the application of tariffs consistent with Section 201 and 301 of the Trade Act of 1974 and Section 232 of the Trade Expansion Act of 1962.

President Reagan deployed similar trade measures when motorcycle and semiconductor imports threatened U.S. industry. His tariff on Japanese motorcycles was 45% and his tariff to shield America's semiconductor industry was 100%.

Hillary Clinton, and her campaign of fear, will try to spread the lie that these actions will start a trade war. She has it completely backwards.

Hillary Clinton unleashed a trade war against the American worker when she supported one terrible trade deal after another – from NAFTA to China to South Korea.

A Trump Administration will end that war by getting a fair deal for the American people.

The era of economic surrender will finally be over.

A new era of prosperity will finally begin.

America will be independent once more.

Under a Trump Presidency, the American worker will finally have a President who will protect them and fight for them.

We will stand up to trade cheating anywhere and everywhere it threatens an American job.

We will make America the best place in the world to start a business, hire workers, and open a factory.

This includes massive tax reform to lift the crushing burdens on American workers and businesses.

We will also get rid of wasteful rules and regulations which are destroying our job creation capacity.

Many people think that these regulations are an even greater impediment than the fact that we are one of the highest taxed nations in the world.

We are also going to fully capture America's tremendous energy capacity. This will create vast profits for our workers and begin reducing our deficit. Hillary Clinton wants to shut down energy production and shut down the mines.

A Trump Administration will also ensure that we start using American steel for American infrastructure.

Just like the American steel from Pennsylvania that built the Empire State building.

It will be American steel that will fortify American's crumbling bridges.

It will be American steel that sends our skyscrapers soaring into the sky.

It will be American steel that rebuilds our inner cities.

It will be American hands that remake this country, and it will be American energy - mined from American resources - that powers this country.

It will be American workers who are hired to do the job.

We are going to put American-produced steel back into the backbone of our country. This alone will create massive numbers of jobs.

On trade, on immigration, on foreign policy, we are going to put America First again.

We are going to make America wealthy again.

We are going to reject Hillary Clinton's politics of fear, futility, and incompetence.

We are going to embrace the possibilities of change.

It is time to believe in the future.

It is time to believe in each other.

It is time to Believe In America.

> This Is How We Are Going To Make America Great Again – For All Americans.
>
> We Are Going To Make America Great Again For Everyone – Greater Than Ever Before.[cxcvii]

I don't know about anyone else but that is a program I can believe in and one that I believe will lead to a rebirth of the American economy.

Hopefully I won't end up living out the words spoken by a character in a book I wrote many years ago who when asked why he supported a disreputable candidate running for president who was a plain-speaking non-politician and the richest man in the world said, "I know he's a liar but I like what he says."

So far I like what he says.

Dispatch Twenty-eight

America Rising

After the greatest upset in American History we have stepped from the precipice of the abyss and now stand upon the threshold of renewal. America's setting sun is rising again.

That hope we voted for was not the victim of a late term abortion. It was not still born in the continuation of corrupt politics, failed policies, and deliberate defeat. Instead we open our eyes on the possibility that after passing through the darkness of the Obamanation on January 20, 2017 we will once again experience the pride and satisfaction of America fulfilling its destiny as the home of the brave and the land of the free.

In the coming months as the Progressives prepare to slink out of the swamp to plot and plan their restoration we must be on guard for the flurry of executive orders, presidential actions, midnight appointments, and pardons that will inevitably spew out of the Oval Office. Now that the Donald has cleared the path and shown the way let us hope that in these waning days of a lame duck administration the Republicans who control Congress will find the courage to stop President Obama from making the swamp that much more malignant.

As we celebrate the great victory let us stand ready to pitch in and help realizing that there will be sacrifices required to flush the bilge and right the ship of state.

Dispatch Twenty-nine

American Pravda and New York's Sixth Crime Family

In America today most people choose only the Corporations Once Known as the Mainstream Media based on the charisma of the news reader, and do not tune into other news options. Do they think they look or sound like authoritative? Are they better looking? Do they have a more pleasing voice? Are they a Male? Are they a female? Are they Gay? Are we not sure? Whatever the reason, it isn't because they say anything different. It often sounds like they all have the same writers and story selectors. The content is no different. It is perhaps the line-up of the stories and that is about it.

Do you want to hear the story about how the Republican Elite is trying to figure out some way to dump Trump before you hear the story about how the Donald is not fit for the highest office in the land or after? Do you want to learn about the latest polls that show the race is already over before or after you hear how much better Hillary's economic plan is than the insane proposals of the racist homophobe misogynist Trump?

When I have a chance encounter and what passes for conversation with so many Kool-Aid drinking low information voters i.e progressive induhviduals the conversation usually goes like this:

Me: What do you think about _____ (fill in the blank)?

Progressive Induhvidual: Repeat what ABC, CBS, NBC, CNN, MSNBC, New York Times, Washington Post, USA Today, Chicago Tribune, etc. has said recently.

Or if they are a Conservative Induhvidual: Repeat what Fox, the Wall Street Journal, the Weekly Standard, National Review, etc. has recently said.

It is almost impossible to find anyone who has actually read any books on topics of importance such as economics, politics, sociology, or the History that ties them all together.

Several times a year I attend meetings that are filled with nothing but PhDs, professors, and university administrators. All content experts in these very subjects as well as many others. The results are basically the same. The death of critical thinking has led us to a deafening silence in the area of actual personal opinion, a dearth of dialogue, and a collapse of conversation. The American people, who at the time of the Founding saw blacksmiths discussing with candle makers the pros and cons of constitutions and the meaning of liberty or carpenters debating with plumbers the need for a free economy versus the need for public works. Just read the Federalist and the Anti-Federalist Papers, look at the level of thought and speech and ask yourself, "How does the public debate, and the newspaper articles of contemporary America match up?" Today the public debate takes place at about a 3rd grade level compared to the graduate school of those earlier days.

What happened? Back then there weren't public schools. Churches and families educated their own. Today after generations of highly funded and severely structured public education we have successfully dumbed ourselves down to the lowest common denominator.

Looking at the Bernie Sanders revolt which was contained by the elite in the Democrat Party and the Trump Revolution which over whelmed the elite in the Republican Party it is obvious that we tax paying entities that inhabit flyover country have had enough of the bi-coastal elite that is driving us over the cliff into the third world. Obviously the elite controlled media has dropped their camouflage of objectivity and is all in to make sure their empty pantsuit carries the day so she can carry the water for the donor class all the way to the bank.

At least there has been one pseudo surprise in the Hollywood scripted replay of Primary Colors the Distaff Edition, all of the frothing at the mouth Bernie supporters who were so brave to boo or turn their backs at the recent Democrat Party Spectacle in Philadelphia are falling into line and surprise surprise they are planning to vote for Hillary. Just as evidence surfaces that yes, the entire primary exercise was rigged from the beginning they are going to stand in line to cast their rationally considered and highly principled vote for the very person who engineered the fix, takes her money and marching orders from the crony capitalists, and is arguably the most corrupt person to ever run for the presidency. Who could have seen this coming except a blind man in a dark room with no media access?

The pre-programmed electorate combined with the usual fraud,[cxcviii] imported voters and all the dead[cxcix] people[cc] who never leave the voting rolls of the corrupt Democrat City fiefdoms,[cci] will march in lockstep to the polls to hand America lock-stock-and-barrel to the Clinton Crime Family.[ccii] Our only hope is that enough people have swallowed the red pill and are willing to at least take a shot at shaking things up before we are swept away by the unregulated immigration invasion and state sponsored outsourcing.

An old saying goes, "There are only two things that are certain in this life, death and taxes." We have all been programmed to accept this as an inevitable truism. Death to be sure is natural and inevitable. If you were born you will die. Taxes however are not a natural thing. They are in actuality the forced expropriation of funds from the productive taken through the use of the state's monopoly on the use of coercive force. And so though they are not natural and they are not inevitable like death or gravity they may in realistic terms given the overwhelming preponderance of government power be unavoidable.

If our country follows the dictates of the elite controlled media America becomes the turf of the Sleazy Donna from Chappaqua whose word parsing motto should be the Bart Simpson anthem, "I didn't do it! Nobody saw me do it! There's no way. You can't prove anything." If the White House once again becomes Bill's love nest and the George Soros puppet in heels moves into the Oval Office with her rolodex of contributors both foreign and domestic let's hope we don't find something else becoming inevitable. Such as critics of the regime joining the ever growing list of questionable deaths that follows New York's Sixth Crime family around like a bad odor.[cciii]

Don't just opt out because the system is obviously going to hell in a handbasket, vote for a change or shall we say, "See you in the camps"?

Dispatch Thirty

Avast There's an Iceberg Ahead!

One of America's greatest philosophers, Yogi Berra once quipped, "A nickel isn't worth a dime today"[cciv] and the inverse logic of that still holds true.

On Sept. 22, 2011 in a speech to business executives Navy Adm. Mike Mullen, chairman of the Joint Chiefs of Staff said, "Debt is the biggest threat to U.S. national security."[ccv] When the leader of the people famous for $800 hammers and $640 toilet seats has to lecture business leaders about the perils of deficit spending we know capitalism in America has jumped the track.

After World War I the world's monetary system was in disarray. The victorious Allies sought to revive the gold standard. However the structure which had been put in place after 1918 collapsed during the Great Depression. Some economists believe that the world's attempt to remain on the gold standard prevented central banks from expanding the money supply enough to revive the world's economies. The problem was they couldn't print enough money if it actually had to be worth something.

Then Came Trump

After World War II, representatives of the once again victorious allies met at Bretton Woods, New Hampshire, to create a new international monetary system. At the time the United States accounted for more than 50% of the world's manufacturing capacity and also held most of the world's gold. Since America was the uncontested economic Superpower these leaders decided to tie world currencies to the dollar. The value of the dollar would in turn be controlled and supported by the fact that the dollar would be tied to gold at $35 per ounce.

While the Bretton Woods System was in force the central banks were given the task of maintaining fixed exchange rates. This was accomplished by massive and continuous intervention in foreign exchange markets. When a country's currency became too expensive in relation to the dollar, that country's central bank would sell its currency for dollars thus driving down the value of its currency. And if the value of a country's money became too low, that country would then aggressively buy its own currency to drive the price up.

This Bretton Woods System worked well until 1971. By then, due to the "Guns and Butter" economic policies of the Johnson and Nixon administration's inflation in the United States and America's rapidly expanding trade deficit undermined the value of the dollar. As a result America urged the now recovered and economically powerful Germany and Japan to increase the value of their currencies. Both nations did not want to do this.

Raising the value of their currencies hurt their exports by increasing the prices for their goods in the United States which was their largest market.

When the pressure became unbearable, when too many nations were redeeming too many dollars against America's dwindling gold supply the United States unilaterally abandoned the fixed gold value of the dollar allowing it to "float." Floating with relationship to money means it is allowed to fluctuate when compared to the currencies of other countries. Immediately the value of the dollar fell substantially when compared to other currencies, especially those of Germany and Japan.

This caused turbulence in the economies of nations and sent shockwaves through the political systems of the world. In consequence the leaders of the major countries made an effort to revive the Bretton Woods system. They came together in 1971, and reached the Smithsonian Agreement which for the first time allowed for the negotiation of fixed exchange rates. However, this attempt soon failed.

In 1973, The United States and the other major economic powers agreed to a new system known as Managed Float. This meant that central banks would still intervene with the buying and selling of their own currencies to eliminate any changes that might be perceived as too dramatic.

How long will this system of floating money, fiat currency, and systemic debt last?

Since I started with a quote from my favorite American philosopher, Yogi Berra I will frame my comments about the end result of America's love affair with monopoly money and ever growing debt with another nugget from this source of double think profundity, "It's tough to make predictions, especially about the future"

You know, I know and anyone who has enough economic awareness to realize you can't spend more than you make forever knows that our present governmental financial framework is unsustainable. Why? Apparently our leaders believe you can spend more than you make forever.

If you have ever tried to manage your Visa payments by charging them to MasterCard you know the end of that game. Our leaders have pawned our grandchildren's future for the votes they buy with social programs, tax giveaways, and bail-outs. However it is hard to lay all the blame on the shoulders of the perpetually re-elected. The government is the people writ large. Almost every household in America is in debt. Almost every business in America is in debt.

Debt is not a bad thing in and of itself. Actually it is one of the most liberating inventions in the world. It allows economic activity to grow based upon future activity instead of just on current holdings. This provides a multiplier effect that has given rise to the modern world.

However, when we spend more of the future than the present can service we have inverted the pyramid and are inviting a correction. Even if the Corporations Once Known as the Mainstream Media are blathering on about how good the stock market is doing, that the pretend unemployment rate is falling, that there is no inflation, and that the President says everything is coming up roses, the alternative media knows the present course is unsustainable. Unsustainable. That word is spoken day after day on Fox and printed multiple times every day online from thousands of blogs, magazines, and newspapers. All it means is it can't last forever, or as an alarmist might say, "A crash is coming!" Or as the economic pirates who sail the crony capitalist seas might say, "Avast there's an iceberg ahead!"

Sure the stock market is flying high. With the Fed pumping 85 billion a month into the banking system why wouldn't it? With that kind of money coming in why not play the Lotto? Sure the unemployment rate is falling as long as you don't count the people who have quit looking for a job. Sure there's no inflation as long as you don't count energy or food. And of course the President says everything is getting better all the time that is what his teleprompter tells him to say.

So, how long will this system of floating money, fiat currency, and systemic debt last? None of us gets to live in the world we grew up in because the world moves too fast. Things change. What was science fiction yesterday is your cell phone today. One thing we can know for sure is that it isn't over till it's over. Yet from a realistic evaluation of the deep hole we have spent ourselves into the future isn't what it used to be and if the world were perfect it wouldn't be.

Is there any way to stop this train wreck before we hit the wall? Can we reign in Washington and stop the money borrowed from the future that the best and the brightest are spending? What do you think? I wish I had an answer to that because I'm tired of answering the question.

What do we know?

We know that the record breaking new people elected to the House in the great Tea Party victories of 2010 and 2014 affirmed Boehner as the leader of the co-opted opposition, voted for multiple debt ceiling increases, and renewed the Patriot Act. Now Mr. Ryan is carrying on the failed tradition bailing out Puerto Rico and reaching across the aisle to pass a 1.1 trillion dollar porkulus budget that funds BHO's fundamental transformation of America. We know that another Progressive Republican à la Romney had no chance to beat BHO and we know it probably wouldn't have made any difference if he did.

Then Came Trump

Now along comes The Donald facing off against a restoration of the Billary interlewd. Is there any chance of turning this Titanic around or at least altering course before we hit the iceberg of insolvency and impotence?

At least with Billary we know where we will be headed, into the dustbin of History. With Mr. Trump we are headed into uncharted waters. Who knows what he will do? I suspect even he doesn't. And as America's greatest philosopher once said, "If you don't know where you are going, you might wind up someplace else."

Dispatch Thirty-one

Back When I was a Boy

I think one of the hardest things about growing old is that you can remember what a pound of hamburger cost fifty years ago ($.45), so when the government assures us over and over there is no inflation we sort of get a disconnect going that seeps into many different areas of our lives.

Wise men say that History repeats itself. Those who have studied the facts and lived long enough to get a seasoned perspective understand that if it doesn't repeat itself it sure does rhyme. Which leads me to an observation made by every generation since time began; every generation believes that the one following it is made up of a bunch of molly-coddled softies who will obviously allow the world to go to hell in a handbasket.

As a still surviving though somewhat battered member of the boomer generation I am beginning to think that when the Greatest Generation thought this about us they may have been right. By every metric imaginable except of course technological toys and wonders we have presided over the decline of America.

Our parents conquered the world and then defended their conquest against that destroyer of hope the USSR for fifty years until that great gulag of nations collapsed under its own weight. Then in 1992 we repudiated those who had won the war and secured the peace. Following a colossal betrayal, "Read my lips," our generation took the reins and proceeded to run the whole thing into the ditch.

First we have the Clinton inter-lewd with its fake prosperity courtesy of the peace dividend, the dot com bubble, and the Contract with America Congress. Then we have George II and endless wars for peace combined with a guns and butter economy at home where couples making a combined income of 40,000 could buy $400,000 houses. This was followed by BHO and his anti-colonialist disdain for all that had made America great combined with a micromanaged centrally-planned economy guaranteed to sweep us into the dystopian trash heap of History.

Then faced with Mrs. "The Last Nail in Our Coffin" Clinton and Mr. "Take a Chance on Me" Trump we chose Mr. Chance who may well end up being the last Boomer president. All of us who chose the chance are now waiting with baited breath praying he will do what he said he would do. If he does, this last Boomer president may well bring back the glory of our parents and we will hand this off to the X Generation and give them a shot at preserving it for those who come after them.

Back to my theory that each generation sees the one following them as the ruin of all that is holy and why that is in reality a truism as old as time.

Then Came Trump

The Greatest Generation was once known as the Silent Generation until we re-christened them because of their stolid plodding through FDR's Great Depression and their solid performance in WWII. They looked askance at the music and the counter-culture of the Boomers. Those few who actually were Hippies did ride a sociological tsunami that did in fact change our culture. The draft dodging flag burning micro minority rose to the top of the political world with the Watergate Congress and hang on to power to this day. The rest of us went to work. Eventually most of us followed the predictable trajectory. The liberal firebrands of youth become the worker drones of middle age and eventually the conservative mossbacks of old age.

Remember the Generation Gap? Today it feels more like a Generation Gulf, or close encounters of the third kind.

Generation X seemed to come out of the womb with an eye for style, a penchant for name brands, and an ability to work for what they wanted. They are mostly moving through the worker drone phase right now. Their younger brothers and sisters of Generation Y or the Millennials are now shedding their youthful fire and entering into middle age. Now come the Centennials or as some of us call them the Snowflake Generation and we see the fruit of our loins terrified of micro-aggressions, seeking safe places, and protesting elections when they didn't even bother to vote. Oh what is the world to do?

Take a beat, take a breath, and step back. Yes, when we see our grandchildren crying because they think someone might have looked at them crossways we wonder about the fate of the Republic. Instead of bemoaning our coming fall once these limp-wristed get a trophy for showing up crybabies take over remember they have several stages of growth coming before they get there. There's nothing like raising kids and working twelve hour days to support them to put a little steel in your spine. Give them time. Their rebellious attitudes and oh so delicate sensibilities will crash upon the reef of 3 AM feedings, paying the bills, buying the house, and worrying whether Social Security will be there when they need it.

The young always act as if youth was some clever thing they invented not knowing that we all were once young, and if we survive we grow old and things generally seem to carry on from there.

The only lesson we learn from History is that we don't learn the lessons of History. As far back as records go every generation has thought the next was going to be a disaster forgetting that they are the ones who raised that next generation and having a little faith in how their example and time would mellow youth into old age.

Remember everything is relative. The next time you find yourself telling some young whippersnapper how you walked to school uphill in both directions in a blizzard without a coat think of the story of two old men. One says, "Why back when I was boy all I had to play with was a stick." The other old man his eyes blazing with jealousy at the frivolous prosperity of others exclaims, "You had a stick!"

Just as an interesting by-the-by:[ccvi]

Average Cost Of New Home
1930 $3,845.00 , 1940 $3,920.00, 1950 $8,450.00 , 1960 $12,700.00 ,
1970 $23,450.00 , 1980 $68,700.00 , 1990 $123,000.00 , 2008 $238,880 , 2013 $289,500

Average Annual Wages
1930 $1,970.00 , 1940 $1,725.00, 1950 $3,210.00 , 1960 $5,315.00 ,
1970 $9,400.00 , 1980 $19,500.00 , 1990 $28,960.00 , 2008 $40,523 , 2012 $44,321

Average Cost of New Car
1930 $600.00 , 1940 $850.00, 1950 $1,510.00 , 1960 $2,600.00 ,
1970 $3,450.00 , 1980 $7,200.00 , 1990 $16,950.00 , 2008 $27,958 , 2013 $31,352

Average Cost Gallon Of Gas
1930 10 cents , 1940 11 cents , 1950 18 cents , 1960 25 cents ,
1970 36 cents , 1980 $1.19 , 1990 $1.34 , 2009 $2.051 , 2013 $3.80

Average Cost Loaf of Bread
1930 9 cents , 1940 10 cents , 1950 12 cents , 1960 22 cents ,
1970 25 cents , 1980 50 cents , 1990 70 cents , 2008 $2.79 , 2013 $1.98

Average Cost 1lb Hamburger Meat
1930 12 cents , 1940 20 cents , 1950 30 cents , 1960 45 cents ,
1970 70 cents , 1980 99 cents , 1990 89 cents , 2009 $3.99 , 2013 $4.68

Then Came Trump

Dispatch Thirty-two

Bart Simpson for President

That ultimate symbol of mischievous scamp Bart Simpson in Season One of the longest running show in TV history when caught red-handed offered up one of his signature phrases, "I didn't do it, nobody saw me do it, there's no way you can prove anything."

This came to mind when I was thinking about Hillary "They'll Never Indict Me" Clinton and her morally challenged obviously corrupt character. Donald Trump has said, "I could stand in the middle of Fifth Avenue and shoot somebody and I wouldn't lose any voters."[ccvii] Hillary could say, "I could stand in the middle of Fifth Avenue and shoot somebody and I wouldn't get indicted."

Everyone in the country knows that if any of us common people did one hundredth of what she has done in the email scandal alone we would have already been indicted along with the ten year Navy Vet indicted for taking a selfie on a submarine.[ccviii] The Obama Justice Department is not going to indict Mrs. Clinton no matter what the FBI recommends. She is above the law and she knows it or as she infamously said in the Benghazi hearing with regard to our four dead heroes, "What does it matter now?"[ccix]

As a person who has been involved with and has closely followed the American political scene for more than fifty years this is the first time in my personal memory or Historical knowledge that a potential candidate for one party has promised to prosecute a potential candidate of the other party if elected.[ccx]

As Secretary of State, Hillary's accomplishments include the failed reset with Russia[ccxi] and of course her debacle in Libya.[ccxii] As a United State Senator what did she accomplish? In eight years she only sponsored three inconsequential laws:[ccxiii]

S.3145, which designated a portion of U.S. Route 20A, located in Orchard Park, N.Y., as the "Timothy J. Russert Highway," after the former "Meet the Press" host.

S. 3613, which renamed the facility of the United States Postal Service located at 2951 New York Highway 43 in Averill Park, New York, as the "Major George Quamo Post Office Building."

S. 1241 which made the brick house of 19th century female union leader Kate Mullany a national historic site.

Her major accomplishment is that she married a man who became the most ethically challenged president in American History. As the wife of Bill Clinton she was deeply involved in smothering the serial bimbo eruptions which grew out of his long history of having affairs, sexually harassing women who worked for him, and assaulting others.[ccxiv]   This is the person who portrays herself as an advocate of women's rights.[ccxv]

To highlight just one of her hypocritical faux stances for women's rights look at her advocacy for equal pay. The Clinton Foundation pays women executives 38% less than their male counterparts.[ccxvi] During her time in the Senate she paid women 72 cents for every dollar she paid men.[ccxvii] According to public records her current campaign pays women staffers less than she pays men. So much for putting your money where your mouth is![ccxviii]

Looking back once more to the email scandal that Hillary so nonchalantly dismisses if as she maintains she never received nor sent any classified material during her entire term as our Secretary of State[ccxix] my question is, what was she doing besides traveling the world at our expense? Was she out of the loop and merely Secretary of State in name only?   It is inconceivable that anyone could be the Secretary of State and not send or receive any classified material. That is beyond belief and a lie so transparent it shows total contempt for those it is meant to fool.

In the current election the Great Impresario likes to label people. In many ways it is an effective form of political shorthand. It sums up the thoughts, accusations, and beliefs about a person and brings them crashing in whenever they hear the catcall. Lyin Ted and Little Marco have taken their toll picked up and repeated by the Corporations Once Known as the Mainstream Media and their pet FOX. Now we have Crooked Hillary. The others were just effective. This one seems appropriate.

If Hillary wins the presidency it will be a watershed just as the election and then re-election of her husband was. As his marked the end of public morality hers will mean the end of the rule of law. It will become evident to anyone observant enough to note the sunrise that enforcement of the bewildering lattice of laws and regulations are only aimed at the common folk not at our masters.

If such a legally challenged individual can fool enough of the people all the time to sit in the oval office it reminds me of what Bart said to Homer after it was revealed he had cheated on an important test, "I cheated on the intelligence test. I'm sorry. But I just want to say that the past few weeks have been great. Me and you have done stuff together. You've helped me out with things and we're closer than we've ever been. I love you, Dad. And I think if something can bring us that close it can't possibly be bad."

Doing bad things for good purposes is the operational rational of Progressive Liberalism. The ends justify the means was the operational rational of all the megalomaniac dictators of world History. Please explain the difference.

Dispatch Thirty-three

Bitter Clingers Hang On

America is suffering through a leadership crisis that threatens to swamp the Ship of State in the shoals of collectivism, cronyism, and corruption. Our leaders dither around acting as if they use Dilbert as a leadership manual destroying the present for a utopian future that will never come to pass. They never seem to realize that their progressive collectivist diktats cause the symptoms they are implemented to cure.

Just as the massive collectivization of America under Hoover and FDR made the Depression great so BHO's stimuli and strangulation regulation has once again proven that you cannot spend your way to prosperity and that taking $10 out of your right hand pocket siphoning off 50% for handling and depositing $5 in your left pocket doesn't make you any richer. In other words government doesn't have anything to give anyone that it doesn't take from someone else.

We are surrounded by monuments of failed and farcical leadership.

Our Dear Leader who will not utter the term "Radical Islamic Terrorism" tells us with a straight face that more people die in bathtub accidents than in terrorist attacks. This may be true however, using the analogy when asked about terrorism was obviously devised to make light of a threat that is real and at least worthy of being named and treated as the death dealing attack upon our nation that it is.

One presidential candidate is a pathological liar grasping for power to do what? Generate even bigger donations from crony capitalists and foreign powers for the Clinton Global Crime Initiative and bigger speaking fees for Bubba.

Speaking of which, what is the difference between Bill Cosby and Bill Clinton? This isn't the set up for a joke it is a legitimate question concerning the comparison between a lecherous former president and a lecherous former TV star. Here's the punchline. Bill Cosby is being tried by a crusading progressive judge for crimes in the past and Bill Clinton is lionized by crusading progressives in the media as our beloved ex-president who was smart enough to take credit for the laws forced upon him by the Gingrich Congress. Bill Cosby gets booked and Bill Clinton books another speaking tour. That's the difference.

We have another presidential candidate who is selling hope and change under the banner of making America great again. Having bought a few pigs in a poke in my life I have an uncanny ability to smell a pig when it walks into my living room. It reminds me of a time when I wanted to refinance a house. I decided to try one of the big online lenders who dominate a large portion of the click-for-cash market. I spend a few days filling out forms and speaking with a friendly customer service person. Then the papers arrived for me to sign and the interest rate was quite a bit higher than we had agreed on. When I called the friendly customer service person they were still really friendly as they advised, "Oh, that's just a typo. Go ahead and sign the papers any way and we'll change the interest rate later." Suddenly a strong pungent odor wafted into my living room and I declined the generous offer to hold the bag. I will recall this story and smell the wind as I vote this November.

The largest 3rd party and the only one that is going to be on the ballot in all fifty states has a candidate who makes boring feel exciting, people stripping naked at their national convention, promotes open borders, free trade and doesn't have a prayer.

The best the political elites have to offer is launching a cypher as an independent candidate that they hope will force the election into the House where their golden boy Paul Ryan could engineer a pyric victory of the status quo.

What's a patriot who believes in limited government, individual freedom, and economic opportunity to do?

Back in April of 2008 before our dear Leader was immaculated he addressed the reaction of the great unwashed in fly-over country by saying, "You go into these small towns in Pennsylvania and, like a lot of small towns in the Midwest, the jobs have been gone now for 25 years and nothing's replaced them. And they fell through the Clinton administration, and the Bush administration, and each successive administration has said that somehow these communities are gonna regenerate and they have not. And it's not surprising then they get bitter, they cling to guns or religion or antipathy toward people who aren't like them or anti-immigrant sentiment or anti-trade sentiment as a way to explain their frustrations."[ccxx]

What was meant as a slur has become a badge of pride to many who proclaim, "I am a bitter clinger." Rejecting the racist projection that anyone who does not embrace the globalist gelding of America we Bitter Clingers may cling to our guns (2nd Amendment) and our religion (1st Amendment). We don't have any antipathy towards those who don't look like us because to even say that we do is assuming that we all look alike and we don't. We're Americans and as such we look like everyone because we and our ancestors came from everywhere. To say we're anti-immigrant is to say you can judge our hearts. We are actually pro-American and believe we should control our borders, decide who we want to join us as citizens, select the best and brightest and move forward. And to say we are anti-trade is like saying we don't shop at Wal-Mart. We are anti-giveaway trade where we get cheap products at the cost of gutting our industrial base and out-sourcing our jobs. We want equitable trade, fair trade not we open our borders to the world and we still have to pay tariffs and fees to sell in other countries' trade.

Trump has uttered the politically-incorrect phrase we bitter clingers believe in America First. At least he has said it and perhaps now we can come in out of the shadows where the PC police have tried to marginalize us. The Silent Majority is silent no more. We want

America First. We want leaders who will restore the Constitution. We want our country back!

So what do we do?

It is time for the bitter clingers to hang on because we are in for a bumpy ride. In the next few years we will either step on the yellow brick road that leads to a return to the greatness Americans once took for granted or we will continue our slide down the shoot into the shabby collectivist hellhole the progressives call utopia.

Keep the Faith. Keep the peace. We shall overcome.

Dispatch Thirty-four

Then Came Trump

So that was Christmas, and what have we done? Another year over and a new one just begun!

In the still sweet morning of December 26, people start preparing for the next blast of holiday cheer. Happy New Year!!!

What will 2017 bring?

The Progressives from George Read-My-Lips Bush through the Clinton Inter-Lewd, George Endless-Wars-For-Peace Bush, and Barack the Destroyer managed to turn Ronaldus Magnus' Morning in America into Mourning in America. We watched a slow motion train wreck as we won the Cold War and seemed to be on the verge of losing the peace as the centralizing finger wagers did their best to snatch defeat from the jaws of victory, and then came Trump.

Think of where we were just a few short weeks ago:

- an unopposed invasion on our southern border
- a collapse taking place in our manufacturing sector
- a loss of allies due to our own unreliability
- a growth of enemies due to our own weakness

- Detroit and other once proud cities decaying before our eyes
- attacks on cops, Christmas, and anything else we held dear becoming common place
- the Progressives where so self-assured that they would pound the last nail in our coffin, Hillary Clinton, they didn't even bother to mount a campaign beyond attack adds

And then came Trump.

The Corporations Once Known as the Mainstream Media as represented in the shrinking megaphone of the ABCCBSNBCCNNMSNBC CABAL and their cable and print sister wives haven't given up. They are doing anything they can to help the Progressives delegitimize The Donald. There is no burden to great, no sacrifice of credibility to shameful, no lie so ridiculous that they will not print or broadcast in their efforts to undermine the draining of the swamp. The silent majority has tried their hope and change, and they want to change it back to what it was before: America. The little people of Big Media thought they had their version of new speak, new thought, group think, PC mind control down pat. And then came Trump.

The cry baby poor losers and their snowflake minions are squawking like a goose getting a mammogram. The celebrity limousine liberals are threatening to leave the country. The neo-cons are plotting and planning to sabotage the agenda people voted for. Every liberal you know repeats the talking points of the DNC pumped out by the pseudo-news anchors and thinks these are their own opinions.   Chicken Little assures us the sky is falling. And then came Trump.

People say, "What if he breaks his promises?"

I say, if I give ten dollars to a charity to do good I have done good. If that charity then takes my ten dollars and throws it away, that is on them. It may be shown that we were naïve. It may be revealed that we were gullible. But I know when I am faced with the choice between the last nail in my coffin and a chance, I will vote for the chance every time.

I also know that I have a promise:

A thousand may fall at your side,

And ten thousand at your right hand;

But it shall not come near you.

Only with your eyes shall you look,

And see the reward of the wicked.

Because you have made the Lord, who is my refuge, even the Most High, your dwelling place,

No evil shall befall you, nor shall any plague come near your dwelling;

For He shall give His angels charge over you, to keep you in all your ways.

The election has come and gone. 2016 has come and gone. Many looked forward to 2017 with dread. We saw nothing before us but the continued decline of our great nation, the last best hope of mankind, managed by the very collectivist Progressives who were orchestrating that decline. We saw ourselves being swamped by the import-a-voter invasion designed to relegate us to nothing more than a tax base for the next dystopian utopia. In Christ we always have hope. In the world our hope was about to be crushed under the juggernaut of New York's Sixth Crime Family and their massive political machine. And then came Trump.

Weeping may endure for a night, but joy comes in the morning. A new day is dawning in America. The Progressives thought we would go with a whimper instead of a bang. However we refused to go gently into that good night. We refused to let hope and change kill our hope so we voted to change the course of History. First came a determination that the nation shall have a new birth of freedom and that government of the people, by the people, for the people, shall not perish from the earth. And then came Trump.

Happy New Year!!

Dispatch Thirty-five

Trump Earthquake Causes Democrat Tsunami

It is not often that we get to witness a true phenomenon.

The Reagan Revolution was exciting but it was not a phenomenon. It was a carefully planned, long fought, and hard won battle between the Conservative wing and the Progressive wing of the Republican Party.

The Reagan Revolution began with The Speech[ccxxi] by Ronaldos Maximus in support of Barry Goldwater delivered on a television program, *Rendezvous with Destiny*. It blossomed during his two successful terms as Governor of California, and sputtered a little in 1976 when he lost the nomination for President to Gerald Ford in the last contested convention in American History. Then after four years of hard grass roots work Reagan's followers, this author included in their ranks, captured the party from precinct captain to national chairman. The next eight years led to many successes, compromises, and a failure culminating in the party being handed over as a prize to George the First and the rest is History. The Bush dynasty ran the brand into the ground.

Then Came Trump

Enter The Donald. Now here is a phenomenon. The last time a non-politician came from nowhere to capture the nomination of one of the major parties was in 1940 when the so-called Miracle in Philadelphia[ccxxii] brought about the surprise nomination of a life-long Democrat who mirrored FDR's positions on most important issues. He came in as a dark horse and through clever manipulation and behind the scenes machinations whisked the nomination out of the hands of the three top contenders: Senator Robert Taft of Ohio (the son of President William H. Taft), Senator Arthur Vandenberg of Michigan, and Manhattan District Attorney Thomas Dewey. Of course this was back in the day when there really were smoke filled backrooms and party bosses and long before primaries and State caucuses.

Here we are a life-time later and the ideological descendants of the Wilkie wonks after turning the Party of Reagan into Democrat Lite were planning on foisting another Bush on their unwilling base. Trump trumped them all. He knocked off one establishment straw man after another as well as the closest thing we will see to Reagan to stand unchallenged for the nomination. No grass roots organization, no army of K-Street consultants, hardly any advertising, just Trump. His triumph over everyone else who should have won is a true political phenomenon.

Now comes the general election at least once the Democrats stop the charade of Hillary losing her way to the nomination and hold their coronation of the Queen of Hearts.

Even relying on the yellow-dog Democrats,[ccxxiii] the dead Democrats[ccxxiv] who continue to vote, and the undocumented Democrats[ccxxv] Hillary is going to face an uphill battle. When you consider she may be ethically challenged,[ccxxvi] personally cold, under threat of indictment, and bringing Slick Willy along her campaign strategy consists of convincing people that her opponent is worse. You can see she may not be the certainty the liberal media make her out to be.

Just look at her record. Everything she has accomplished has been because she said "I do" to Bubba. While he was playing hound dog and doing some government jobs on the side she was busy covering up his serial abuse of women and smoothing out the wrinkles from his frequent bimbo-eruptions.[ccxxvii] Then after they left the White House, looting it on the way out the door,[ccxxviii] she ran for the Senate in a state where the Democrats own the vote. She spends a term and a half accomplishing nothing and is appointed as Secretary of State. The judgment of her tenure as America's leading diplomat has yet to be adjudicated. She is a poor campaigner at best. And she's bringing Bill back to the scene of his crimes. This is not the recipe for the Clinton Crime Family to recapture the capitol.

If that isn't enough we do have Hillary's top scandals as reported in World Net Daily (this is an abbreviated version):[ccxxix]

1. Benghazi: Four American lives lost: On Sept. 11, 2012, while Hillary was secretary of state, Islamic militants attacked a U.S. special mission in Benghazi, Libya, and murdered U.S. Ambassador

J. Christopher Stevens and U.S. Foreign Service Information Management officer Sean Smith. Two CIA contractors, Tyrone Woods and Glen Doherty, were also killed. In the months leading up to the attack, Hillary's State Department cut security in Libya. Sen. Ron Johnson, R-Wis., accused Hillary of "dereliction of duty" that led to the deaths of the four Americans. "The State Department not only failed to honor repeated requests for additional security, but instead actually reduced security in Libya," Johnson wrote in the Milwaukee Journal Sentinel. "Although no one can say with certainty, I firmly believe a relatively small contingent of armed military guards would have prevented the attack, and those four lives would not have been lost." As WND reported, a security decision finalized personally by Hillary may have unwittingly doomed the Americans in Benghazi. Hillary herself signed waivers that allowed the facility to be legally occupied, since it did not meet the minimum official security standards set by the State Department. The waiver legally allowed the CIA annex to be housed in a location about one mile from the U.S. special mission. According to accounts from Benghazi survivors, the delayed response time by those at the CIA annex may have cost the lives of Stevens and the three other Americans killed at the special mission. If the CIA annex had been co-located with the U.S. special mission, a rapid response team would have been on site during the initial assault in which Stevens was killed. Clinton's waiver allowed the CIA annex to be housed at the separate location. As WND also reported, State Department emails show Clinton knew while the attack was under way that it was being carried out by terrorists. Judicial Watch has obtained previously classified documents from the U.S. Department of Defense and the Department of State revealing that DOD almost immediately reported that the attack on the U.S. Consulate in Benghazi, Libya, was planned and carried out by al-Qaida and Muslim Brotherhood-linked terrorists. A federal court ordered the government hand over more than 100 pages of previously secret documents that showed then-Secretary of State Hillary Clinton and other senior Obama officials were given reports within hours of the Sept. 11, 2012, attack. In those memos, the DOD described details of a plan 10 days in advance "to kill as many Americans as possible." Nonetheless, Hillary falsely blamed it on "rage and violence over an awful Internet video" when she spoke at a ceremony at Andrews Air Force Base on Sept. 14, 2012, as the remains of the four Americans were returned to the U.S.

2. Clintons turn IRS into 'gestapo': Individuals singled out for audits during the administration included Clinton paramours Gennifer Flowers and Liz Ward Gracen, sexual assault accusers Paula Jones and Juanita Broaddrick, fired White House Travel Office Director Billy Dale and attorney Kent Masterson Brown. Fox News' Bill O'Reilly, an

outspoken critic of both Bill and Hillary Clinton, said he was audited three times during the Clinton presidency. A 1996 survey by the Washington Times could not identify a single liberal public policy organization that had been audited during the entire Clinton administration.

3. Filegate: FBI files on GOP enemies: The Clinton duo was involved in a scandal known as "Filegate" in which they illegally obtained FBI files on perceived adversaries, most of whom served in previous Republican administrations. The scandal was first detected by the House Government Reform and Oversight Committee, which investigated the Clintons' Travelgate caper. The committee found that the FBI files had been improperly accessed by Craig Livingstone, a former bar bouncer Hillary had hired to work in the White House Counsel's Office. However, Hillary called the whole affair a "completely honest bureaucratic snafu."

4. Travelgate: The staff of the White House travel office was fired to make way for Clinton cronies, including Bill's 25-year-old cousin, who was reportedly promised the position of office director. Hillary allegedly fired seven employees and gave the positions to her Arkansas friends. According to the Washington Post,[ccxxx] there was

an effort to award a White House airline contract to a Clinton friend. Also, Hillary reportedly had the FBI investigate the former head of the travel office, Billy Dale, who was fired without notice and removed from the White House grounds. Dale was charged with embezzlement but found not guilty of the crime in 1995. He was later audited by the IRS.

5. Landing under sniper fire' in Bosnia: In her March 17, 2008, foreign-policy speech on Iraq, then-Sen. Hillary Clinton recalled a trip she made to Tuzla, Bosnia, in 1996. "I remember landing under sniper fire," Hillary said of her visit while she was first lady. "There was supposed to be some kind of a greeting ceremony at the airport, but instead we just ran with our heads down to get into the vehicles to get to our base." But news footage of her visit revealed her "sniper fire" claim wasn't just exaggerated. It was completely false. And Hillary had repeated the claim several times, including during her time on the presidential campaign trail in 2007. Rather, Hillary landed on a tarmac and greeted a crowd, including an 8-year-old child who gave her a poem, under no duress. According to the Washington Post, a review of more than 100 news articles revealed no security threats to Hillary at the time.

6. Hillary's 'missing' law firm billing records: In 1994, federal investigators subpoenaed Hillary's billing records from her days as a partner in the Rose Law firm during the Watergate scandal. The White House said it didn't have the 115 pages of files. While Hillary claimed she had a minor role in the affair, the Washington Examiner reported that "when the records mysteriously turned up in the White House in 1996, they showed she met repeatedly with key figures in the scandal."[ccxxxi]

7. Pardongate: Hillary Senate contributions: Before Bill Clinton left the White House in 2001, he granted numerous controversial pardons – including to convicted tax evader Marc Rich, whose wife made significant contributions to Hillary's 2000 Senate campaign and the Clinton presidential library. The Associated Press reported that Rich had been "indicted by a U.S. federal grand jury on more than 50 counts of fraud, racketeering, trading with Iran during the U.S. Embassy hostage crisis and evading more than $48 million in income taxes – crimes that could have earned him more than 300 years in prison." Rich fled to Switzerland in 1983 after his indictment and remained on the FBI's Most Wanted List until President Clinton pardoned him. Also, Hillary's brothers, Tony and Hugh Rodham, reportedly received large amounts of money from people who were pardoned by Bill Clinton. Hillary said she and Bill were unaware of the scheme. Accuracy in Media reported, "Hugh

Rodham, Hillary's brother, was taking money and promising access to help get pardons. Two such high profile cases were those of drug kingpin Carlos Vignali and convicted swindler Glenn Braswell. Rodham received hundreds of thousands of dollars from each, and they were both granted pardons. Rodham was quoted as telling a top White House aide that the pardon for Vignali was 'very important' to Hillary."[ccxxxii]

8. Hillary's cash cows and 9,987 percent profit: In March 1994, it was revealed Hillary – with no previous experience – had made massive profits from cattle futures trading between 1978 and 1979, when Bill Clinton's salary as Arkansas attorney general had been modest. She reportedly made $99,537 in profit on a $1,000 investment (a 9,987 percent profit) in just nine months because of a highly placed connection at Tyson Foods, which was the largest employer in Arkansas and a big Clinton donor. The New York Times reported: "During Mr. Clinton's tenure as Governor, Tyson benefited from several state decisions, including favorable environmental rulings, $9 million in state loans, and the placement of company executives on important state boards. ... The commodities trades were the most successful investment the Clintons ever made. The nearly $100,000 profit enabled them to buy a house, invest in securities and real estate and provide a nest egg for their daughter, Chelsea."[ccxxxiii]

9. Clinton body count: 'You find dead people' "The Clinton body count," first published in WND and later circulated by Linda Tripp to Monica Lewinsky, is a collection of names of people associated with Clinton administration scandals who have died mysterious and often violent deaths. Reporter David Bresnahan broke the story of the list during the summer of 1997 while researching his book, "Cover Up: The Art and Science of Political Deception." "I started looking into all the various deaths of people that were involved in various Clinton scandals," Bresnahan said. "I started to investigate the entire picture instead of just one focused event. Nobody out there was putting it all together," he said. "If you look at one scandal, you'll find one dead guy. When you investigate all Clinton scandals, you find similarities, you find common tactics, you find common actions and you find dead people." The list was not just a source of terror among sworn enemies of the administration. It was an even greater terror for those close to Clinton – for those closest, it appeared, died younger and more inexplicably than those on the outside looking in. In his research, Bresnahan came up with more than one list. "Not only did I find a list of dead people, but I also found that there are over 100 people who have refused to testify," he said at the time. "There is also a list of people who have gone to jail. There are 45 people who have gone to jail, some of them White House staff, Cabinet members

as well as people from the Justice Department. So many of those (lists) developed when I started to pursue the big picture."

10. Watergate: Fired for being a 'liar' Hillary actually played a role in the Watergate saga, and her actions as a young attorney may have set the tone for her career. The 27-year-old Clinton was fired from the staff of the House Judiciary committee investigating the Watergate scandal in 1974. She was fired by her supervisor, lifelong Democrat Jerry Zeifman, who called her a liar and much worse. "She was an unethical, dishonest lawyer," he said. "She conspired to violate the Constitution, the rules of the House, the rules of the committee and the rules of confidentiality." Zeifman also refused to give Clinton a letter of recommendation, making her one of only three employees he snubbed during his 17-year career.

Who knows maybe she will get indicted before the coronation and save the democrats all this baggage. Then they could parachute in Biden and Warren to save the day. Or maybe they will nominate the man who is winning so many of their primaries and instead of a red queen go for a red king.

Believe it or not Bernie's their best chance and he's a Socialist. I know his <u>useful idiots</u> repeat the party line, "He's not a Socialist. He's a Democratic Socialist." This is like Hitler reassuring the Germans with, "I'm not a Fascist I'm a National Socialist." A statist is a statist, central planning is central planning, and collectivism is collectivism. To put it in terms the philosophical among Bernie's supporters might understand Capitalism is the thesis, Socialism is the anti-thesis, and Progressivism is the synthesis.

At least he would bring the enthusiasm for anything but the status quo to the support of the Democrat ticket. If they nominate anyone else a large percentage of that vote may well end up crossing over from the dark side and support Trump.

However, try as they may, the Democrats are on the wrong side of History in this election cycle. Their rule-by-decree culture of corruption coupled with the Neo-Conns and their nation-building wars for peace have brought us to the precipice. The political class ensconced in their gated communities and safe behind the beltway moat may not know it or they may not care, but the once secure middle-class in the rustbelt flyover country know it and Trump has managed to convincingly play the marshal for this parade. He has ridden the wave of discontent into the nomination and the phenomenon that is the Trump earthquake is about to cause a tsunami for the Democrats.

I just pray that everyone remembers that while a rising tide may lift all boats a crashing tidal wave submerges the whole coast and anything less than freedom isn't freedom.

Keep the faith. Keep the peace. We shall overcome.

Dispatch Thirty-six

Trump or Clinton Life or Death

There will be no end to History until there is an end to events. Current events are the History of the future. However History can be lost. People can ignore their past, live only in the now, and leave their future to chance. History provides the opportunity to learn from the mistakes of others as well as the chance to build upon what others have learned. To ignore these two paths to success gives life to the notion that failure to plan is planning to fail.

All Americans should cherish their History. We left a known and secure world for a new one. We turned an untamed land into one bustling with enterprise and development. We stood against the world's greatest superpower to assert that all men are created equal and are endowed by their Creator with certain unalienable rights and that among them are life, liberty, and the pursuit of happiness. We made it through a sectarian war and clawed our way from the outskirts of an Atlantic culture to the pinnacle of global dominance. Our industry, our education, our health care system, our culture, and our military became the epitome of western civilization and the envy of the entire world.

Then Came Trump

There was a time in America when every child was infused with the story of America rising from nothing to the apex of power, a time when everyone was taught in Civics class about the declaration of Independence, the Constitution, and the melting pot that made us the embodiment of E pluribus unum: out of many, one.

Today after the Progressives and that destroyer of education the Department of Education has worked for generations to dumb us down from individuals using personal freedom to succeed to induhviduals using a pack mentality to follow the herd to a ride in the entitlement hammock. Now we glory in being a smelting pot where the cheerleaders of fragmentation parrot "Diversity is our strength" as we unravel into warring factions. Hyphenated Americans of every color, creed, and ethnicity now jockey for their place in the que as government goodies are doled out to preferred groups.

Where we are today:

A culture of death swallows a culture of life. A terminally ill California woman determined to be with her four young children for as long as she could was reportedly denied an expensive chemotherapy treatment — but won approval for a lethal drug to legally end her life. We even have a presidential candidate who says we have to ban guns to save the children yet we need to keep partial birth abortions legal to kill the babies, and no one in the media has the insight or the integrity to call her on it.

Not only is New York's Sixth Crime Family guilty of pay to play they are also guilty of bribe to walk: The charge - A Hillary Clinton ally donated almost $500,000 to the campaign of the wife of an FBI official who helped oversee the agency's probe of Clinton's email server. The particulars - Virginia Gov. Terry McAuliffe, a longtime ally of Bill and Hillary Clinton, donated almost $500,000 to the campaign of Dr. Jill McCabe, wife of Federal Bureau of Investigation deputy director Andrew McCabe.[ccxxxiv] A serial liar, unindicted co-conspirator with a notoriously philandering husband is going to win the votes of millions of low information voters, government dependents, and dead people.

Early voting has started and not only is the expected fraud showing up immediately the imported voters are turning out en mass for open borders and an end to America as America: Residents of at least two cities in Texas are complaining that they voted for Donald Trump only to see the voting machine switch their ballot to Hillary Clinton.[ccxxxv] And illegal immigrants have been caught on tape stuffing ballot boxes during early voting.[ccxxxvi]

Corruption is accepted as the norm in today's America, with a totally corrupt Hillary Clinton presented as a viable presidential candidate. Bill Clinton's type of lewd behavior once considered unacceptable is swept under the rug as our culture sinks to its lowest common denominator. Life is being swallowed by death and a shining city on the hill is being remade into a squalid third world hell hole that will use our grandchildren as beasts of burden to support the human debris of failed states.

The America of "Give us liberty or give us death" has morphed into "Give me bread and circuses." Throw a six pack over the fence and beam a game to the flat screen and the descendants of the pioneers are ready to roll over and cash their next government check.

This may be the trail chosen for us by the blind guides of the left. This may be the end of western civilization and the death of life conjured up by the globalist puppet masters who pull the strings in this final act of the Progressive Putsch; however, I choose another way.

I choose to vote for Donald Trump. I choose to vote for America first.

Two things ring in my mind as I contemplate this election:

"I call heaven and earth as witnesses today against you, *that* I have set before you life and death, blessing and cursing; therefore choose life, that both you and your descendants may live; [20] that you may love the Lord your God, that you may obey His voice, and that you may cling to Him, for He *is* your life and the length of your days; and that you may dwell in the land which the Lord swore to your fathers, to Abraham, Isaac, and Jacob, to give them."

And "And if it seems evil to you to serve the Lord, choose for yourselves this day whom you will serve, whether the gods which your fathers served that *were* on the other side of the River, or the gods of the Amorites, in whose land you dwell. But as for me and my house, we will serve the Lord."

Dispatch Thirty-seven

Trump Tames Billary

Back in the days of the peace dividend, "Read my lips," and "It's the economy stupid" we were told we got two for the price of one. And we sure did. One president to chase skirts in the Oval Office and one harridan to persecute his victims: Billary, the corrupt couple from Whitewater. Remember back in the Sleazy Nineties when the Clinton interlewed between George I and George II lowered the standards for what was acceptable public conduct. Remember all the fun we had with these two madcap political savants: Chinagate, Travelgate, Whitewater, Vince Foster, Filegate, the Cattle Futures Miracle, Lootergate, Drug Dealer Donor Scandal, Ponzi Scheme, and the Political Favor Scandal.[ccxxxvii]

Then in 2000 AlGore their trusty assistant failed in his bid to continue their legacy of lunacy. After two terms of Bushness the female side of Billary was in the Senate not passing legislation just screeching enough to keep her name in the headlines, approving wars she would later repudiate, and condemning Bush for believing phony intelligence she believed before she doubted. In the meantime Bubba was flying off on the Lolita Express[ccxxxviii] to Orgy Island[ccxxxix] for a little RR with underage sex slaves.[ccxl]

Along comes 2008 and she and her con-conspirator Bill lined up for a re-run of the bimbo eruption express. A funny thing happened on the way to her coronation. Barack Hussein Obama erupted from who knows where, and reminiscent of the sainted JFK who defeated Tricky Dick he vanquished the Duality of Deception and just as JFK's media facilitators built Camelot he built Chicago-on-the-Potomac. This is a wondrous place where America gets fundamentally transformed from the Unipolar Hegemon of the World into a banana republic whose Tin Pot rules by decree, the borders are erased, the New Normal says .05% growth is the best we can do, and our Dear Leader bows to foreign despots and apologizes for who we were.

All that was just a bump in the road.

Along comes 2012 and after four years as a figurehead Secretary of State handing out re-set buttons that didn't work, presiding over the massacre in Benghazi, and setting up an illegal private server so Bubba could solicit pre-election bribes she is ready to ride the backs of a complicit media back into the White House. A funny thing happened on her way to her second coronation. Crazy Bernie after years of being a Socialist back bencher became a Democratic Socialist and started winning primaries. His brand of "From each according to their ability to each according to their need" Marxism appealed to the everyone-gets-a-trophy-for-showing-up generation and Billery started taking on water.

As the BOGO candidate failed to put away the crazy guy on the left they traded promises to give everyone everything, to punish business, and humble, humiliate, and cripple America even more than BHO. Just because she is universally known to be an inveterate liar people seemed to believe the crazy one more than the sleazy one.

Crazy Bernie's crowds filled stadiums and she was lucky to fill gymnasiums. In an honest contest crazy would have beaten sleazy but it wasn't anywhere near a fair fight. The media carries water for the Duality of Debauchery and the super delegates in the Democrat system make the voters merely cover for smoke-filled rooms.

In the old days Bill would bite his lip and tell us, "I did not have sex with that woman," or Hillary would remind us she is a woman and that would settle the matter. Just like prosecutors believe they can indict a ham sandwich the media believed they could foist any type of incompetent dishonest lecher and his less than better half on the great unwashed. Then along came Trump.

The Donald upended the calculations of the Perpetually Reelected- Mainstream Media-Crony Capitalist Cartel. The political hacks are confounded not knowing how to counter his counter punches. The Media can't help themselves. They have to cover everything he says since he pushes their ratings which have been taking a beating from alternative online sources. They may spend more time trying to destroy him than anything else, but it turns out there is no such thing as bad press and they do spell his name right. And the Crony Capitalists? He's one of their own, so if they haven't already jumped on the Trump Train they will, because they know which side of their bread is buttered and they always end up on the winning side.

There are still many interesting things to look forward to in this unusual election cycle.

Billary will go over the top even if she loses California, but Crazy Bernie won't go away. He's like the goofy old uncle who always shows up. Sometimes you aren't even sure how he is related to you, but he always shows up.

Then we have the 2016 Republican National Convention which will be held in Cleveland, Ohio at the Quicken Loans Arena July 18-21, 2016. It will be the *GREATEST SHOW ON EARTH* complete with all-star entertainment, suspense and drama. This will break records for ratings and launch Trump the Magnificent onto the world stage as the anointed leader of the millionaires and billionaires who are going to save the forgotten man.

Next comes the 2016 Democratic Convention that will be held at the Wells Fargo Center in Philadelphia July 25th-28th, 2016. That will either be a snoozefest or Chicago 1968 on steroids. After this gathering of give-away artists have done all they can to whip their disparate interest groups into line, bribe the covetous, and fool the rest, after more than a year of preliminaries we finally will arrive at the actual election campaign.

Ah, the 2016 election this should be a show worth watching. Billary will try everything. Bill will bite his lip and Hillary will remind everyone she's a woman. The Media will do their best to paint her as a St. Hillary of Arch riding in to save us from the Trump monster.

Then Came Trump

This should be Kabuki of the highest order. Billary will flail around using the same Democrat playbook as always and hurl baseless charges through their media megaphone like they did with Romney, "He hasn't paid taxes in years" or "He gave someone a wedgie back in seventh grade." Bill will bite his lip and Hillary will still be a woman.

Mr. Trump will counterpunch so effectively Bill will be calling her Crooked Hillary before he's done. They won't know what hit them. They are busy building up the Clinton Library and Message Parlor with bribes, I mean donations, from the misogynistic oil slicks and anyone else who wants to get on the waiting list to rent the Lincoln Bedroom or get a pardon. Having made millions giving 20 minute speeches about nothing Billary has no conception of what a person who really builds things and is a mover and shaker based on their achievements not their connections can move and shake. They'll have PTSD by the time the election results add their name to Goldwater and McGovern in the list of also rans.

Dispatch Thirty-eight

Trump Triumph Now Do What You Said You Would Do

I was a house painter for many years. In a profession famous for drunks who show up late, finish late, and inflate prices in between I found that if I did what I said I was going to do when I said I was going to do it for the price agreed upon I never ran out of work. As a matter of fact I was always the highest priced and most sought after painter in every market I ever entered with a six month waiting list and satisfied customers.

I give the same advice to President-Elect Donald Trump that I gave myself, do what you said you would do, when you said you would do it and for the price agreed upon.[ccxli]

Don't take a bite out of the poison apple that has betrayed every wave election since 2010. Don't twist yourself into a pretzel reaching across the aisle to the very Progressives you vowed to repudiate and who your followers voted to retire.

The Democrats are masters at snatching victory from the jaws of defeat. Look at 2010, the great Tea Party wave election. President Obama comes out the next day and says we got shellacked and then proceeds to act as if he had won and the Republican leadership fell into line reauthorizing the Patriot Act, passing the continuing resolutions and generally acting like a water boy for the Progressive first string. In 2012 the Republican nominee won the first debate and then virtually conceded the next two agreeing with almost everything his opponent said. Then he disappeared for the last two weeks of the campaign. In 2014 another wave gave the Republicans the Senate to go along with the House and what have they done?

Mr. Trump don't let the Pollyannas lead you down the primrose path. Stand strong. To paraphrase Winston Churchill: your victory is not the end. It is not even the beginning of the end. It is but the end of the beginning. Now is the time that tests men's souls. Now is the time to be resolute in the face of the Progressives of Left and Right, their propaganda arm in the media, and their bully-boys in the streets. These are the very people who have been trying to destroy you for eighteen months and trying to subvert and transform our nation for a century. Now is not the time to try and compromise our way to unity with everything the movement you lead has been trying to push off the stage.

Rush Limbaugh uses the example of the Second World War in the Pacific. We did not compromise our way to unity with Japan. We demanded unconditional surrender. They offered to negotiate and we continued to demand unconditional surrender. It was not until they laid down every weapon and surrendered unconditionally that we welcomed them back into the family of nations. Japan repudiated their fascist system, embraced democracy and capitalism, and we are still united with them to this day.[ccxlii]

Pat Buchanan uses the examples of FDR and LBJ as presidents who used their landmark victories to launch America in new directions that have left indelible marks and shaped the course of our nation for generations. He also used the example of Nixon in 1968 who failed to seize the initiative instead trying to compromise and appease the Progressives. A decision he regretted the rest of his life. Reagan is another example of a president who successfully used the momentum of victory to change the course of America. And he only had one house of Congress. You have two.[ccxliii]

Step out boldly onto the stage of History and make a place for yourself as one of the greatest presidents of all time.

You are the consummate business man. You took a loan of one million dollars and turned it into billions. A feat which I am sure sounds much easier than it is. You wrote the book on thinking big, deal making, getting rich, and never giving up. You have surrounded yourself with the best and the brightest. Work this transition like no one has since FDR, and when your hand comes off that Bible move decisively from the Obamanation to Trump Triumph.

Have a second Scalia picked, vetted and ready to nominate. Announce an all-star cabinet with marching orders to clear the path for a return to limited government, personal freedom, and economic opportunity. Untie the hands of our border patrol, give us a time table for building the wall, and give ICE the green light to start deporting those illegals who have been convicted of crimes. Cut of all federal funds for sanctuary cities. Having coordinated with Congressional leadership introduce bills to repeal and replace Obamacare, repeal Dodd-Frank, pass a new Glass–Steagall Act, and open the door for the re-patriation of American corporate profits held off shore. Begin the work of untangling the nightmare the Neo-con Progressive axis has made of our foreign policy. And make all of BHO's unconstitutional executive orders null and void.

In other words, do what you said you would do, when you said you would do it and for the price agreed upon. What was the price? We give you the presidency and you give us our country back. Now is not the time for a bunt. This is the time to swing for the bleachers.

Don't crack your back leaning across the aisle or you might end up with people looking back at all you have promised and trying to read your lips. If that happens in four years the very movement that has catapulted you to the pinnacle of power may end up saying, "You're fired."

Dispatch Thirty-nine

Trump Triumph to Dream the Impossible Dream

According to Albert Einstein, "Insanity is doing the same thing over and over and expecting different results."[ccxliv]

If *We the People* want to restore the Republic we will have to rise above the shop worn politics presented by the two-headed party of power and as described by the Corporations Once Known as the Mainstream Media.

We cannot be diverted into the channels of thought and discussion that inevitably lead to the same conclusions. We debate where and when we should intervene in overseas adventures not if we should intervene. We debate how much money the Fed should create not if the Fed should create money or if there should be a central bank at all. We debate how big the deficit should be instead of should we run deficits at all. As long as we allow the advocates of big government to dictate the debate we lose before the first words are spoken because the answers are prescribed by the questions.

In an article as short as this I cannot cover all the many schemes, swindles, and boondoggles that have led us to the precipice. Let me examine one that is rarely thought about, barely understood, and never mentioned in political campaigns.

Fractional Reserve Banking is the prescription that causes the disease. The attempt to create prosperity by inflating bubbles leads inevitably to the bursting of bubbles. This bubble blowing is a result of the so-called "multiplier effect. According to Investopedia:[ccxlv]

> The multiplier effect is the expansion of a country's money supply that results from banks being able to lend. The size of the multiplier effect depends on the percentage of deposits that banks are required to hold as reserves. In other words, it is the money used to create more money and is calculated by dividing total bank deposits by the reserve requirement.

BREAKING DOWN 'Multiplier Effect'

> To calculate the effect of the multiplier effect on the money supply, start with the amount banks initially take in through deposits, and divide this by the reserve ratio. If, for example, the reserve requirement is 20%, for every $100 a customer deposits into a bank, $20 must be kept in reserve. However, the remaining $80 can be loaned out to other bank customers. This $80 is then deposited by these customers into another bank, which in turn

must also keep 20%, or $16, in reserve but can lend out the remaining $64.

This cycle continues as more people deposit money and more banks continue lending it until finally the $100 initially deposited creates a total of $500 ($100/0.2) in deposits. This creation of deposits is the multiplier effect.

Required Reserves

The reserve requirement is set by the board of governors of the Federal Reserve System, and it varies based on the total amount of liabilities held by a particular depository institution. For example, as of 2016, institutions with more than $110.2 million in deposits are required to hold 10% of their total liabilities in reserve.[ccxlvi]

Ten percent! That is all the banks are required to keep out of every dollar deposited. No wonder there are so many balls in the air at once, and no wonder they periodically come crashing down. For every one hundred dollars deposited the banks make another 609 dollars appear as if by magic. How could this ever go wrong? When the music stops there never seems to be a chair for everyone, and as the dominos tumble they always take down the next in line.

Enter the government which legalized Fractional Reserve Banking to begin with to solve the problems caused by

Fractional Reserve Banking. After George Bush II declared, "I've abandoned free market principles to save the free market system"[ccxlvii] and went on to bail out the main perpetrators of the government mandated sub-prime loans, for some reason the 99% became upset.

All the little people who pay the bills burned out on bail outs. It was time for the next dog and pony show, so the government steps in to fix the situation they caused by trying to fix the situation they caused passing the Dodd-Frank Bill. In classic government cure the disease by amplifying the infection mode Dodd-Frank actually enshrines too big to fail and sets the stage for the next big bail out of the crony capitalists who are one of the three legs of the Washington fascist economy. A classic case of doing what feels good instead of doing what is good. Some may think that my use of the word fascist to describe the current American economy is hyperbole. It is not. A fascist economic system, also known as Corporatism, is a union of the government, crony capitalists, and big unions. Sound familiar?[ccxlviii]

From a rigged economic system to a rigged political system our once proud Republic has devolved from a nation of the people by the people and for the people to a dysfunctional oligarchy masquerading as a functional democracy.

If you listen to the Corporations Once Known as the Mainstream Media and their cable network step sisters we are poised to elect the most corrupt person to have ever run, the head of a crime family, and the wife of the defiler of the oval office. No matter what the next scandal, no matter the prospect of a failed presidency racked by serial investigations these bought and paid for pundits act as if her victory is inevitable.

I don't think so. As I have predicted since January 31 I believe the Donald will win in the greatest landslide since Reagan in 1984. After decades of Progressives who have sold us down the river and regaled us with lies such as "If you like your doctor you can keep your doctor" we finally have a man who inspires us with his dream of making America great again.

In a recent speech Mr. Trump said we should dream big. He said that if we will unlock the potential of the American people no dream will be beyond our reach. I have always been a dreamer and now like someone waking up from the fever dream of the Obamapocalypse I am joining with Donald Trump to dream the impossible dream: to make America great again.

To dream the impossible dream

To fight the unbeatable foe

To bear with unbearable sorrow

To run where the brave dare not go

To right the unrightable wrong

Then Came Trump

To be better far than you are

To try when your arms are too weary

To reach the unreachable star

This is my quest, to follow that star

No matter how hopeless, no matter how far

To be willing to give when there's no more to give

To be willing to die so that honor and justice may live

And I know if I'll only be true to this glorious quest

That my heart will lie peaceful and calm when I'm laid to my rest

And the world will be better for this

That one man scorned and covered with scars

Still strove with his last ounce of courage

To reach the unreachable star

Let us join together on November 8th to elect Donald J. Trump as the next president of the United States. Let us dream the impossible dream. Let us stop doing the same thing over and over expecting a different result. Let us make that impossible dream possible once again. Let us make America great again.

Dispatch Forty

Trump Trumps Never-Trump

The Perpetually Re-elected Progressive Elite, the Corporations Once Known as the Mainstream media, and their pet poodle pundits make fun of Trump by calling him a "Reality TV Star." They just don't get it. Half the country wishes they were reality TV Stars. They say he is brash, uncouth, and disrespectful to the army of political hacks he has been and will confront. They just don't get it. People want someone who will stand up for the Country Party in the face of the Government Party that has controlled both major parties for so long.

The list of disconnects between the imperial rulers in Chicago-on-the-Potomac and the great unwashed out here in fly-over country is massive. It is easily more than enough to define a complete breakdown in the social contract of a limited government. A social contract forged in the Declaration of Independence and enshrined in the Constitution which defines the legitimacy of the current regime.

The Progressive megaphones tell us this is the strongest economy in American History and that President Obama is the greatest chief executive of modern times. They even fantasize about the "Obama Boom." Working people laugh when you try to sell them this obvious propaganda. The government tells us that we have reached full employment. Anyone who reads should know that over ninety-three million able bodied Americans no longer work and only a little over 150 million are working. Yet the government tells us there is 5% unemployment when the numbers say it is closer to 40%. Our leaders tell us there is no inflation no matter how many trillions of fiat dollars they print, and all of us who shop for our own food, buy our own clothes, or pay utility bills know otherwise.

They tell us we won the war in Iraq. We may have won it by the time King George II left but since Prince Obama got his hands on it ISIS tells us we haven't. Our leaders say we have won in Afghanistan. Everyone in the world knows that the minute we leave the Taliban roll right back into Kabul and the sock puppets we have been supporting all these years as the leaders of a democratic Afghanistan will be flying to Switzerland in 747s filled with American taxpayer's cash. We are told Obamacare is a great success. Anyone who had insurance before it started knows that if you like your doctor you can keep your doctor has to be tempered by increased fees, increased deductibles, increased co-payments, and decreased covered services.

They tell us and they tell us and they tell us, we just don't believe them anymore.

If these belchers of beltway bromides think every day working Americans swallow any of this they have seriously underestimated our intelligence, our interest, and our attention spans.

Then Came Trump

I have the opportunity to travel the country throughout the year. I take what some call back roads, the secondary roads that parallel America's vast Interstate system and that still goes through small towns instead of bypassing them and homogenizing everywhere in to anywhere. I try to stop at Mom-and-Pop restaurants and take every opportunity possible to talk with people about the issues of the day. Here's what I find, Trump, Trump, Trump.

I believe the polls are skewed. Perhaps people don't want to say they are for Trump because they know the pollsters will look down on them as simple country bumpkins, racists, or reactionary supporters of old dead white guys. Perhaps they are talking to those who are at home when the workers are busy working. Whatever the reason I believe, and I predict that Trump is going to beat Hillary like a drum. He is going to win in a landslide, and he is going to drag the Republican Party that tried to reject him along for the ride. I am predicting that due to his wave election coattails the Republicans will increase their majorities in the House and the Senate.

What is the cause of this phenomenon? Generations of politicians who run as outsiders and who become insiders as soon as they enter the moral and patriotic black hole and before they start swirling in the DC drain to their life-time pensions. Generations of politicians who sold us out in so-called free trade deals that gave others a free pass into our markets while keeping their own locked to us. Generations of politicians who have spent us into oblivion, printed more money that there is paper, and borrowed so much money from other nations that we are now the world's greatest debtor.

So who is to blame for the coming over throw of the twin headed bird of prey that is the Government Party of Power: the politicians themselves. Living in their bubble asking why those who have no bread don't eat cake they have no idea of what is coming. Their pollsters are polling themselves and providing the information their paymasters want to see. And all the while out here in the Heartland a tsunami is brewing that will wash them all away.

To paraphrase what Phil Ochs said so long ago,

In tattered tuxedos they faced the new heroes
And crawled about in confusion
All the hands raised, they stood there amazed
In the shattering of their illusions[ccxlix]

Many of the nattering nabobs of negativism who dominate the 24 hour news cycle have been waiting expectantly for Trump to make one mega-gaff that will destroy his campaign. To hear them crow you would believe he made it when he resurrected the phrase, "America First."

First used as the name of a widely based organization that sought to keep us out of World War Two. Then it was used in the nineties by Pat Buchanan in his prescient campaign to save America from the one-worlders. The left has done their best to make this a catch phrase for defeat because they hate not only what it says but what it implies. The Elite political class has sought to make it an unutterable phrase condemned by political correctness and exiled because in their minds to even say America First is to defile their one world religion. They may believe they have tarnished the concept with 75 years of negative propaganda and indoctrination but still 57% of American citizens believe in America First, they want an America First foreign policy, an America First trade policy, and an America First immigration policy. They want an America First president.

My prediction: After all is said and done, after all the dust settles, after Crooked Hillary goes home to lick her wounds, after the neo-con talking heads and their K-Street financiers realize the prize has slipped from their hands it will end up that Trump Trumps Never-Trump.

Dispatch Forty-one

Trump Vote is a Vote for Hope

Marching out of Yorktown to surrender the British Army played the song "The World Turned Upside Down." As I drive to Meg Lo Mart to make my latest deposit of monopoly money in a Chinese savings account all I can do is mumble the final tag-line of the Wicked Witch of the West, "What a world. What a world."

There is a massive unspoken problem in America today, floating like the iceberg in front of the Titanic waiting to sink the unsinkable ship. Founded by revolutionaries crying "No taxation without representation!" the Republic these revolutionaries devised has devolved into a society where more than 40% of the people pay no Federal income tax[ccl] and the number of people receiving government benefits is even higher. What incentive would these non-paying receivers have to reign in an overbearing and intrusive government? This unseen and unspoken problem is a cancer in the body politic.

Self-serving professional politicians buy votes by exempting non-productive people from personal financial responsibility while providing ever-expanding benefits at the expense of the productive. This is not the right versus left, conservative versus liberal, Democrat versus Republican he-said-she-said endless debate that devours the chatocracy of cable's wall-to-wall talking-heads. This is not an academic exercise that pointy-headed Political Science and History majors with dueling pocket protectors debate for hours in their mother's basement as they post their latest scoop on their samizdat blogs. If it is not any of these things what is it? It is a dagger pointing directly at the heart of our civilization.

Western Civilization awoke from the slumber of the Dark Ages enlightened and empowered by a belief, based in the Judeo-Christian tradition that humanity has an innate right to be free and a natural right to excel. Rights and freedoms are given by God not bestowed at the whim of some legend-in-his-own-mind Leader. This civilization gathered steam in Europe exploding upon the world stage through an energetic period of exploration.

In America after a revolution fought by farmers and merchants against the greatest empire of the day the Founders, dared to declare "We hold these truths to be self-evident, that all men are created equal, that they are endowed by their Creator with certain unalienable rights, that among these are Life, Liberty and the pursuit of Happiness."[ccli] After centuries of government thugs standing on the windpipe of everyday people these self-sacrificing giants observed that in a civilized world government was not imposed by the strong upon the weak it was instead built upon a social contract between the governed and those entrusted with the privilege to govern when they said, "That to secure these rights, Governments are instituted among Men, deriving their just powers from the consent of the governed."[cclii]

Today this bold and unique experiment in freedom is being devoured from within and challenged from without. Those who believe the collective should reign over the individual, those who believe in the suffocating sameness of socialism over the rough-and-tumble of capitalism have worked for generations building a culture of dependency which has tempered the steel will of the pioneers into the sloppy demands of the couch-potato slacker waiting for someone to find their remote as they guzzle some refreshments and wait for the game as bread and circuses take the place of innovation and accomplishment. Schools teaching 2+2 might = 5, trophies for everyone, politically correct new-speak and affirmative action promotions have sapped the vitality from the citizens of our Republic. Politicians and their fellow-travelers use a system of cronies[ccliii] and sweet-heart deals to reward each other for siphoning trillions from the public treasury promising the dumbed-down descendants of revolutionaries that they just might win the lotto before they have to declare bankruptcy so they might as well re-elect the same old grafters once again.

There comes a time when those who are raising the sails and paddling the boat have to admit to themselves the ballast down in steerage weighs more than the cargo. There comes a time when even the most non-confrontational and loyal among us begin to ask, "Who is John Galt" as Atlas tires of his thankless job and shrugs the burden of dead-weight into the dustbin of history. As the perpetually-reelected and the propaganda spewing Corporations Once Known as the Mainstream Media trumpet the inevitability of government rationed health-care, cap-n-trade industrial suicide, comprehensive import-a-voter immigration reform and the surrender of sovereignty through treaties supposedly designed to deliver so-called free trade and deal with mythical global warming there shines a light in a bell tower, one if by land and two if by sea.

Voting for Hillary is voting for the final nail in our coffin. Four more years of open borders, give-away trade deals, and unilateral disarmament and the United States we have known and loved will be merely a memory as Obama's promise to fundamentally transform America[ccliv] will have been realized and we become the United Socialist States of America.

A vote for Donald Trump is a vote for hope. As a person who has been politically aware and involved since 1960 I can say without exaggeration that several of Mr. Trump's speeches, specifically his Economic Speech,[cclv] his America First Speech,[cclvi] and his Gettysburg Address[cclvii] were among the clearest and most inspirational I have ever heard. They rank right up there with the epic speech of Ronald Reagan to the 1976 Republican Convention. I have waited my whole life to hear a leader who wants to serve America first. If his Contract with America[cclviii] is implemented it will create a pathway to make America great again. Get out and vote. Vote for Donald Trump. Vote for hope.

Without hope you're hopeless and I refuse to allow the unbelievable changes currently assaulting our economy and our political system to bring about my own personal Great Depression. Those who believe in the Devil believe he comes to steal, kill and destroy. I believe if he can't steal your joy he can't keep your stuff and weeping may endure for a night but joy comes in the morning. Don't despair pray. Why worry when you can pray? Don't give up, give it up to God. Let me ask you, "Do you have hope?" I hope so. Personally as for me and my house we will trust the Lord for our hope is in Christ.

Then Came Trump

Dispatch Forty-two

Who Do You Believe When You Can't Believe Anyone?

An old joke goes like this, "How do you know when a politician is lying?" answered by, "When their lips are moving." One of my favorite Chicago post-construction philosophers puts it this way, "All politicians lie. The good ones do it convincingly." This is what passes for trust in our leaders in America today.

America is easily distracted. The majority of the population is hooked on the bread and circus sports world. They can tell you the minutest details about the lives and statistics of their favorite team but they don't know how many Supreme Court Justices rule their lives.

They spend countless hours transfixed watching cars run around a track, people hit balls, pass balls, dunk balls, slap pucks, and try for a hole in one. While they doze on the couch cheering for this side against that they have never watched a congressional hearing, don't have time to read a book, and forgot even the minimal civics education they were force fed at the government run school.

Try to share anything you have learned from hours of research and you are greeted with, "I don't think that's right," or "I never heard that before," about anything that contradicts or doesn't line up with what the Progressive-controlled ABCCBSNBCCNNMSNBC cartel extrude as truth.

Our leaders lie to get elected. They lie to us after they are elected. And we lie to ourselves about what is going on. No matter how bad it gets the media megaphones and the public screwals continue to tell us we are the freest most prosperous and most powerful country on earth. But are we?

According to the Legatum Prosperity Index's findings for 2016[cclix] America has slipped to number fifteen when it comes to freedom and number eleven when it comes to prosperity. According to the 2016 Index of Economic Freedom we rank number eleven.[cclx] Our military is the best of the best. However they are committed to no-win wars hamstrung at every turn by politicians who use the blood, sweat, and tears of our heroes for props in their political theater. Sure we are better than many places, but we used to be number one, and now our rankings are falling constantly.

Why?

Because America's leaders no longer look out for America they look out for number one. Our trade deals are good for everyone but us. Our military is sent on peace keeping missions that end in body bags and wounded warriors fighting for everyone else's protection while our own country is being overwhelmed by an invasion through open borders.

When we elect traitors who appoint traitors what do we expect to get?

Looking at the issue of traitors from another perspective we now live in a country where the government can listen to and record everything you say without a warrant and the person who tells us about it is branded a traitor by the Elite Regime and its media sycophants.

We know Hillary is a serial liar. From Whitewater through Travelgate, from the Rose Law firm, through her emails we know she even lies about lying. The Clinton Crime Family routinely gets away with things that would land a mere mortal in jail.

Looking at The Donald everyone tells me he is a liar too. They say electing him instead of the Hillary, the tool of Oligarchs, would be electing one of the oligarchs instead.

"They" may be right. However, I have been waiting my whole life, or at least since the last time Pat Buchanan ran for president, to hear someone say that they were going to put America First. I have been waiting my whole life, or at least since Ronaldus Magnus brought us morning in America, to hear someone say they were going to unshackle the economy and let freedom ring.

Donald Trump has said these things.

When I give to a charity and that charity is later exposed as taking more of the money for administration than for doing the work I gave them the money to do that is on them, I gave out of my generosity and that is on me. If I believe someone who tells me they will secure our borders, stop the endless wars for peace, and free the economy, and then they do something else that is on them.

I try to live my life with clean hands and a pure heart. If I head North and things go South at least I know I used my mind, followed my heart, and voted my conscious. For this reason I once again endorse Donald Trump for president.

Who do you believe when you can't believe anyone? I say believe the one who is saying what you want to hear and then pray they are telling the truth.

Some might say this is naive. Some might say this is foolish. Some might even say this is another case of "I know they are lying but I like what they say." None of that worries me in the least.

Why worry when you can pray?

Dispatch Forty-three

Why Should Obama Declare Martial Law

If you turn on, tune in, browse or otherwise peruse the alternative media you will undoubtedly come across the question, "Will President Obama declare Martial Law?" or one of its many variants: "Can President Obama use martial law to stay in the White House?" "What is Obama's plan to declare martial law?" "President Obama signs martial lar order." "President Obama will suspend 2016 election and impose martial law." And of course there has to be an exposé with international implications, "Obama instigating war to declare Martial Law and stay in power for a THIRD term?"

Now I love a good conspiracy theory as well as the next person however, after reading these and a gazillion other variations on the theme I have come to the conclusion, why should President Obama declare martial law when he is already ruling by decree, refusing to enforce any laws he disagrees with, nationalizing local police forces, signing treaties by-any-other-name without ratification by the Senate, legislating by fiat, and in general acting like any other tin-pot dictator in a banana republic. In other words his actions are already imposing martial law and no one is connecting the dots. This isn't conspiracy. This is observation.

We are witnessing the culmination of the Progressive's long march from Trust Busting Teddy, through Whites Only Woodrow, Hoover's unrecognized New Deal seed bed, FDR's New Deal corporatist take-over[cclxi] which Joseph Goebbels, Hitler's propaganda chief, in 1933, spoke of as the way for National Socialism to follow, LBJ's Great Society safety net hammock vote buying scheme,[cclxii] Nixon's "We are all Keynesians now"[cclxiii] George I's compassionate conservative read-my-lips betrayal,[cclxiv] Clinton's dot Com bubble panty raid,[cclxv] George II's "we must abandon free market principles to save the free market,"[cclxvi] to Obama's war upon all that is good.

This has taken more than 100 years. The Progressives have kept their eye on the ball. To them it was always a game of two steps forward then one step back. First they set out to capture education. Then they captured the mainstream media and entertainment. Along the way they picked up the courts and infiltrated the leadership of both big box parties. Today we face a monolith that has brainwashed generations, distorted our culture, and makes even the most ardent supporters of freedom accept the seeming inevitability of their final triumph with the coming victory of Hillary "The Nail in Our Coffin" Clinton.

Given the electoral map, the unified media support, the guaranteed votes of the Kool-Aide drinking generational Democrats who may disagree with everything their leaders say but still vote that way, illegals driving to the polls on motor-voter, felons who can vote for those who let them out and restore their voting privileges, the massive government payroll that now outnumbers manufacturing employees by 9,932,000 who will vote for someone who wants to increase the size of government, those riding the government hammock, and of course all the dead who cast their zombie votes in the Democrat controlled wastelands we used to call alabaster cities gleaming undimmed by human tears.

Look at the vast number of disillusioned Democrats who fell for Bernie's the burn out is real ersatz eruption which Rush said all along was just a front to make Hillary look like she had some competition in what we now know for sure was a rigged illusion.[cclxvii] Look at the record breaking crowds that the Donald continues to gather in stadiums and arenas while hiding Hillary has a hard time filling a phone booth and it becomes apparent there is a groundswell for something besides the corrupt corporatist system we have today.

If this is thwarted by the rigging in the system, this ship of state may sail off a cliff. The present rule-by-decree tin pot may ride off into the sunset but another would take and ignore the same oath and the regime will go on. They have elections in China too. They have a new president every 5 – 10 years however the regime goes on.

So why should President Obama declare martial law? He shouldn't. Why bother. The sheeple may bah-bah about wanting change. They may rally and demand change. However the regime believes if they pat us on our heads and have a mock election that changes nothing we will settle back down and play nice while they import a new population that is used to their authoritarian dreams.

Maybe they're right and maybe they're wrong. November is coming fast. What are you going to do? The only way the Donald, our only hope for change, wins is by a landslide. Anything close and the perpetually elected will find enough bags of votes in the basement to win. It must be a landslide. It must be such an overwhelming crushing defeat that the Progressives will not dare to thwart the will of the people or ... the regime goes on.

Dispatch Forty-four

Why the Progressives Want a Recount They Know They Will Lose

The recount in Wisconsin and the coming ones in Michigan and Pennsylvania will not change the outcomes in any of those states. Even though the party of Mayor Daley, Boss Tweed, and their big city machines are famous for winning recounts by finding bags of votes in candy store basements no recount has ever changed thousands of votes let alone tens of thousands. I do not believe changing the outcome is the purpose. It is instead changing the perception of it.

I predict that they will demand the recounts are done by hand. This would make them take so long these three pivotal States would not certify their results by the last day possible for directing their Electors how to vote. If all three states miss the deadline, Trump is at 260, Hillary at 232. No one hits 270.

Then, according to the Constitution, the election would go to Congress. The House votes with one vote per State. The Republican House would then elect Donald Trump as the 45th president. The Republican Senate would elect Pence Vice President.

This has happened before. In 1824, though Andrew Jackson had more popular votes and more electoral votes John Quincy Adams won in the House. President Adams made a deal with the Speaker of the House Henry Clay who Adams then named as his Secretary of State, which at the time was considered the stepping stone to the presidency. This was immediately termed the Corrupt Bargain by supporters of Jackson.[cclxviii] The antagonistic presidential race of 1828 began practically before Adams took office. To the Jacksonians the Adams-Clay alliance symbolized a corrupt system where elite insiders pursued their own interests without heeding the will of the people.

This is Hillary and the Progressives strategy to place the mantel of corrupt elite insiders on the Republicans now that they see the nation is incensed against the circle of Progressive power brokers who led us from the pinnacle of prosperity to the brink of bankruptcy. This is akin to how the Democrats have successfully placed the mantel of racist on the party of Lincoln and the Emancipation Proclamation. What a masterful stroke of political maneuvering that convinced the descendants of slaves that their natural allies are the descendants of Jim Crow.

If this goes to the US House and Senate, and the result is the same as the result from the Electoral College without the recounts, why do it? The answer is to make Trump seem completely illegitimate. They and their obedient shills in the media will tell us every day and at every opportunity that Trump did not win the popular vote saying he lost by over 2.1 million ignoring the fact that millions of illegals voted. He did not win the Electoral

College since in this scenario he would not have attained 270. They will say just as they did about Bush the Younger that he was not elected he was selected by members of his own party in Congress.

However, there is one wrinkle in this strategy. If a state never gets to name electors, the number needed to win does not remain the 270 needed if every state names every elector. In that case it would once again be a majority of those named. Even with 260-232, Trump would still win. Then again the thugs on the left are sending death threats to electors already named trying to frighten some of them into becoming faithless electors who do not vote as instructed by their States. I don't foresee this happening. The number of faithless electors in American History doesn't make a handful.

So if after all these devious machinations Trump still wins without the election being thrown into Congress this would only be used by the Sandernistas and the Clintonites to cry rigged system. They would keep their bully boys from Black Lives Matter and Move On in the streets for years while they hope and pray that Trump's policies don't make America great again which could solidify his hold over the working men and women throughout the nation.

No matter how this evil strategy plays out, whether the election is thrown into Congress or if Trump wins with a majority of a short electoral count, we will have four years of the Democrats calling this another Corrupt Bargain. They will try to disrupt the inauguration. They will have protestors outside the White House from day one. They will have demonstrations everywhere

President Trump goes. They may even try to incite mass marches and violence in the rotted hulks of our once magnificent cities they control like medieval fiefdoms. Using their big megaphone in the media they will use print, broadcast, movies, and songs to agitate their followers for the 2020 rematch between the Donald and perhaps Senator Elizabeth Warren or whoever they can scrape up to be the new face for their shopworn collectivist movement.

In other words they know the recount won't change anything but they hope it will be enough to energize their low information base for a restoration of corporate socialism in four more years.

Then Came Trump

Dispatch Forty-five

Donald Dumps Bubba Dashes Dowager's Dreams

The Dowager dreamed of doing great things

Importing voters

And taxing your bling

Her dupes in the media played right along

Planning on 90 minutes singing the same song

When the first question asked

About trash talk and jibes

Was answered with reminders

Of Bubba's philandering crimes

The sycophants changed tracks

Interrupting Donald and proving their hacks

One against three

The battle exposed

He wins on the issues

Hillary Billary Sleazy Media deposed.

Dispatch Forty-six

Crooked Hillary Revealed

In the cesspool known as Washington DC filled with corruption the Clintons take it to new depths. Operating with the functional immunity granted by the compromised Obama Justice Department and the FBI they blatantly skim millions as they take pay-to-play to levels that would have made Chicago's Mayor Daley green with envy.

Here are three examples that could serve as representative of what we should expect if corruptions number one power couple and New York's Sixth Crime Family once again occupy the White House.

The overlap between Hillary Clinton's State Department, her family's foundation, and a consulting firm run by members of her inner circle has reaped a windfall for all involved, steering tens of millions of dollars to the Clinton Family and generating lucrative contracts for a consulting practice run by a close confidante.[cclxix]

Newly released emails show that Hillary Clinton's top State Department adviser, Huma Abedin, granted access to the then-Secretary of State during overseas diplomatic visits based upon Clinton Global Initiative (CGI) donor status.[cclxx]

In a 12-page memo sent by Clinton's former aide Doug Band in 2011 to Bill Clinton, his daughter Chelsea, several board members of the Clinton Foundation, its lawyers and then special advisor John Podesta details how Band helped run what he called 'Bill Clinton Inc.'

In the memo Band revealed that he and another aide helped secure $66 million from ventures, including speaking fees, according to the memo.

He wrote that using his role as the president of his own consulting firm Teneo, Band worked to raise funds for the Foundation and Clinton personally.

Band also wrote that he helped obtain 'in-kind services for the President and his family – for personal, travel, hospital, vacation and the like.'

'Throughout the past almost 11 years since President Clinton left office, I have sought to leverage my activities, including my partner role at Teneo to support and raise funds for the Foundation,' Band wrote.

'This memorandum strives to set forth how I have endeavored to support the Clinton Foundation and President Clinton personally.'

Under a section called 'For-Profit Activity of President Clinton (i.e. Bill Clinton, Inc)' Brand said he and another aide, Justin Cooper brought Clinton all four of his advisory arrangements at the time.

These yielded more than $30million in personal income – with a further $66million to be paid out over the next nine years should he continue with them. ... Band also said that Teneo was responsible for negotiating a number of speaking fees for Clinton, including $1.15million from Ericson and $900,000 from UBS. The full article and all the sordid details are found in the Daily Mail.[cclxxi]

For a more detailed look at the legacy Hillary drags around like Marley's chains see the World Net Daily article <u>Hillary's 22 Biggest Scandals Ever</u>.[cclxxii]

For an in-depth look at what WikiLeaks has so far revealed see the article <u>21 Things We've Learned About Hillary Clinton from Wikileaks That the MSM Won't Share...But YOU Can!</u>.[cclxxiii]

The Donald may have some baggage but like an invading army Hillary travels with a baggage train.

The Wall Street Journal calls the Clintons Grifters-in-Chief saying the Clintons don't draw lines between their 'charity' and personal enrichment.[cclxxiv]

Don't be fooled by the wall-to-wall propaganda vomited out by the Corporations Once Known as the Mainstream Media. To these committed Progressive pseudo-journalists it isn't what the leaks reveal it is all about how they were revealed. Go to drrobertowens.com and see the article <u>Don't Look at Hillary the Russians Did It</u>. The WikiLeaks revelations continue to pour out and the Clinton campaign crew never dispute what is revealed they instead shoot the messenger.

Returning the two heads of the Clinton Crime Family to the White House would be like paying criminals to return to the scene of the crime, guaranteeing a pardon for all future crimes and then looking the other way.

Vote Trump and drain the swamp.

Then Came Trump

Dispatch Forty-seven

Obama The Bad Santa

Pretending to gives he really takes

Pretending to love he really hates

Supposed to leave he's going to stay

Supposed to be quiet he'll have plenty to say

Instead of a present he'll leave us in debt

Instead of fond memories we'll come to regret

The Bad Santa who came promising hope and change

The Bad Santa who left but stays on the stage

Twas the night after the election and all through land

We're still hoping for change we pray is at hand

Ding Dong the Witch is dead

Billy Bongs still sleazy and Uncle Bernie's a red

Pocahontas and Michelle wait in the wings

The Donald must deliver or in four years the Fat Lady sings

Dispatch Forty-eight

The December Revolution

What the Democrat cry-baby sore losers and their snowflake generation supporters are calling for is nothing less than a coup. They are attempting to intimidate Electors into breaking faith with the citizens of their States. In many cases they are attempting to con these Electors into breaking the laws of their States. All of these machinations in a desperate attempt to steal the election fairly won by Donald Trump and hand it to someone else in a December Revolution. Failing to install either their own failed candidate or someone who will play ball with them they seek to through the election into the House to delegitimize The Donald.

They just can't believe that the voters in enough States to win the electoral vote were so stubborn, so heard-headed, so intent on salvaging their country they successfully resisted the Progressive's wall-to-wall propaganda driven attempt to pound the last nail in our own coffin. Progressives can never admit they lost because people rejected their ideas or programs. No, it's always because of the vast right-wing conspiracy, the trickery of the Republicans, the stupidity of the voters.

Or this year's newly minted excuse, the Russians. It can never be because people see through their shop-worn rehash of Soviet era collectivism.

I hate to be the bearer of bad news but I voted for Trump and no Russian told me to do it.

When President Clinton won overwhelming media support and because Ross Perrot split the vote, that was considered fair. When President Obama won, with overwhelming media support, with "Hope and Change" that was fair. When he won, with overwhelming media support, because "If you liked your plan you could keep your plan" that was fair. However when Trump wins against the odds, attacked by every side that is beyond the pale.

And forget about that, "She won the popular vote" smokescreen. If you study motor voter on the Left Coast alone you will see that more than enough illegal immigrants were granted voting rights to turn that around.[cclxxv]

They are now blaming the Electoral System. If you read the Constitution there is no mention of the people voting for the president at all. All that is mentioned is the legislatures of the several States choosing Electors who then choose the president. In the election of 1824 there were States where the people never did vote, just the State legislatures and their chosen Electors.

The Electoral College wasn't designed to make sure not that unqualified people didn't become president as the media tells us today. It was designed to make sure presidents were elected by a majority of the States and not just by the most populous ones.

Electoral majorities do not appear spontaneously like clouds before a shower. They are constructed by national political parties that build them with an eye to the Electoral College's enforced need for a diverse coalition of States. Therefore, the Electoral College system demands that the winning majority are not geographically confined to a few populous States but are instead reflections of a nation-wide decision as opposed to a mere majority of the Citizens of New York, California, Texas and Florida.

This election is no singularity. Of the forty-eight elections since 1824 eighteen resulted in presidents who won less than 50% of the vote. In 1860, Abraham Lincoln, received 39.9 percent. In 1912, Woodrow Wilson won just 41.8 percent of the popular vote. In 1992, Bill Clinton won 43 percent of the popular vote. This has happened before and it will likely happen again.

What may never happen again is this mass movement of patriotic Americans who have risen up and demanded that the Progressives quit engineering and managing our decline. We demanded that the silent majority be heard instead of being drowned out by the Progressives and the aggressive ABCCBSNBCCNNMSNBC propaganda machine.

We demanded that someone lead us out of the wilderness and back to the mountain top. We have demanded an America first administration dedicated to making America great again.

This is no fluke. This is no mistake. This is a new beginning. This is the true December Revolution. It is scheduled to happen today. Let the bells ring and the choirs sing. This is the culmination of the Tea Party revolt of 2010 and the repudiation of the Progressives and their collectivist ways. This is the dawn of a rebirth for limited government, personal freedom and economic opportunity. Mark this day down in your calendars and your minds. This is a day you will want to tell your grandchildren about. This is a day when the people triumphed over the political elites and marched with their pitchforks and torches to drain the swamp.

Today Donald Trump will be officially elected president of the United States! This is the day the Lord has made!

Dispatch Forty-nine

Trump Offices Attacked by Thugs

Thugs vandalize Donald Trump's Denver campaign office.[cclxxvi] His offices in North Carolina have been repeatedly attacked[cclxxvii] so quite naturally the Democrats under Hillary "The Nail in Our Coffin" Clinton accuse Trump of being a Nazi. For one thing the Nazis are more accurately known as the extreme leftist National Socialist German Workers Party which is what the German acronym Nazi stands for.

A second point is that it is the Democrats who are sending undercover operatives into Trump rallies to incite violence so that their propaganda arm (read Mainstream Media) can then accuse Trump of inciting violence. As a follow on I seriously doubt that it is anyone besides the bully boys from the left who are trashing Trump offices and physically attacking Trump supporters. This isn't a case of the pot calling the kettle black this is a case of thugs trying to silence anyone who disagrees with them.

Dispatch Fifty

Trump the Chumps and Choose the Heroes

No one in the Corporations Once Known as the Mainstream Media and their step-sisters in the cable news industry shrink from giving their critique of President-elect Trump's cabinet choices. They still have the same talking heads who got everything wrong for the last year telling us what we are supposed to think.

As someone who began predicting Trump's victory last January, I feel I have a right to at least make some suggestions for those positions still unannounced. I believe that Mr. Trump and his team of political savants will in the end make the best choices however here are my suggestions just in case anyone is interested.

Secretary of Veteran Affairs – Sarah Palin

Secretary of Homeland Security – Sherriff Joe Arpaio

Director of ICE and Immigration Services – Sherriff David Clarke

Press Secretary - Monica Crowley

Chairman of the Economic Advisors - Larry Kudlow

Director, Office of Management and Budget (OMB) – David Stockman

Director, Environmental Protection Agency - Myron Ebell

Secretary of Agriculture - Forrest Lucas

Director of National Intelligence - Admiral Mike Rogers

Secretary of State - Gen. David Petraeus

Secretary of Energy - Myron Ebell

Secretary of Housing and Urban Development – Ben Carson

For RICO charges – The Clinton Foundation or as I see it New York's Sixth Crime Family

For Prisoner 0000000000000001 – Hillary Clinton

For retirement and the dustbin of History – BHO

Our coming "Let the Chips Fall Where They May" 45th President will call the tune. We just need some patriots who are ready to sing off the same sheet of music and Make America Great Again!

Dispatch Fifty-one

Trump Triumph Tour Takes America By Storm

The Donald showed with his surprise (to some / I started predicting it in January) upset election that he is the consummate political strategist in America today. In addition, he has shown with the unprecedented work to save jobs before he is even inaugurated that he will deliver on his promises to Make America Great Again.

His speech in Ohio last night was a real barn burner. It set the crowd on fire and inspired millions across the fruited planes. I can't imagine what he will give as an inaugural speech that could top that. I am sure multiple millions of us will tune in to find out. I would also suggest tuning in to the rest of his Triumph Tour speeches. Last night he had a surprise announcement that he couldn't make but he told us all in advance. I'd share it here but it is a secret….;--)

With the Impresario himself to orchestrate and with Kellyanne Conway and the team to advise I firmly believe we are on track to Make America Great Again.

However, as one lone voice hunkered in the bunker out here on the prairie I would like to add my wish list to the long dreamed of, long fought for, and much anticipated restoration administration:

Counter the VAT taxes the rest of the world uses to put tariffs by another name on us and to subsidize their exports with a VAT tax of our own on all imports.

Quit the WTO, the IMF, and the UN.

Make America the most business friendly place on earth with lower corporate taxes, reduced taxes on repatriated money, cut the noose of regulations that strangles our productivity.

Repeal and replace that job killing destroyer of the American healthcare system; Obamacare.

Re-negotiate or leave NAFTA and every other one-way trade deal the globalists have devised to make America just one among many.

In other words Mr. Trump do what you said you would do. You laid out a plan to make America Great Again and enough of us bought into it to elect you to be our president. Now deliver on those promises. Fulfill that vision and watch as the snowflake demonstrators turn into supporters once they learn that these policies will bring jobs, prosperity and the satisfaction of earning your own way instead of riding on the backs of others. If you do this and you will not only Make America Great Again you will go down in History as one of America's greatest presidents. As the Historian of the Future I can guarantee that with a promise of my own.

Dispatch Fifty-two

Trump's Gettysburg Address Needs Secret Sauce to Succeed

If this election has revealed one thing it is the existence of the Government-Media-Crony Capitalist-Dependent Class-Imported Voter Complex that sees this as their final act in the seizure of total power. Four more years continuing down the road of an imperial president ruling by decree, open borders and international capitulation, and America's fate as a declining power will be sealed. This is not a debate or power struggle between Internationalists and Isolationists.

This is a life or death battle between Globalists and Nationalists. They want us to be one vote among many, one province of a world government. We want the United States to remain an independent country. They want to submerge our institutions in a Soviet style rule from the center socialist dystopia. We want the Land of the Free and the Home of the Brave to become again a federal republic with a limited government, personal liberty, and economic freedom for all.

The twin headed bird of prey that is the government party of the Republicrats will have succeeded in perverting the greatest experiment in human freedom in the History of the World into one more centrally-planned kleptocracy where those with the levers of power reward those who support them by pilfering the wealth produced by those who innovate and strive.

"Who is John Galt" will ring out from the throats of millions who no longer see any reason to work to feed those who oppress them as America will embrace the old Soviet saying, "They pretend to pay us so we pretend to work."

Ultimately the Deplorables will see that their nation has been stolen and delivered to the millions of dumbed down economic parasites our government has indoctrinated at home and the invading hordes from the third world.

The Corporations Once Known as the Mainstream Media colludes openly to drag a political hack who would be 20 points down if it weren't for their propaganda megaphone across the finish line before she collapses under the weight of her own corruption.

Mark Twain said, "If you don't read the papers you're uninformed. If you do read them, you're misinformed."[cclxxviii]

So turn off the ABCNBCCBSCNNMSNBC New York Times Wall Street Journal LA Times cabal and think for yourself!

Winston Churchill said, "If you will not fight for right when you can easily win without bloodshed; if you will not fight when your victory is sure and not too costly; you may come to the moment when you will have to fight with all the odds against you and only a precarious chance of survival. There may even be a worse case. You may have to fight when there is no hope of victory, because it is better to perish than to live as slaves."

Now is the time for all good citizens to come to the aid of their country. Hillary will seal the doom of an independent, prosperous America. Look at The Donald's contract with America as outlined in his Gettysburg Speech and you will see the outline of a plan to make America great again.[cclxxix] We can do it! All we have to do is do it. So just do it. Vote Trump and you vote to give us one more chance.

And here is the secret sauce the only thing that can make all this work. "If My people who are called by My Name will humble themselves, and pray and seek My face, and turn from their wicked ways, then I will hear from heaven, and will forgive their sin and heal their land."

Conclusion

Dispatch Fifty-three

Are We as Dumb as They Think We Are

I've been called a fascist by communists and a communist by fascists. I've been called a pagan by Christians and a Christian by pagans. I've been called an optimist by pessimists and a pessimist by optimists. All of us have been labeled by others. We've all been called this by that and that by this, we've all had people try to insult us by how they refer to us, but when people insult our intelligence they are usually showing their ignorance.

The actions of the second-stringers, stand-ins, and understudies from the theater of the absurd who now pass for leadership in our Republic not only insult our intelligence, they act as if the American people have the IQ of a potted plant and the attention span of someone riddled with ADD. There is one good thing about people who insult our intelligence; they're probably misunderestimating the true level of our understanding.

Looking back our President told us that killing the Keystone Pipeline was no big deal. Instead he told us

"However many jobs might be generated by a Keystone pipeline, they're going to be a lot fewer than the jobs that are created by extending the payroll tax cut and extending unemployment insurance." Making decisions that kill the opportunity to create real jobs is offset by the jobs created by extending payments made to those who are unemployed. That doesn't make sense to anyone outside the beltway

While Mr. Obama may work day and night to kill projects that might actually provide some work for the rest of us he has no problem investing billions of our dollars in green energy boondoggles that turn a profit for his donors and cronies. Then when the flimflams are about to be exposed as the money pits they are, or on the eve of an election, the Energy Department which turned a blind eye to the initial foolish investment suddenly becomes involved and the announcement is delayed until after the marks, I mean voters, have cast their ballots.

In foreign policy our Commander-in-Chief announced the date for our withdrawal from Afghanistan at the same time he announced the same type of surge he was against in Iraq. The he decides it's time to negotiate with the Taliban. Are we supposed to believe these highly dedicated, highly motivated, and religiously fanatic battle hardened warriors will rush to make concessions? Didn't they instead hang tough, demand concessions, waiting to pick up the pieces as our leader leads our valiant, though under-cut warriors, for the door? Does anyone doubt that our creatures in Kabul will be on a jumbo jet filled with American dollars before our last soldier gets home? All this is presented as a rational settlement instead of an abject surrender and jaded political maneuver.

There's no inflation. At least that's what the Federal Government wants us to believe. Everyone who goes to the supermarket buys gas or pays to heat their home can evaluate the reliability of that piece of government information for themselves.

Looking at today Hillary says she didn't blame the video when she spoke at the return of the coffins.[cclxxx] All it takes is one click of the mouse to find a video that shows her doing it[cclxxxi] yet the Corporations Once Known as the mainstream Media and their cable twin sisters never mention that as they debate endlessly whether she is lying or not.

Bernie isn't a socialist. This what we are told yet once again one click of the mouse produces so much evidence that socialist is putting it mildly. In addition, this supposed voice for the working man never had a job until he was in his forties and he has been a professional agitator or politician all his life. He has never had a real job yet the multimedia never mention this at all though the information is once again merely a mouse click away.

On the other hand... Marko is all in for controlling immigration as exposed by his gang of eight debacle. Ted is going to fight the big corporations that control government by taking loans to get elected from the same people he wants to fight. Kasich is going to solve all our problems caused by the professional politicians because he is a professional politician. And of course the Big Kahuna is going to fight the very establishment he has been a part of for more than 40 years.

How could anyone ever see through any of this unless of course they have at least the IQ of that potted plant mentioned earlier? This may be insulting, it may show us what the perpetually re-elected think of their constituents, but it also shows that they're giving us an advantage. We're smarter than they think we are so we should be able to blind side them with organizational skills and motivational abilities far beyond what they'll expect.

They are counting the Tea Party out because we aren't holding mass rallies any more. They believe they've won the organizational battle because they were able to mobilize the occupy everywhere crowd to gather for a street party and pollute some major cities. They believe that since the conservative vote is currently split the GOP will commit suicide in a brokered convention that ignore their own voters and nominates the next Bob Dole/John McCain/Mitt Romney moderate to play the part of the Washington Generals in a Harlem Globe Trotter game: good but never quite good enough. In 2016 they see the Republicans, like the Washington Generals, there to provide a platform for the chosen winner to shine.

Then Came Trump

The parties of power treat us with such disdain it's obvious they believe we're the sheep they work so hard to make us. They believe Americans have been dumbed down enough and fattened with enough entitlements that we'll barely bah bah bah as they lead us to the shearing shed one more time. Our Progressive leaders in both parties see that this election is the one that counts. This is the election that will either drive us over the cliff into the shabby abyss of collectivist conformity or will give us one last opportunity to return to limited government, personal liberty, and economic freedom.

We may not be demonstrating in the streets. We may not be organizing boycotts. We may not be united behind one candidate. However, we are awake. We are educating ourselves. We are determined that this great experiment in human freedom shall not perish from the face of the earth. Vote for the Constitution. Vote for personal liberty. Vote for economic freedom. If we all do what we can we will accomplish what must be done. We will keep the faith. We will keep the peace. We shall overcome!

Or are we as dumb as they think we are?

Dispatch Fifty-four

Do You have Hope?

Marching out of Yorktown to surrender the British Army played the song "The World Turned Upside Down." As I drive to Meg Lo Mart to make my latest deposit of monopoly money in a Chinese savings account all I can do is mumble the final tag-line of the Wicked Witch of the West, "What a world? What a world?"

There is a massive unspoken problem in America today, floating like the iceberg in front of the Titanic waiting to sink the unsinkable ship. Founded by revolutionaries crying "No taxation without representation!" the Republic these revolutionaries devised has devolved into a society where more than 40% of the people pay no Federal Income Tax[cclxxxii] and the number of people receiving government benefits is even higher.[cclxxxiii] What incentive would these non-paying receivers have to reign in an overbearing and intrusive government? This unseen and unspoken problem is a cancer in the body politic.

Self-serving professional politicians buy votes by exempting non-productive people from personal financial responsibility while providing ever-expanding benefits at the expense of the productive. This is not the right versus left, conservative versus liberal, democrat versus republican he-said-she-said endless debate that devours the chatocracy of cable's wall-to-wall talking-heads. This is not an academic exercise that pointy-headed political science and history majors with dueling pocket protectors debate for hours in their mother's basement as they post their latest scoop on their samizdat blogs. If it is not any of these things what is it? It is a dagger pointing directly at the heart of our civilization.

Western Civilization awoke from the slumber of the Dark Ages enlightened and empowered by a belief, based in the Judeo-Christian tradition that humanity has an innate right to be free and a natural right to excel. Rights and freedoms are given by God not bestowed at the whim of some Legend-in-his-own-mind Leader. This civilization gathered steam in Europe exploding upon the world stage through an energetic period of exploration.

In America after a revolution fought by farmers and merchants against the greatest empire of the day the Founders, dared to declare, "We hold these truths to be self-evident, that all men are created equal, that they are endowed by their Creator with certain unalienable rights, that among these are Life, Liberty and the pursuit of Happiness." After centuries of government thugs standing on the windpipe of everyday people these self-sacrificing giants observed that in a civilized world government was not imposed by the strong upon the weak it was instead built upon a social contract between the governed and those entrusted with the privilege to govern when they said, "That to secure these rights, Governments are instituted among Men, deriving their just powers from the consent of the governed."

Today this bold and unique experiment in freedom is being devoured from within and challenged from without. Those who believe the collective should reign over the individual, those who believe in the suffocating sameness of socialism over the rough-and-tumble of capitalism have worked for generations building a culture of dependency which has tempered the steel will of the pioneers into the sloppy demands of the couch-potato slacker waiting for someone to find their remote as they guzzle some refreshments and wait for the game as bread and circuses take the place of innovation and accomplishment. Schools teaching 2+2 might = 5, trophies for everyone, politically correct new-speak and affirmative action promotions have sapped the vitality from the citizens of our Republic. Politicians and their fellow-travelers use a system of cronies and sweet-heart deals to reward each other for siphoning trillions from the public treasury promising the dumbed-down descendants of revolutionaries that they just might win the lotto before they have to declare bankruptcy so they might as well re-elect the same old grafters once again.

There comes a time when those who are raising the sails and paddling the boat have to admit to themselves the ballast down in steerage weighs more than the cargo. There comes a time when even the most non-confrontational and loyal among us begin to ask, "Who is John Galt" as Atlas tires of his thankless job and shrugs the burden of dead-weight into the dustbin of history. As the perpetually-reelected and the propaganda spewing Corporations Once Known as the Mainstream Media trumpet the inevitability of government rationed health-care, cap-n-trade industrial suicide, comprehensive import-a-voter immigration reform and the surrender of sovereignty through treaties supposedly designed to deal with mythical global warming there shines a light in a bell tower, one if by land and two if by sea.

Without hope you're hopeless and I refuse to allow the unbelievable changes currently assaulting our economy and our political system to bring about my own personal Great Depression. Those who believe in the Devil believe he comes to steal, kill and destroy. I believe if he can't steal your joy he can't keep your stuff and weeping may endure for a night but joy comes in the morning. Don't despair pray. Don't give up, give it up to God. Let me ask you, "Do you have hope?" I hope so. Personally as for me and my house we will trust the Lord for our hope is in Christ.

Then Came Trump

Dispatch Fifty-five

How Do We Get back to Where We Were?

It's hard to be a conservative when there's little left to conserve. The increasing pace of America's progression from free markets to a command economy has reached such a pace and become so obvious that way back in 2009 the Russian Prime Minister used his spotlight time at the World Economic Forum to warn America not to follow the socialist path. The Russian newspaper Pravda, once the leading communist voice on earth published an article entitled, "American capitalism gone with a whimper." People around the world can see the individual decisions of producers and consumers are being replaced by the form letters of a faceless central-planning bureaucracy even if the Obama boosters still haven't swallowed the red pill and watched the matrix dissolve.

Pushed by the breathtaking speed of America's devolution into a command economy some conservatives have entered the ranks of the radicals. They're beginning to think about how to cure the systemic political problems precipitating the November Revolution of 2008. One solution some are embracing is known as the Sovereignty Movement. This is a movement of citizens and state representatives attempting to right the listing ship-of-state by appealing to the 10th Amendment which says, "The powers not delegated to the United States by the Constitution, nor prohibited by it to the States, are reserved to the States respectively, or to the people."

The 10th Amendment addressed one of the most hard-fought points in the establishment of a central government. The States even though they surrendered some of their sovereignty didn't want to lose it all. Specifically they didn't want to lose the power to make internal decisions. They did not want to be powerless before a distant national bureaucracy. So as the capstone of the Bill of Rights the 10th Amendment was meant to reassure the States they would remain sovereign within their borders. However, since the 1830s, court rulings have garbled the once universally accepted meaning of the 10th Amendment as the Federal Government extended its authority from roads to schools to GM to Health Care to whatever they want.

Now some are turning to a resurrection of the straightforward meaning of the 10th Amendment as a way to mitigate the ever expanding power of centralized-control and social engineering combined with perpetual re-election and runaway pork-barrel deficit spending. But, is this enough?

Then Came Trump

As a Historian I always believe even a little history might help push back the darkness swirling around us. In 1787, at the close of the Constitutional Convention, as Benjamin Franklin left Independence Hall a lady asked "Well Doctor what have we got a republic or a monarchy." "A republic" replied Franklin "if you can keep it."

Many have the mistaken idea that the United States is a democracy. It's not. It's a representative republic. The Framers distrusted unfettered democracy therefore they inserted several mechanisms into the Constitution which added some innovations between direct democracy and the power to rule.

One of the great innovations the Framers built into our system is the federal concept. Since this is an important component of our political legacy that has been overlooked in our contemporary education system let me define what is meant by federal. A federal system is a union of states with a central authority wherein the member states still retain certain defined powers of government.

According to the Constitution the Federal Government cannot mandate policies relating to local issues such as housing, business, transportation, etc. within the States. At least this was how the Constitution was interpreted by President James Madison, the Father of the Constitution. He expressed this clearly in a veto statement in

1817.^{cclxxxiv} In that there has never been anyone more qualified to address the original intent of the framers I believe it is important to bring his entire statement into this article:

To the House of Representatives of the United States:

> Having considered the bill this day presented to me entitled "An act to set apart and pledge certain funds for internal improvements," and which sets apart and pledges funds "for constructing roads and canals, and improving the navigation of water courses, in order to facilitate, promote, and give security to internal commerce among the several States, and to render more easy and less expensive the means and provisions for the common defense," I am constrained by the insuperable difficulty I feel in reconciling the bill with the Constitution of the United States to return it with that objection to the House of Representatives, in which it originated.
>
> The legislative powers vested in Congress are specified and enumerated in the eighth section of the first article of the Constitution, and it does not appear that the power proposed to be exercised by the bill is among the enumerated powers, or that it falls by any just interpretation within the power to make laws necessary and proper for carrying into

execution those or other powers vested by the Constitution in the Government of the United States.

"The power to regulate commerce among the several States" cannot include a power to construct roads and canals, and to improve the navigation of water courses in order to facilitate, promote, and secure such a commerce without a latitude of construction departing from the ordinary import of the terms strengthened by the known inconveniences which doubtless led to the grant of this remedial power to Congress.

To refer the power in question to the clause "to provide for the common defense and general welfare" would be contrary to the established and consistent rules of interpretation, as rendering the special and careful enumeration of powers which follow the clause nugatory and improper. Such a view of the Constitution would have the effect of giving to Congress a general power of legislation instead of the defined and limited one hitherto understood to belong to them, the terms "common defense and general welfare" embracing every object and act within the purview of a legislative trust. It would have the effect of subjecting both the Constitution and laws of the several States in all cases not specifically exempted to be superseded by laws of Congress, it being expressly declared "that the Constitution of the United States and laws made in pursuance thereof shall be the supreme law of the land, and the judges of every State shall be bound thereby, anything in the constitution or laws of any State to the contrary notwithstanding." Such a view of the Constitution, finally, would have the effect of excluding the judicial authority of the United States from its participation in guarding the boundary between the legislative powers of the General and the State Governments, inasmuch as questions relating to the general welfare, being questions of policy and expediency, are unsusceptible of judicial cognizance and decision.

A restriction of the power "to provide for the common defense and general welfare" to cases which are to be provided for by the expenditure of money would still leave within the legislative power of Congress all the great and most important measures of Government, money being the ordinary and necessary means of carrying them into execution.

If a general power to construct roads and canals, and to improve the navigation of water courses, with the train of powers incident thereto, be not possessed by Congress, the assent of the States in the mode provided in the bill cannot confer the power. The only cases in which the consent and cession of particular States can extend the power of

Congress are those specified and provided for in the Constitution.

I am not unaware of the great importance of roads and canals and the improved navigation of water courses, and that a power in the National Legislature to provide for them might be exercised with signal advantage to the general prosperity. But seeing that such a power is not expressly given by the Constitution, and believing that it cannot be deduced from any part of it without an inadmissible latitude of construction and a reliance on insufficient precedents; believing also that the permanent success of the Constitution depends on a definite partition of powers between the General and the State Governments, and that no adequate landmarks would be left by the constructive extension of the powers of Congress as proposed in the bill, I have no option but to withhold my signature from it, and to cherishing the hope that its beneficial objects may be attained by a resort for the necessary powers to the same wisdom and virtue in the nation which established the Constitution in its actual form and providently marked out in the instrument itself a safe and practicable mode of improving it as experience might suggest.[cclxxxv]

This is an eloquent expression of how the Constitution was meant to be understood. However, through expansive interpretations by activist judges this gradually morphed into almost limitless Federal control of the domestic affairs of the States.

Another vital component of our Constitutional heritage is the protection provided by a system of "Checks and Balances" wherein each level or branch of government acts as a barrier to other levels or branches of government from acquiring too much power. The most important check on the power of the Federal Government in relation to the constituent States was the Senate. In the Constitution the people directly elected the House of Representatives to represent their interests, the various State legislatures elected the members of the Senate to represent the individual states.

The adoption of the Seventeenth Amendment in 1913 mandating the popular election of Senators fatally damaged this system. Since then, the States have been reduced from equal partners with the Federal Government to a group of individual lobbyists. Before this amendment senators remained in office based upon how they upheld the rights of their state. The hot-and-cold winds of populist considerations didn't compromise the Senator's ability to serve. This freedom to vote against populist sentiment allowed the Senators to balance the directly-elected House.

Now we have two houses of Congress trying to spend enough of other people's money to make political profits for themselves. So what do I propose? Resurrect the 10th Amendment, repeal the 17th and while we're at it we should drive a stake through the heart of the 16th which allows progressive taxation and all that's still on the conservative side of radicalism.

Restore the balance and save the Republic!

Dispatch Fifty-Six

A Parallel Universe Without Progressives

An astrophysicist, Ranga-Ram Chary at the European Space Agency's Planck Space Telescope data center at CalTech says he may have found evidence of alternate or parallel universes by looking back in time to just after the Big Bang more than thirteen billion years ago.

Then there is always the possible parallel universe of dark matter. As researchers learn more about dark matter's complexities, it seems possible that our galaxy lives on top of a shadow galaxy without us even knowing it.

I have often heard it said the universe is so large that anything we can imagine exists somewhere. Taking that as a starting point for a flight of fancy, let's imagine a parallel universe without Progressives.

We wouldn't have had the 16th amendment. Therefore we would still have a land without personal income tax and the Federal Government would have lived on fees and tariffs as it always did before the Progressives secured a source of money large enough to spend us into oblivion.

We wouldn't have had the 17th amendment and the senators would still be selected by the State legislators. This was one of the checks and balances the Founders embedded in the original Constitution to protect the federal nature of the Federal Government. The House represents the people and the Senate was supposed to represent the States.

We wouldn't have had the Creature from Jekyll Island, the Federal Reserve System, and America's representative of the international banking cartel. Without the Fed to mismanage the money supply there would never have been the banking crisis of the early 1930s. This is crisis that set the stage for the re-boot of America's free economy as a centrally-planned command and control machine used to transform every sector of American life.

We wouldn't have had Woodrow Wilson to take us into the War to End all Wars that ended up building up the three largest empires in the world and setting the stage of WWII.

We wouldn't have had FDR to impose fascist economic forms on America extending what would have been a recession into the Great Depression.

We wouldn't have had JFK to lose his nerve in 1961. Thus the Castro brothers and their murderous savagery would have fallen with the successful Bay of Pigs invasion.

We wouldn't have had LBJ to build a Great Society safety net that has become a hammock entrapping uncounted millions and generations in the snare of dependency.

We wouldn't have had BHO to fundamentally transform America into a falling empire and a soon to be third world backwater.

And we wouldn't have HRC campaigning for president as Mrs. Santa Clause promising to give everyone who doesn't work everything they want while she seeks to take the Second Amendment from the rest of us.

Think about this; look at how our government treats citizens now as taxing units or dependent voting units and we are armed to the teeth. Imagine how they will treat us once we are disarmed. Many believe the Second Amendment makes all the others possible.

Just imagine a parallel universe without Progressives. It's easy if you try.

Dispatch Fifty-seven

Trump Makes America Great Again – Why Wait

I know the snowflakes and their geriatric leaders are freaking out because they have lost the keys to the gravy train. However, out here where Americans work every day to pay the bills our President, The Donald isn't waiting to take the oath to fulfill his oath to us.

Just like the interminable hostage crisis that Jimmy Malaise Carter couldn't solve solved itself when the Gipper took the oath of office. As Ronaldus Magnus placed his hand on the bible and raised his hand the Ayatollahs deiced, "We don't want to mess with him," and sent them home. So too as BHO's death grip on the throat of American enterprise weakens people begin to see the light at the end of the collectivist tunnel. Just the promise of fewer regulations, tax relief, and the Commissars returning to their faculty lounges is enough to inspire entrepreneurs to hope again. It is enough to ignite America's Can-do class to once again plan and project growth instead of stagnation.

Just look at what has already been announced and imagine what will happen once the assault on American enterprise has finally ended.

As reported by Warner Todd Huston in Breitbart:

Ford: 700 Jobs to Start

As January began, Ford Motor Company went public to tell Donald Trump that they are ready to deal with the new administration and also noted that at least 700 new jobs were on the table with more to come as the year rolls onward.

SAP SE: 400 Jobs

German business-software maker SAP SE is adding nearly 400 jobs to its Pittsburgh and suburban Philadelphia facilities, according to *The Philadelphia Inquirer*.

Amazon.com: 100,000 Jobs

Amazon is eyeing a huge expansion starting this year and recently announced it intended to add up to 100,000 workers to its retail staff in new facilities across the nation.

Many of these jobs will be in brand new fulfillment centers the online giant plans to begin building this year.

Lockheed Martin: 1,800 Jobs

Aeronautics leader Lockheed Martin told President-elect Trump that it intends to hire over 1,800 new workers in the coming months.

Indeed, Lockheed feels that its expansion will bring even more jobs indirectly. CEO Marillyn Hewson said of the new jobs, "when you think about the supply chain across 45 states in the U.S., it's going to be thousands and thousands of jobs."

GM: 1,500 Jobs and $1 Billion Investment

General Motors said this month that it is looking to re-invest in factories in the U.S.A. and will add some 1,500 or more jobs to its roster of workers. The plans will include a one-billion-dollar plan to build new manufacturing lines in the U.S.

Bayer AG: $8 Billion Investment

The Trump transition team is touting a commitment by German-based Bayer AG pharmaceutical company to invest an additional $8 billion in the U.S.A. in research and development in cooperation with Monsanto AG.

The announcement came on the heels of a "very productive meeting" between the Trump team and Bayer CEO Werner Baumann and Monsanto chief Hugh Grant.

Walmart: 10,000 Retail Jobs, 24,000 Construction Jobs

Retail giant Walmart is eyeing an expansion plan to build new stores that will eventually amount to some 10,000 new jobs in outlets across the country. But it will also mean up to 24,000 jobs for construction workers needed to build the new stores.

Walmart intends to build at least 59 new stores in fiscal year 2017, according to a statement by the company.

LKQ: 150 Jobs and New HQ in Tennessee

Publicly traded automotive company LKQ Corp is establishing a new headquarters in the Nashville, Tennessee, area. It is a sign that the company feels that the automotive industry in the U.S. is on track to grow in the age of Trump.[cclxxxvi]

Add to that other announced industry expansions: Carrier 1,100; US Steel 10,000; IBM 25,000; Soft Bank 50,000; Dow Chemical 1,000; Tesla 1900; Sprint 5,000; One Web 3,000; Black & Decker 100; Chrysler 2,000; Toyota 5,000; and Apple 2,000 and it becomes apparent how much change some real hope can inspire.

During the tenure of our Regulator-in-Chief it is estimated that 107,000 jobs were created or saved per year. Since the unexpected victory of Himself and even before the official beginning of the Trump Revolution by my estimation he has added 220,650. Not bad for a prequel. Just imagine the growth we will see in the coming years.

Remember the Democrat controlled Creature from Jekyll Island will do its best to slow or sink the economy. The rent-mob Progressive grass-roots simulation will do its best to agitate. The nomenclature in Congress and the bureaucracy will do its best to malign, de-legitimize and possibly impeach The Donald. However, I believe that they will not be able to get the lightening back in the bottle. I believe that unlike the Reagan Revolution this re-birth of the American Spirit will not be betrayed and sold out by a thousand points of light and led into decades of darkness.

Keep the faith. Keep the peace. We shall overcome.

Dispatch Fifty-eight

The Hope That Does Not Disappoint

Listening to the lies of the politicians as presented by the prattle of the biased it is easy to lose hope in a secular sense. My hope in an eternal sense is founded on the rock of an unshakable faith in Jesus, and so it cannot be shaken. However, in the secular resting, as it must upon the shifting sands of man in America today, hope as a measured commodity is all too often hopeless. Seeking for hope in current events, a diamond among the discards and a point of light in a sea of darkness, is seeking something positive among the gathering gloom of an empire in eclipse.

I don't know about you, but I cannot focus on the negative trends of our current situation for long without at least contemplating depression and I don't mean the economic kind. I am thankful I have a peace that passes all understanding and a hope that cannot be taken away, and I am also glad that I have a sense of History which gives me a context to frame the Now. For if all we have is the Now it can always be changed with the next headline, the next news bulletin, or the next press release. Having a historical context brings things into focus fitting the events of today into flow of time from yesterday to tomorrow.

Truth often becomes the victim of expediency. For what seems true at the moment may end up as the lie of the hour. Politicians bend truth like gravity bends light: the heavier the perceived need the greater the unperceived distortion. Lies can become so widely believed that truth is swallowed in truism. Lies become the accepted wisdom of professional pundits chattering endlessly, supporting that which ultimately must fall for those who seek to surf a tsunami into a safe harbor. The news is filled with half-truths and as my second favorite philosopher, Anonymous, once said, "Beware of half-truths, you may have gotten the wrong half."

We live in a twilight time. Twilight by definition is a time when two sources of light pierce the gloom. It is that quivering moment when both the sun and the moon hold back the darkness. The darkness of confusion is dispelled by the brightness of the sun of truth, but it is disputed by refracted light of the moon of opinion masquerading as truth.

Casting about for something solid in the midst of the swirling fog of conflicting facts, shifting observations, and contradictory visions in the secular sense I must focus on one thing: the people. I trust the American people. I trust them to make the right choice when presented with unvarnished reality. I trust them to do what must be done to preserve the bequest of our forefathers for the inheritance of our posterity.

The Declaration of Independence was written to proclaim the righteousness of the actions of "One people" with the courage to declare to a world sold into bondage that our liberty was founded upon truth. "We hold these truths to be self-evident, that all men are created equal, that they are endowed by their Creator with certain unalienable Rights that among these are Life, Liberty and the pursuit of Happiness."

We the People wrote the Constitution in order to perfect that which had been founded upon the truth. "We the People of the United States, in Order to form a more perfect Union, establish Justice, insure domestic Tranquility, provide for the common defense, promote the general Welfare, and secure the Blessings of Liberty to ourselves and our Posterity, do ordain and establish this Constitution for the United States of America."

It is to this one people, this "We the people" that I look for secular hope, political peace, and the eventual solution to our current cultural conundrum. The popular definition of a conundrum is a problem without a solution. However it also has another meaning: a riddle whose answer is or involves a pun. Since I am referring to the second meaning I will present the riddle, "How is liberalism the solution to the problem of liberalism?"

In our through-the-looking-glass world, politicians use actual truth to obscure the obvious truth. Congressman Joe Early (D-Mass) at a press conference to answer questions about the House Bank scandal said, "They gave me a book of checks. They didn't ask for any deposits."[cclxxxvii] While I'm sure it is true he was given a book of checks, obviously one needs to make deposits if one is to honestly write checks. In this same manner the leaders of our free country promote socialism as the solution to the problems socialism has caused knowing that you cannot honestly write checks if you don't make deposits. Capitalism makes the deposits and socialism wants to write the checks. As Churchill said "Socialism is a philosophy of failure, the creed of ignorance, and the gospel of envy, its inherent virtue is the equal sharing of misery."[cclxxxviii]

We are awash in polls. Every campaign and every major news source constantly trumpet polls many of which contradict each other. No matter what the polls say I believe that the American people still believe in freedom. I believe they still believe in the equality of opportunity and the opportunity of equality. We all aren't the same. Each of us is born with a particular set of talents and each of us uses those talents in a certain way.

It is my belief, that given the level playing field of personal freedom, individual liberty and economic opportunity, the vast majority of Americans will work hard to earn what they deserve. This is my secular hope. Heaven on earth is not possible but given personal freedom, individual liberty and economic opportunity freedom inherently promised in the perfect union we the people sought to create we can at least avoid remaining in the hell of socialism the Progressives are currently foisting upon us, as Churchill also said "If you're going through hell, keep going."[cclxxxix]

Oh, by the way, the answer to the riddle is that Classical Liberalism promotes the general welfare by promoting the limitation of government and the liberty of the individual in order to better serve the whole. Welfare Liberalism erodes the general welfare by expanding the government at the expense of the individual in order to better serve the individual. Thus Classical Liberalism is the solution to the problems caused by Welfare Liberalism. And that's the truth which brings me to one last Churchill quote for the day, "The truth is incontrovertible. Malice may attack it. Ignorance may deride it. But in the end, there it is."[ccxc]

Hope and change may have convinced our fellow citizens to sell their birthright of freedom for the savory red stew of give me more; however, another November is coming and things may change. At least we can hope.

What we need is the hope that does not disappoint and that is found in adversity and tried in the furnace of persecution. This is not the first time good people have been subjected to the rule of those dedicated to plunder and dominance. It is an old story that has repeated itself ad infinitum throughout time. Hope lies in the fact that we will never be tested beyond what we can endure and that with each test there is a way of escape. This is so true and so common it has been written in our hearts and if we allow it blazes in our spirit. That, having been justified by faith, we have peace with God through our Lord Jesus Christ, through whom also we have access by faith into this grace in which we stand, and rejoice in hope of the glory of God. And not only that, but we also glory in tribulations, knowing that tribulation produces perseverance; and perseverance, character; and character, hope. Now hope does not disappoint, because the love of God has been poured out in our hearts by the Holy Spirit who was given to us.

Above all if we know He has said, if My people who are called by My name will humble themselves, and pray and seek My face, and turn from their wicked ways, then I will hear from heaven, and will forgive their sin and heal their land.

Reject the culture of death and the society of depravity that have gained ascendance in our land. Seek out the good and cling to that. Stand forthrightly in the face of persecution, pray for renewal and live a renewed life. Refuse to be a part of the plunder mentality which manages our decline and discards the future of our children for the repose of the moment.

Don't be discouraged by the blather of the pontificating politicians or confused by the conflicting ruminations of the professional talkers. When all is said and done if we will trust God we can trust us. *We the People* will eventually come down on the side of truth, justice, and the American way. Freedom will be reborn just as surely as night follows day for tears may come at night but joy comes in the morning.

Then Came Trump

Endnotes

[i] Think Exist.com, http://thinkexist.com/quotes/ruth_bader_ginsburg/ Accessed 1-19-17
[ii] Frontline http://www.pbs.org/wgbh/pages/frontline/shows/target/etc/modern.html Accessed 1-17-17
[iii] Ibid.
[iv] What Makes Islam So Different http://www.thereligionofpeace.com/pages/articles/opinion-polls.aspx Accessed 1-17-17
[v] CNN http://www.cnn.com/2011/WORLD/asiapcf/05/02/osama.timeline/ Accessed 1-17-17
[vi] History-World.org http://history-world.org/islam4.htm Accessed 1-17-17
[vii] What Makes Islam So Different http://www.thereligionofpeace.com/pages/muhammad/peace-war.aspx Accessed 1-17-17
[viii] Dreher, Rod, The American Conservative "Is ISIS Islamic? How Would We Know?" http://www.theamericanconservative.com/dreher/isis-islamic-apocalypse/
[ix] Ibid.
[x] Ibid.
[xi] Historical Atlas of the Mediterranean, "The Birth of Islam in Arabia," http://explorethemed.com/mohammed.asp Accessed 1-17-17
[xii] Dreher, Rod, The American Conservative "Is ISIS Islamic? How Would We Know?" http://www.theamericanconservative.com/dreher/isis-islamic-apocalypse/
[xiii] Ibid.
[xiv] Wood, Graeme, Atlantic, "What ISIS Really Wants," http://www.theatlantic.com/magazine/archive/2015/03/what-isis-really-wants/384980/ Accessed 1-17-17
[xv] Dreher, Rod, The American Conservative "Is ISIS Islamic? How Would We Know?" http://www.theamericanconservative.com/dreher/isis-islamic-apocalypse/
[xvi] Ibid.
[xvii] How Islamic is the Islamic State, https://www.youtube.com/watch?v=DhkP--UV9yk Accessed 1-17-17
[xviii] Ibid.
[xix] Ibid.

[xx] Dreher, Rod, The American Conservative "Is ISIS Islamic? How Would We Know?" http://www.theamericanconservative.com/dreher/isis-islamic-apocalypse/
[xxi] How Islamic is the Islamic State, https://www.youtube.com/watch?v=DhkP--UV9yk Accessed 1-17-17
[xxii] Ibid.
[xxiii] Dreher, Rod, The American Conservative "Is ISIS Islamic? How Would We Know?" http://www.theamericanconservative.com/dreher/isis-islamic-apocalypse/
[xxiv] Cauchon, Dennis, USA Today, "Leap in U.S. debt hits taxpayers with 12% more red ink" http://usatoday30.usatoday.com/news/washington/2009-05-28-debt_N.htm Accessed 1-17-17
[xxv] https://www.youtube.com/watch?v=Tmi8cJG0BJo Accessed 1-17-17
[xxvi] Wegmann, Philip, The National Interest, "America's Real Debt Shocker: $100 Trillion Owed in Unfunded Liabilities," http://nationalinterest.org/blog/the-buzz/americas-real-debt-shocker-100-trillion-owed-unfunded-16581 Accessed 1-17-17
[xxvii] Rutz, Jim, World Net Daily, "Brother, can you spare $65 trillion?" http://www.wnd.com/2006/07/37167/ Accessed 1-17-17
[xxviii] Beech, Eric, Reuters, "U.S. government says it lost $11.2 billion on GM bailout," http://www.reuters.com/article/us-autos-gm-treasury-idUSBREA3T0MR20140430 Accessed 1-17017
[xxix] Isidore, Chris, CNN, "GM cars sold: 12 million. Recalled: 13.8 million," http://money.cnn.com/2014/05/21/news/companies/gm-recall-nightmare/ Accessed 1-17-17
[xxx] Whoriskey, Peter, The Washington Post, "Under Restructuring, GM To Build More Cars Overseas," http://www.washingtonpost.com/wp-dyn/content/article/2009/05/07/AR2009050704336.html Accessed 1-17-17
[xxxi] Fox News Insider, http://insider.foxnews.com/2016/04/10/chris-wallace-challenges-obama-isis-comments-and-bathtub-deaths Accessed 1-17-17
[xxxii] 2nd Amendment Library, http://www.madisonbrigade.com/g_mason.htm Accessed 1-17-17
[xxxiii] 2nd Amendment Library, http://www.madisonbrigade.com/t_jefferson.htm Accessed 1-17-17
[xxxiv] The Founder's Constitution, The 2nd Amendment, http://press-pubs.uchicago.edu/founders/documents/amendIIs10.html Accessed 1-17-17
[xxxv] Good Reads, http://www.goodreads.com/quotes/tag/demographics Accessed 1-17-17
[xxxvi] Judicial Watch, http://www.judicialwatch.org/document-archive/camteleconference/ Accessed 1-17-17

[xxxvii] White, Jeremy B., The Sacramento Bee, "California immigrants soon can seek driver's licenses," http://www.sacbee.com/news/politics-government/article4486973.html Accessed 1-17-17

[xxxviii] _____, Sacramento Bee, "Half a million California immigrants seek licenses, exceeding projections," http://www.sacbee.com/news/politics-government/capitol-alert/article17313002.html Accessed 1-17-17

[xxxix] Picket, Kerry, The Daily Caller, "Former DOJ Official: Non-Citizens Registered To Vote Through Motor Voter Registration Forms," http://dailycaller.com/2015/04/08/former-doj-official-non-citizens-registered-to-vote-through-motor-voter-registration-forms/ Accessed 1-17-17

[xl] Coffman, Keith, Reuters, "Denver hires teachers who came to U.S. illegally as children," http://www.reuters.com/article/us-usa-colorado-immigrants-idUSBREA3A1RP20140411 Accessed 1-17-17

[xli] Study Guide The Rights of Refugees, http://hrlibrary.umn.edu/edumat/studyguides/refugees.htm Accessed 1-17-17

[xlii] Rasmussen Reports, "Immigration Update," http://www.rasmussenreports.com/public_content/politics/current_events/immigration/immigration_update Accessed 1-17-17

[xliii] Dinan, Stephan, The Washington Times, "Judge accuses Obama lawyers of misleading him, refuses to restart amnesty," http://www.washingtontimes.com/news/2015/apr/7/obama-motion-immediately-restart-amnesty-rejected-/#ixzz3ZOm9FcsM Accessed 1-17-17

[xliv] Ibid.
[xlv] Ibid.
[xlvi] Ibid.
[xlvii] Ibid.
[xlviii] Ibid.

[xlix] May, Caroline, Brietbart, "More than A Half Million Social Security Numbers Issued To Illegal Immigrants Granted Amnesty," http://www.breitbart.com/big-government/2015/04/14/over-a-half-million-social-security-numbers-issued-to-illegal-immigrants-granted-amnesty/ Accessed 1-17-17

[l] Catholic Online, "Social Security numbers issued to more than half a million illegal immigrants in U.S." http://www.catholic.org/news/politics/story.php?id=59827 Accessed 1-17-17

[li] May, Caroline, Brietbart, "More than A Half Million Social Security Numbers Issued To Illegal Immigrants Granted Amnesty," http://www.breitbart.com/big-government/2015/04/14/over-a-half-million-social-security-numbers-issued-to-illegal-immigrants-granted-amnesty/ Accessed 1-17-17

[liiiii] Bureau of Labor Statistics, https://data.bls.gov/timeseries/LNS14000000 Accessed 1-18-17
[liii] Viam, Invenium, MN Progressive Project, "Obama's Economic Policies Achieve Full Employment During Record 61 Straight Months of Private Sector Job Growth," http://mnprogressiveproject.com/obamas-economic-policies-achieve-full-employment-during-record-61-straight-months-of-private-sector-job-growth/ Accessed 1-18-17
[liv] The People's View, http://www.thepeoplesview.net/main/2015/1/9/the-roaring-obama-recovery-from-bottom-falling-out-to-full-employment Accessed 1-18-17
[lv] Snyder, Michael, The Economic Collapse, "Federal Reserve Money Printing Is The Real Reason Why The Stock Market Is Soaring," http://theeconomiccollapseblog.com/archives/federal-reserve-money-printing-is-the-real-reason-why-the-stock-market-is-soaring Accessed 1-18-17
[lvi] Kasperowicz, Pete, The nHill, "GOP bill lets Congress sue Obama over failure to enforce laws," http://thehill.com/blogs/floor-action/government-oversight/195353-gop-bill-lets-congress-sue-obama-over-failure-to Accessed 1-18-17
[lvii] Boaz, David, Reason.com "Hitler, Mussolini, Roosevelt," https://reason.com/archives/2007/09/28/hitler-mussolini-roosevelt Accessed 1-18-17
[lviii] Gordon, David, Mises Institute, "Three New Deals: Why the Nazis and Fascists Loved FDR," https://mises.org/library/three-new-deals-why-nazis-and-fascists-loved-fdr Accessed 1-18-17
[lix] Boaz, David, Reason.com "Hitler, Mussolini, Roosevelt," https://reason.com/archives/2007/09/28/hitler-mussolini-roosevelt Accessed 1-18-17
[lx] Ibid.
[lxi] Ibid.
[lxii] Ibid.
[lxiii] Ibid.
[lxiv] Ibid.
[lxv] Ibid.
[lxvi] Ibid.
[lxvii] Ibid.
[lxviii] Ibid.
[lxix] Ibid.
[lxx] Quizlet, https://quizlet.com/44529016/fdr-flash-cards/ Accessed 1-18-17
[lxxi] Discover the Networks, "THE PROGRESSIVE ERA'S LEGACY: FDR'S NEW DEAL," http://www.discoverthenetworks.org/viewSubCategory.asp?id=1228 Accessed 1-18-17

[lxxii] Gordon, David, Mises Institute, "Three New Deals: Why the Nazis and Fascists Loved FDR," https://mises.org/library/three-new-deals-why-nazis-and-fascists-loved-fdr Accessed 1-18-17
[lxxiii] Ibid.
[lxxiv] Discover the Networks, "THE PROGRESSIVE ERA'S LEGACY: FDR'S NEW DEAL," http://www.discoverthenetworks.org/viewSubCategory.asp?id=1228 Accessed 1-18-17
[lxxv] Boaz, David, Reason.com "Hitler, Mussolini, Roosevelt," https://reason.com/archives/2007/09/28/hitler-mussolini-roosevelt Accessed 1-18-17
[lxxvi] Ibid.
[lxxvii] Ibid.
[lxxviii] Ibid.
[lxxix] Ibid.
[lxxx] Ibid.
[lxxxi] Ibid.
[lxxxii] Ibid.
[lxxxiii] Ibid.
[lxxxiv] Lee, Carol E., Politico.com, "Obama makes FDR comparison," http://www.politico.com/story/2009/05/obama-makes-fdr-comparison-023031 Accessed 1-18-17
[lxxxv] Raasch, Chuck, USA Today, "Obama aspires to a transformational presidency," http://usatoday30.usatoday.com/news/opinion/columnist/raasch/2009-04-16-raasch-column-04162009_N.htm Accessed 1-18-17
[lxxxvi] You Tibe, https://www.youtube.com/watch?v=KrefKCaV8m4 Accessed 1-18-17
[lxxxvii] Armarillo Globe-News, "Khrushchev prediction slowly coming true," http://amarillo.com/opinion/letters-editor/2012-10-08/letter-khrushchev-prediction-slowly-coming-true Accessed 1-18-17
[lxxxviii] Ibid.
[lxxxix] Brainy Quote, https://www.brainyquote.com/quotes/quotes/n/nikitakhru115027.html Accessed 1-18-17
[xc] Ibid.
[xci] Duran, Nicole, The Washington Examiner, "Obama asks people to read TPP deal themselves," http://www.washingtonexaminer.com/obama-asks-people-to-read-tpp-deal-themselves/article/2575999 Accessed 1-18-17
[xcii] Ibid.
[xciii] Public Citizen, "Trans-Pacific Partnership (TPP): Expanded Corporate Power, Lower Wages, Unsafe Food Imports," http://www.citizen.org/TPP Accessed 1-18-17

[xciv] Citizen.org http://www.citizen.org/documents/tpp-nafta-on-steroids-infographic.png Accessed 1-18-17
[xcv] Public Citizen, http://citizen.org/Page.aspx?pid=3595 Accessed 1-18-17
[xcvi] Public Citizen, "Corporate-Rigged Trade Deals: Undermining Wall Street Reform," http://www.citizen.org/Page.aspx?pid=6474 Accessed 1-18-17
[xcvii] You Tube https://www.youtube.com/watch?v=OoqI5PSRcXM Accessed 1-18-17
[xcviii] You Tube https://www.youtube.com/watch?v=KrefKCaV8m4 Accessed 1-18-17
[xcix] Fox News, "Obamacare Regulations Two and a Half Times as Long as the Bible," http://nation.foxnews.com/obamacare/2012/02/29/obamacare-regulations-two-and-half-times-long-bible Accessed 1-18-17
[c] Kauffman, Bill, The American Conservative, "Still America First," http://www.theamericanconservative.com/articles/still-america-first/ Accessed 1-18-17
[ci] You Tube, https://www.youtube.com/watch?v=txukr5zgHnw Accessed 1-18-17
[cii] Yale Law Schools, "Washington's Farewell Address 1796," http://avalon.law.yale.edu/18th_century/washing.asp Accessed 1-18-17
[ciii] National Priorities Project, "Federal Spending: Where Does the Money Go," https://www.nationalpriorities.org/budget-basics/federal-budget-101/spending/ Accessed 1-18-17
[civ] Richman, Sheldon, The Future of Freedom Foundation, "We Were Warned about the Rise of Empire," http://www.fff.org/explore-freedom/article/tgif-we-were-warned-about-the-rise-of-empire/ Accessed 1-18-17
[cv] Anslow, Matt, Life Remixed, "what is an "empire"?" https://liferemixed.net/2011/08/17/what-is-an-empire/ Accessed 1-18-17
[cvi] Inspiring Quotes.com http://www.inspiringquotes.us/author/2687-garet-garrett Accessed 1-18-17
[cvii] Bureau of Labor Statistics, https://data.bls.gov/timeseries/LNS14000000 Accessed 1-18-17
[cviii] Ibid.
[cix] Labor Statistics, http://www.dlt.ri.gov/lmi/laus/us/usadj.htm Accessed 1-18-17
[cx] Tyrrell, Patrick, The Daily Signal, "By One Measure, 95.5 Million Are Dependent on the Federal Government," http://dailysignal.com/2015/12/18/by-one-measure-95-46-million-are-dependent-on-the-federal-government/ Accessed 1-18-17
[cxi] Samples, John, Cato Institute, "On the Motor Voter Act and Voter Fraud," https://www.cato.org/publications/congressional-testimony/motor-voter-act-voter-fraud Accessed 1-18-17

[cxii] corporatism: the organization of a society into industrial and professional corporations serving as organs of political representation and exercising control over persons and activities within their jurisdiction
[cxiii] Freiling, Nicholas, Values and Capitalism, "Minimum Wage: Good Intentions, Bad Policy," http://www.valuesandcapitalism.com/minimum-wage-good-intentions-bad-policy/ Accessed 1-18-17
[cxiv] Riedl, Brian M., Heritage Foundation, "Why Government Spending Does Not Stimulate Economic Growth," http://www.heritage.org/research/reports/2008/11/why-government-spending-does-not-stimulate-economic-growth Accessed 1-18-17
[cxv] Schroeder, Paul W., The American Conservative, "The Case Against Preemptive War," http://www.theamericanconservative.com/articles/the-case-against-preemptive-war/ Accessed 1-18-17
[cxvi] Paul, Ron, The Free Foundation, ""Beware The Consequences of Pre-Emptive War, http://www.the-free-foundation.org/tst2-11-2013.html Accessed 1-18-17
[cxvii] Brainy Quotes, https://www.brainyquote.com/quotes/quotes/n/napoleonbo161968.html Accessed 1-20-17
[cxviiicxviii] The Quotation Page, http://www.quotationspage.com/quotes/Voltaire Accessed 1-20-17
[cxix] History News Network, http://historynewsnetwork.org/article/1328 Accessed 1-20-17
[cxx] _____, http://historynewsnetwork.org/article/1328 Accessed 1-20-17
[cxxi] Neusys, Inc. "Chains of the Constitution," http://www.neusysinc.com/columnpublication.html Accessed 1-20-17
[cxxii] The Washington Post, "Breyer says understanding foreign law is critical to Supreme Court's work," https://www.washingtonpost.com/politics/courts_law/breyer-says-understanding-foreign-law-is-critical-to-supreme-courts-work/2015/09/12/36a38212-57e9-11e5-8bb1-b488d231bba2_story.html Accessed 1-20-17
[cxxiiicxxiii] Good Reads, "Quotes about Taxation," http://www.goodreads.com/quotes/tag/taxes Accessed 1-20-17
[cxxiv] _____, http://www.goodreads.com/author/quotes/63859.James_Madison Accessed 1-20-17
[cxxv] True Blue http://truebluevigilance.blogspot.com/2012/04/james-madison-and-some-thoughts-on.html Accessed 1-20-17
[cxxvi] Ibid.

[cxxvii] Debatepedia, http://www.debatepedia.com/en/index.php/Argument:_Progressive_taxation_is_socialist_wealth_redistribution_and_state_theft Accessed 1-20-17
[cxxviii] Ibid.
[cxxix] Ibid.
[cxxx] Ibid.
[cxxxi][cxxxi] The Foundation for Economic Education, https://fee.org/articles/the-progressive-income-tax Accessed 1-20-17
[cxxxii] Mcann, Steven, The American Thinker, http://www.americanthinker.com/articles/2011/03/confiscate_americans_wealth_to.html Accessed 1-20-17
[cxxxiii] http://www.f169bbs.com/bbs/news/178996-if-the-irs-grabbed-100-of-everyones-income-over-1-million-the-take-would-be-just-616-billion Accessed 1-20-17
[cxxxiv] Cover, Matt, CNS News, "Warren Buffett's Taxing the Rich Won't Solve Deficit, Says Tax Foundation," http://www.cnsnews.com/news/article/warren-buffett-s-taxing-rich-wont-solve-deficit-says-tax-foundation Accessed 1-20-17
[cxxxv] Hayek, Fredrick, Wikiquote, The Constitution of Liberty, https://en.wikiquote.org/wiki/The_Constitution_of_Liberty Accessed 1-20-17
[cxxxvi] Debatepedia, http://www.debatepedia.com/en/index.php/Argument:_Progressive_taxation_is_socialist_wealth_redistribution_and_state_theft Accessed 1-20-17
[cxxxvii] Ibid.
[cxxxviii] Ibid.
[cxxxix] Eddlem, Thomas R., The New American, "Before the Income Tax," http://www.thenewamerican.com/culture/history/item/14268-before-the-income-tax Accessed 1-21-17
[cxl] Colorado Alliance for Immigration Reform, "Anchor babies, birthright citizenship, and the 14th Amendment," http://www.cairco.org/issues/anchor-babies Accessed 1-21-17
[cxli] Coulter, Ann, Human Events, "Justice Brennan's Footnote Gave Us Anchor Babies," http://humanevents.com/2010/08/04/justice-brennans-footnote-gave-us-anchor-babies/ Accessed 1-21-17
[cxlii] Noble, S., The Independent Sentinel, "Can Birthright Citizenship Be Overturned Without A Constitutional Amendment," http://www.independentsentinel.com/can-birthright-citizenship-be-overturned-without-an-amendment/ Accessed 1-21-17
[cxliii] The Tenth Amendment Center, "2nd Amendment: Original Meaning and Purpose," http://tenthamendmentcenter.com/2014/09/22/2nd-amendment-original-meaning-and-purpose/ Accessed 1-21-17

[cxliv] Lundy, Alan L., Keep and Bear Arms, "A Lesson in Anti-Federalism," http://www.keepandbeararms.com/information/XcIBViewItem.asp?ID=1266 Accessed 1-21-17

[cxlv] Sowell, Thomas, Newsmax, "Obama Seeks to Knock US Down a Peg," http://www.newsmax.com/ThomasSowell/Obama-US-redistribution-wealth/2012/10/01/id/458210/ Accessed 1-21-17

[cxlvi] White House Dossier, "Obama Has Bowed Eight Times as President," http://www.whitehousedossier.com/2012/06/20/obama-bowed-eight-times-president/ Accessed 1-21-17

[cxlvii] Snyder, Michael, The Economic Collapse, "Have You Heard About The 16 Trillion Dollar Bailout The Federal Reserve Handed To The Too Big To Fail Banks?," http://theeconomiccollapseblog.com/archives/have-you-heard-about-the-16-trillion-dollar-bailout-the-federal-reserve-handed-to-the-too-big-to-fail-banks Accessed 1-21-17

[cxlviii] Bandler, Aaron, Town Hall, "Record 93.8 Million Americans Out of the Labor Force," http://townhall.com/tipsheet/aaronbandler/2015/08/07/record-937-million-americans-out-of-the-labor-force-n2036061 Accessed 1-21-17

[cxlix] Statista, "Monthly number of full-time employees in the United States from November 2015 to November 2016 (in millions, unadjusted)," https://www.statista.com/statistics/192361/unadjusted-monthly-number-of-full-time-employees-in-the-us/ Accessed 1-21-17

[cl] Trading Economics, "United States Labor Force Participation Rate," http://www.tradingeconomics.com/united-states/labor-force-participation-rate Accessed 1-21-17

[cli] Case Briefs, "U.S. Term Limits, Inc. v. Thorton," http://www.casebriefs.com/blog/law/constitutional-law/constitutional-law-keyed-to-sullivan/national-powers-and-local-activities-origins-and-recurrent-themes/u-s-term-limits-inc-v-thorton/ Accessed 1-21-17

[clii] Ibid.

[cliii] de Vogue, Ariane, ABC News, "Arizona Immigration Law: Enforcement Blocked by Circuit Court," http://abcnews.go.com/Politics/arizona-immigration-law-enforcement-blocked-circuit-court/story?id=13350124 Accessed 1-21-17

[cliv] Ibid.

[clv] TSA Blog, "Texas House of Representatives Seeking to Ban Current TSA Pat-Down," http://blog.tsa.gov/2011/05/texas-house-of-representatives-seeking.html Accessed 1-21-17

[clvi] Levy, Robert A., The CATO Institute, "The Taxing Power of Obamacare," https://www.cato.org/publications/commentary/taxing-power-obamacare Accessed 1-21-17

[clvii] Somin, Ilya, The Volokh Conspiracy, "Number of States Challenging the Constitutionality of Obamacare Rises to 28," http://volokh.com/2011/01/19/number-of-states-challenging-the-constitutionality-of-obamacare-rises-to-28/ Accessed 1-21-17

[clviii] Allahpundit, Hotair, "Federal judge rules ObamaCare is unconstitutional in its entirety," http://hotair.com/archives/2011/01/31/federal-judge-rules-obamacare-is-unconstitutional-in-its-entirety/ Accessed 1-21-17

[clix] Think Exist, http://thinkexist.com/quotation/-if_you_tell_a_lie_big_enough_and_keep_repeating/345877.html Accessed 1-21-17

[clx] Fox Nation, "'Dude, This Was Two Years Ago!': Former WH Security Spox Blusters Over '#TBT' Benghazi, Said Obama Not in Situation Room," http://nation.foxnews.com/2014/05/01/dude-was-two-years-ago-fmr-wh-security-spox-blusters-over-tbt-benghazi-said-obama-not Accessed 1-21-17

[clxi] Fox News, "'Not even a smidgen of corruption': Obama downplays IRS, other scandals," http://www.foxnews.com/politics/2014/02/03/not-even-smidgen-corruption-obama-downplays-irs-other-scandals.html Accessed 1-21-17

[clxii] CBS DC, "Report: More Than 92 Million Americans Remain Out Of Labor Force," http://washington.cbslocal.com/2014/05/02/report-more-than-92-million-americans-remain-out-of-labor-force/ Accessed 1-21-17

[clxiii] Levinson, Alexis, The Daily Caller, "Clinton on Benghazi story confusion: 'What difference at this point does it make!?'," http://dailycaller.com/2013/01/23/clinton-on-benghazi-story-confusion-what-difference-does-it-make-video/ Accessed 1-21-17

[clxiv] Allen, Jonathan, VOX, "House Republican says Benghazi committee was "designed" to hit Clinton," http://www.vox.com/2015/10/15/9539481/republican-benghazi-committee-designed Accessed 1-21-17

[clxv][clxv] Armstrong Economics, https://www.armstrongeconomics.com/uncategorized/covering-up-obama-boehner-conspiracy/ Accessed 1-21-17

[clxvi] The History P{lace, http://www.historyplace.com/unitedstates/impeachments/nixon.htm Accessed 1-21-17

[clxvii] Dinan, Stephan, The Washington Times, "House Republicans find 10% of tea party donors audited by IRS," http://www.washingtontimes.com/news/2014/may/7/house-republicans-find-10-of-tea-party-donors-audi/ Accessed 1-21-17

[clxviii] Howley, Patrick, The Daily Caller, "Ten IRS Scandal Excuses That Are Now Completely Discredited," http://dailycaller.com/2014/05/04/ten-irs-scandal-excuses-that-are-now-completely-discredited/ Accessed 1-21-17

clxix Rushing, J. Taylor, Daily Mail, "Benghazi victim's father: Hillary told me maker of film about prophet Mohamed would be arrested 'for causing my son's death'," http://www.dailymail.co.uk/news/article-3287090/Benghazi-victim-s-father-Hillary-told-maker-film-prophet-Mohamed-arrested-causing-son-s-death.html Accessed 1-21-17

clxx Wilson, Stan, CNN, "Producer of anti-Islam film arrested, ordered held without bail," http://www.cnn.com/2012/09/27/world/california-anti-islam-filmmaker/ Accessed 1-21-17

clxxi Bordelon, Brendan, National Review, "Benghazi Committee Bombshell: Clinton Knew 'Attack Had Nothing to Do with the Film'" http://www.nationalreview.com/article/425933/benghazi-committees-bombshell-e-mails-clinton-knew-attack-had-nothing-do-film-brendan Accessed 1-21-17

clxxii You Tube, https://www.youtube.com/watch?v=bOjX-o9axmw Accessed 1-21-17

clxxiii Nolte, John, Breitbart, "Benghazi Family Hits Back: Hillary Clinton Lied About Us To George Stephanopoulos," http://www.breitbart.com/big-government/2015/12/10/benghazi-family-hits-back-hillary-clinton-lied-about-us-to-george-stephanopoulos/ Accessed 1-21-17

clxxiv Lifson, Thomas, The American Thinker, "Hillary now denies blaming video to Benghazi victims' families," http://www.americanthinker.com/blog/2015/12/hillary_now_denies_blaming_video_to_benghazi_victims_families_comments.html Accessed 1-21-17

clxxv YouTube, https://www.youtube.com/watch?v=hAZ_O07PXkg Accessed 1-21-17

clxxvi Best, James D., What Would the Founders Think, "The Founders on a Living Constitution," http://www.whatwouldthefoundersthink.com/the-founders-on-a-living-constitution Accessed 1-21-17

clxxvii Ibid.
clxxviii Ibid.
clxxix Ibid.
clxxx Ibid
clxxxi Ibid.
clxxxii Ibid.

clxxxiii The Sovereign Investor Daily, "America's Decadence Signals End of an Empire," http://thesovereigninvestor.com/us-economy/americas-decadence-signals-end-empire/ Accessed 1-21-17

clxxxiv Stockman, David, The Mises Institute, "The Mythical Banking Crisis and the Failure of the New Deal," https://mises.org/blog/mythical-banking-crisis-and-failure-new-deal Accessed 1-21-17

[clxxxv] Ibid.
[clxxxvi] Ibid.
[clxxxvii] Brainy Quote, https://www.brainyquote.com/quotes/authors/r/rahm_emanuel.html Accessed 1-21-17
[clxxxviii] History Matters, http://historymatters.gmu.edu/d/5057/ Accessed 1-21-17
[clxxxix] YouTube, https://www.youtube.com/watch?v=7TOV1m2IgcA Accessed 1-21-17
[cxc] Ibid.
[cxci] History Matters, http://historymatters.gmu.edu/d/5057/ Accessed 1-21-17
[cxcii] The National Conference of State Legislatures, "Separation of Powers—Delegation of Legislative Power," http://www.ncsl.org/research/about-state-legislatures/delegation-of-legislative-power.aspx Accessed 1-21-17
[cxciii] Good Reads http://www.goodreads.com/quotes/112295-a-nation-that-cannot-control-its-borders-is-not-a Accessed 1-17-17
[cxciv] Ron Paul Quotes http://ronpaulquotes.com/concordance/non-intervention.html Accessed 1-17-17
[cxcv] Politico, http://www.politico.com/story/2016/06/full-transcript-trump-job-plan-speech-224891 Accessed 2017
[cxcvi] YouTube, https://www.youtube.com/watch?v=_NiDay86Ft0 Accessed 1-21-17
[cxcvii] Politico, http://www.politico.com/story/2016/06/full-transcript-trump-job-plan-speech-224891 Accessed 2017
[cxcviii] Discover the Networks, http://www.discoverthenetworks.org/viewSubCategory.asp?id=2216 Accessed 1-21-17
[cxcix] Goldstein, David, CBS Los Angeles, "Investigation Uncovers Votes Being Cast From Grave Year After Year," http://losangeles.cbslocal.com/2016/05/23/cbs2-investigation-uncovers-votes-being-cast-from-grave-year-after-year/ Accessed 1-21-17
[cc] Ballotopedia, "Dead People Voting," https://ballotpedia.org/Dead_people_voting Accessed 1-21-17
[cci] Goldstein, David, CBS Los Angeles, "Investigation Uncovers Votes Being Cast From Grave Year After Year," http://losangeles.cbslocal.com/2016/05/23/cbs2-investigation-uncovers-votes-being-cast-from-grave-year-after-year/ Accessed 1-21-17
[ccii] Murdock, Deroy, National Review, "The Clintons: New York's Sixth Crime Family," http://www.nationalreview.com/article/435968/hillary-clinton-bill-clinton-crime-family-where-politics-and-mafia-meet" Accessed 1-21-17
[cciii] Kosar, The Political Insider, "Another Clinton Associate Found DEAD, Bill & Hillary's Body Count Increases!,"

http://www.thepoliticalinsider.com/another-clinton-associate-found-dead-bill-hillarys-body-count-increases/ Accessed 1-21-17
[cciv] Yogi Berra Quotes, http://www.mindspring.com/~hsstern/maewest/y_berra.htm Accessed 1-22-17
[ccv] CNN, http://www.cnn.com/2010/US/08/27/debt.security.mullen/ Accessed 1-22-17
[ccvi] The People's History, http://www.thepeoplehistory.com/70yearsofpricechange.html Accessed 1-22-17
[ccvii] The Guardian, https://www.theguardian.com/us-news/2016/jan/24/donald-trump-says-he-could-shoot-somebody-and-still-not-lose-voters Accessed 1-22-17
[ccviii] Larter, David, Navy Times, "Sailor faces charges for submarine photos on cell phone," http://www.navytimes.com/story/military/crime/2015/08/01/kristian-saucier-alexandria-submarine-pictures-john-walker/30907091/ Accessed 1-22-17
[ccix] YouTube, https://www.youtube.com/watch?v=ny3bOmey-BE Accessed 1-22-17
[ccx] Giaritelli, Anna, The Washington Examiner, "Trump: As president, I would prosecute Clinton," http://www.washingtonexaminer.com/trump-as-president-i-would-prosecute-clinton/article/2583925 Accessed 1-22-17
[ccxi] Ernst, Douglas, The Washington Times, "Russia's Sergey Lavrov says failed 'reset' was 'invention of Hillary Clinton,'" http://www.washingtontimes.com/news/2015/jun/3/russian-fm-sergey-lavrov-failed-reset-was-inventio/ Accessed 1-22-17
[ccxii] Yasmeh, Joshua, The Daily Wire, "Libya Was Hillary's War. Here's The Proof," http://www.dailywire.com/news/3398/libya-was-hillarys-war-heres-proof-joshua-yasmeh Accessed 1-22-17
[ccxiii] Guest, Steve, The Daily Caller, "Just 3 Bills Sponsored By Sen. Hillary Clinton Became Law," http://dailycaller.com/2015/12/30/just-3-bills-sponsored-by-sen-hillary-clinton-became-law/ Accessed 1-22-17

[ccxiv] Kessler, Glenn, The Washington Post, "A guide to the allegations of Bill Clinton's womanizing," https://www.washingtonpost.com/news/fact-checker/wp/2015/12/30/a-guide-to-the-allegations-of-bill-clintons-womanizing/ Accessed 1-22-17
[ccxv] Nolte, John, Breitbart, "Rap Sheet: The Women Who Claim to Be Victims of Bill and Hillary Clinton," http://www.breitbart.com/big-government/2015/12/31/rap-sheet-the-women-who-claim-to-be-victims-of-bill-and-hillary-clinton/ Accessed 1-22-17

[ccxvi] Benson, Guy, Town Hall, "Of Course: Clinton Foundation Pays Female Executives 38 Percent Less Than Male Counterparts," http://townhall.com/tipsheet/guybenson/2016/04/14/of-course-clinton-foundation-pays-female-executives-38-percent-less-than-male-counterparts-n2148105 Accessed 1-22-17

[ccxvii] Kelleher, Seamus, Independent Journal Review, "Hillary Clinton Demands Equal Pay But Doesn't Put Her Money Where Her Mouth Is," http://ijr.com/2015/02/257200-hillary-clinton-paid-female-staff-28-percent-less-men/ Accessed 1-22-17

[ccxviii] Scher, Brent, Washington Free Deacon, "Hillary Clinton's Campaign Has a Gender Pay Problem," http://freebeacon.com/politics/hillary-clintons-campaign-has-a-gender-pay-problem/ Accessed 1-22-17

[ccxix] Richter, Greg, NewMax, "Hillary: Truth 'Hasn't Changed,' I 'Never Sent or Received' Classified Material Emails" , http://www.newsmax.com/Headline/hillary-clinton-email-server-inspector/2016/01/20/id/710214/ Accessed 1-22-17

[ccxx] YouTube, https://www.youtube.com/watch?v=DTxXUufI3jA Accessed 1-22-17

[ccxxi] The Speeches of Ronald Reagan, "The Speech," https://secure3.convio.net/reagan/site/SPageServer/?pagename=Speech_Page_Redesign&gclid=CImM4Ln-4MwCFZWMaQodYaMCcw Accessed 1-22-17

[ccxxii] Jasper, William J., New American, "Wendell Willkie: The "Miracle Man" of 1940," http://www.thenewamerican.com/culture/history/item/21537-the-miracle-man-of-1940 Accessed 1-22-17

[ccxxiii] Political Dictionary, http://politicaldictionary.com/words/yellow-dog-democrats/ Accessed 1-22-17

[ccxxiv] Byrne, Dennis, The Barbershop, "About 1.8 million dead people listed as active voters," http://www.chicagonow.com/dennis-byrnes-barbershop/2012/02/about-1-8-million-dead-people-listed-as-active-voters/ Accessed 1-22-17

[ccxxv] von Spakovsky, Hans A., The National Review, "The Obama Administration Wants to Make Sure Non-Citizens Vote in the Upcoming Election," http://www.nationalreview.com/article/431676/obama-administration-enabling-noncitizen-voting Accessed 1-22-17

[ccxxvi] YouTube, https://www.youtube.com/watch?v=-dY77j6uBHI Accessed 1-22-17

[ccxxvii] Thrush, Glenn and Maggie Habermann, Politico, "What Is Hillary Clinton Afraid Of?," http://www.politico.com/magazine/story/2014/05/hillary-clinton-media-105901_Page2.html#.WITyLH3ko20 Accessed 1-22-17

ccxxviii The Los Angeles Times, "Clintons Began Taking White House Property a Year Ago," http://articles.latimes.com/2001/feb/10/news/mn-23723 Accessed 1-22-17
ccxxix Worldnet Daily, "Here they are: Hillary's 22 biggest scandals ever," http://www.wnd.com/2015/05/here-they-are-hillarys-22-biggest-scandals-ever/#RseZsduoqEsC4YlG.99" Accessed 1-22-17
ccxxx Locy, Toni, The Washington Post, "For White House Travel Office, a Two-Year Trip of Trouble" http://www.washingtonpost.com/wp-srv/politics/special/whitewater/stories/wwtr950227.htm Accessed 1-22-17
ccxxxi The Washington Examiner, "A brief guide to Clinton scandals from Travelgate to Emailgate," http://www.washingtonexaminer.com/a-brief-guide-to-clinton-scandals-from-travelgate-to-emailgate/article/2562906 Accessed 1-22-17
ccxxxii Irvine, Reed and Cliff Kincaid, Accuracy in Media, "The Pardongate Report," http://www.aim.org/media-monitor/the-pardongate-report/ Accessed 1-22-17
ccxxxiii Labaton, Stephen, The New York Times, "Hillary Clinton Turned $1,000 Into $99,540, White House Says," http://www.nytimes.com/1994/03/30/us/hillary-clinton-turned-1000-into-99540-white-house-says.html?pagewanted=1 Accessed 1-22-17
ccxxxiv Bunker, Theodore, NewsMax, "Gov. McAuliffe Donated Almost $500K to Campaign of FBI Official's Wife," http://www.newsmax.com/Politics/Terry-McAuliffe-Donated-Campaign-FBI-Official/2016/10/24/id/755054/ Accessed 1-22-17
ccxxxv Watson, Paul Joseph, Infowars, "Votes Switched From Trump to Hillary in Texas," http://www.infowars.com/report-votes-switched-from-trump-to-hillary-in-texas/ Accessed 1-22-17
ccxxxvi YouTube, https://www.youtube.com/watch?v=Gh0Wc5hsV8U Accessed 1-22-17
ccxxxvii Fox, Brad, MRC TV, "10 Scandals Involving Hillary Clinton You May Have Forgotten," http://www.mrctv.org/blog/10-scandals-involving-hillary-clinton-you-may-have-forgotten Accessed 1-22-17
ccxxxviii The Daily Mail, "All aboard the 'Lolita Express': Flight logs reveal the many trips Bill Clinton and Alan Dershowitz took on pedophile Jeffrey Epstein's private jet with anonymous women," http://www.dailymail.co.uk/news/article-2922773/Newly-released-flight-logs-reveal-time-trips-Bill-Clinton-Harvard-law-professor-Alan-Dershowitz-took-pedophile-Jeffrey-Epstein-s-Lolita-Express-private-jet-anonymous-women.html Accessed 1-22-17
ccxxxix Ibid.
ccxl Ibid.

[ccxli] Kelly, Anita, NPR, "Here Is What Donald Trump Wants To Do In His First 100 Days," http://www.npr.org/2016/11/09/501451368/here-is-what-donald-trump-wants-to-do-in-his-first-100-days Accessed 1-22-17
[ccxlii] The Rush Limbaugh Show, " I'm Getting Nervous About All These Calls for Trump to Unify with the Losers," https://www.rushlimbaugh.com/daily/2016/11/10/i_m_getting_nervous_about_all_these_calls_for_trump_to_unify_with_the_losers/ Accessed 1-22-17
[ccxliii] Patrick J. Buchanan Official Site, "Memo to Trump: 'Action This Day!'," http://buchanan.org/blog/memo-trump-action-day-125997 Accessed 1-22-17
[ccxliv] Brainy Quote, https://www.brainyquote.com/quotes/quotes/a/alberteins133991.html Accessed 1-22-17
[ccxlv] Invetopedia, "Fractional Reserve Banking," http://www.investopedia.com/terms/f/fractionalreservebanking.asp Accessed 1-22-17
[ccxlvi] Ibid.
[ccxlvii] YouTube, https://www.youtube.com/watch?v=Tmi8cJG0BJo Accessed 1-22-17
[ccxlviii] Calomiris, Charles, Allan H. Meltzer, The Hoover Institute, "How Dodd-Frank Doubles Down on 'Too Big to Fail'," http://www.hoover.org/research/how-dodd-frank-doubles-down-too-big-fail Accessed 1-22-17
[ccxlix] Metro Lyrics, http://www.metrolyrics.com/ringing-of-revolution-lyrics-phil-ochs.html Accessed 1-22-17
[ccl] Tax Policy Center, "Who Doesn't Pay Federal Taxes?," http://www.taxpolicycenter.org/resources/video-who-doesnt-pay-federal-taxes Accessed 1-22-17
[ccli] America's Founding Documents, https://www.archives.gov/founding-docs Accessed 1-22-17
[cclii] Ibid.
[ccliii] Cost, Jay, The Weekly Standard, "Crony Capitalism Has Deep Roots," http://www.weeklystandard.com/crony-capitalism-has-deep-roots/article/804847 Accessed 1-22-17
[ccliv] YouTube, https://www.youtube.com/watch?v=KrefKCaV8m4 Accessed 1-22-17
[cclv] Charles, J. Brian, The Hill, "Transcript of Donald Trump's economic policy speech to Detroit Economic Club," http://thehill.com/blogs/pundits-blog/campaign/290777-transcript-of-donald-trumps-economic-policy-speech-to-detroit Accessed 1-22-17

[ccvi] Beckwith, Ryan Teague, Time, "Read Donald Trump's 'America First' Foreign Policy Speech," http://time.com/4309786/read-donald-trumps-america-first-foreign-policy-speech/ Accessed 1-22-17
[ccvii] Trump Pence, "DONALD J. TRUMP DELIVERS GROUNDBREAKING CONTRACT FOR THE AMERICAN VOTER IN GETTYSBURG," https://www.donaldjtrump.com/press-releases/donald-j.-trump-delivers-groundbreaking-contract-for-the-american-vote1 Accessed 1-22-17
[ccviii] Deroy Murdock, Deroy, "Trump's Gettysburg Address Overflows with Conservative Ideas," http://www.nationalreview.com/article/441458/donald-trump-contract-american-voter-gettysburg-address Accessed 1-22-17
[ccix] THE LEGATUM PROSPERITY INDEX, http://www.prosperity.com/ Accessed 1-22-17
[ccx] 2016 Index of Freedom, http://www.heritage.org/index/ranking Accessed 1-22-17
[ccxi] Marina, William, History News Network, "Corporatism: FDR's 'Right Path,' is Alive and Well," http://historynewsnetwork.org/blog/64898#sthash.mk2GCDe0.dpuf" Accessed 1-22-17
[ccxii] Thorner, Nancy, Champion News Net, "The 'War on Poverty' has increased, not decreased government dependency," http://www.championnews.net/?p=13412 Accessed 1-22-17
[ccxiii] The Wall Street Journal, "We're All Keynesians Now," http://www.wsj.com/articles/SB120062129547799439 Accessed 1-22-17
[ccxiv] Meris, Frideriki A., Inquiries, "The Bush Tax Cuts: A Lasting Legacy," http://www.inquiriesjournal.com/articles/279/the-bush-tax-cuts-a-lasting-legacy Accessed 1-22-17
[ccxv] Baker, Dean, The Huffington Post, "There Is No Santa Claus and Bill Clinton Was Not an Economic Savior," http://www.huffingtonpost.com/dean-baker/there-is-no-santa-claus-a_b_2362845.html Accessed 1-22-17
[ccxvi] Miller, Jonathan, Matrix Blog, http://www.millersamuel.com/sec-inaction-defined-serious-economic-consequences/ Accessed 1-22-17
[ccxvii] http://imgur.com/JasfaS6 Accessed 1-22-17
[ccxviii] U. S. History, http://www.ushistory.org/us/23d.asp Accessed 1-22-17
[ccxix] Markay, Lachlan, The Washington Free Beacon, "Clinton Aide's Memo Details Ties Between Consulting Firm and Clinton Foundation," http://freebeacon.com/politics/clinton-aides-memo-details-ties-consulting-firm-clinton-foundation/ Accessed 1-22-17
[ccxx] Ross, Chuck, The Daily Caller, "Huma Abedin Granted Access To Hillary Based On Clinton Global Initiative Donor Status," http://dailycaller.com/2016/10/26/huma-abedin-granted-access-to-hillary-based-upon-clinton-global-initiative-donor-status/ Accessed 1-22-17
[ccxxi] Daily Mail.com, "Inside Bill Inc: Aide lays out how the former president raked in tens of millions of dollars through a series of deals while Hillary was

Secretary of State in a memo unearthed by Wikileaks," http://www.dailymail.co.uk/news/article-3877062/Inside-Bill-Clinton-Latest-hacked-email-details-aides-helped-rake-millions-former-president.html Accessed 1-22-17

[cclxxii] World Net Daily, "Here they are: Hillary's 22 biggest scandals ever," http://www.wnd.com/2015/05/here-they-are-hillarys-22-biggest-scandals-ever/ Accessed 1-22-17

[cclxxiii] Luther, Daisy, LewRockwell.com, "21 Things We've Learned About Hillary Clinton from Wikileaks That the MSM Won't Share...But YOU Can!," https://www.lewrockwell.com/2016/10/daisy-luther/21-things-weve-learned-hillary/ Accessed 1-22-17

[cclxxiv] Strassel, Kimberly A., The Wall Street Journal, "Grifters-in-Chief," http://www.wsj.com/articles/grifters-in-chief-1477610771 Accessed 1-22-17

[cclxxv] Lachman, Samantha, The Huffington Post, "Jerry Brown Signs Automatic Voter Registration In California," http://www.huffingtonpost.com/entry/automatic-voter-registration-california_us_561680d5e4b0082030a15119 Access 1-22-17

[cclxxvi] Matthews, Mark K., The Denver Post, "Vandals hit Donald Trump's Denver campaign office," http://www.denverpost.com/2016/11/04/vandals-hit-donald-trumps-denver-campaign-office/ Accessed 1-22-17

[cclxxvii] Hoggard, DeJuan, ABC 11 News, "Photo of suspect in Alamance County Republican Party headquarters vandalism released," http://abc11.com/politics/alamance-county-republican-party-headquarters-vandalized/1589680/ Accessed 1-22-17

[cclxxviii] Quotefish, http://quotefish.blogspot.com/2016/10/if-you-dont-read-papers-youre.html Accessed 1-22-17

[cclxxix] Daily Mail.com, "Trump's 'Gettysburg address' makes closing argument for choosing him and unveils first-100-days agenda as he promises 'the kind of change that only arrives once in a lifetime'," http://www.dailymail.co.uk/news/article-3861392/Trump-prepares-Gettysburg-address-unveiling-100-days-agenda-aides-say-Hillary-just-waiting-clock.html Acessed 1-22-17

[cclxxx] Benson, Guy, Town Hall, "Hillary: No, I Didn't Blame the Video in My Meeting With Benghazi Families," http://townhall.com/tipsheet/guybenson/2015/12/08/whoa-hillary-says-benghazi-families-are-wrong-she-didnt-blame-attacks-on-internet-video-n2090274 Accessed 1-22-17

[cclxxxi] YouTube, https://www.youtube.com/watch?v=QSooz2wXpes Accessed 1-22-17

[cclxxxii] Hill, Catey, Market Watch, "45% of Americans pay no federal income tax," http://www.marketwatch.com/story/45-of-americans-pay-no-federal-income-tax-2016-02-24 Accessed 1-22-17

[cclxxxiii] Boyd, Kevin, Independent Journal Review, "Percentage of Americans Now on Welfare Paints a Disturbing Picture of the State of Our Economy," http://ijr.com/2014/08/170299-percentage-americans-welfare-will-shock/ Accessed 1-22-17
[cclxxxiv] Sweet Speeches, http://www.sweetspeeches.com/s/142-james-madison-veto-message-on-the-internal-improvements-bill Accessed 1-22-17
[cclxxxv] Ibid.
[cclxxxvi] Huston, Warner Todd, Breitbart, "Trump Jobs Boom Continues Before Inauguration Day," http://www.breitbart.com/big-government/2017/01/17/trump-jobs-boom-continues-inauguration-day/ Accessed 1-22-17
[cclxxxvii] Funny Quotes, http://cmgm.stanford.edu/~lkozar/Famous_Quotes.html Accessed 1-22-17
[cclxxxviii] Churchill Quotes, https://www.brainyquote.com/quotes/quotes/w/winstonchu111291.html Accessed 1-22-17
[cclxxxix] Ibid.
[ccxc] Brainy Quote, https://www.brainyquote.com/quotes/quotes/w/winstonchu129864.html Accessed 1-22-17

Made in the USA
Columbia, SC
24 July 2021